THE NEW DICTIONARY OF LEGAL TERMS

By
IRVING SHAPIRO

Looseleaf
Law Publications, Inc.
43-08 162nd Street
Flushing, NY 11358

Published By
LOOSELEAF LAW PUBLICATIONS, INC.
43-08 162nd Street
Flushing, NY 11358
www.LooseleafLaw.com

ISBN 0-930137-01-9

FOREWORD

Words constitute the skin and bones of the law. Often legal rights and liabilities will turn upon the construction of a single word. Anyone with a reason to read, write or interpret legal documents needs a handy source for the immediate definition of the all important legal word.

This dictionary fills that need with clear, concise and succinct definitions. The fluid quality of legal language is reflected throughout, and contemporary terms are emphasized.

It is a formidable task to put together such a book. It is a job expertly done by Irving Shapiro, a highly qualified author who loves the legal profession and loves his work. This dictionary will be of tremendous assistance to all, and all will find it a treasure.

Judge Vito J. Titone
NYS Court of Appeals

ABOUT THE AUTHOR

Irving Shapiro has been a member of the New York State Bar for 60 years. For nearly 30 years he worked for the NYS Supreme Court, Second Judicial Department during which time he founded *Court Careers* – known as one of New York's preeminent organizations which assists court personnel in successfully preparing for competitive promotion examinations. During this time as a court official he lectured extensively as well as participating as an instructor in the courts training program and was a volunteer arbitrator in Small Claims court.

Along with numerous well-received articles appearing in professional journals he has authored the best selling and highly effective Shapiro's Explanatory Quizzers for New York's Penal Law, Criminal Procedure Law and Civil Practice Law & Rules.

In 1974 he retired from court employment and began his next career as a Professor of criminal justice and court management at St. John's University, Jamaica, New York and as an adjunct professor at Adelphi University, Garden City, New York.

From 1993 until 1997 he served as an elected Town Justice in Hillsdale, New York.

His extensive experience as a lawyer, court official and professor has given him a broad perspective for the design of a dictionary for the 21st Century law professional.

PREFACE

Busy practitioners, paralegals, legal secretaries, court reporters and other court officials, law enforcement agents and law students need a quick and direct answer when they seek the meaning of a word. This dictionary is designed to fill that need.

Obsolete material has been screened out both to reflect the fluid quality of legal language and to emphasize terms and definitions in current use. The definitions employ simple words, requiring no further search for meaning.

Case references and citations have not been used, in recognition of variances in interpretation and statutory definition in different jurisdictions.

For the convenience of users and with the consent of its publisher, terms and definitions are included from the U.S. Bureau of Justice Statistics, *Dictionary of Criminal Justice Data Terminology: Terms and definitions proposed for interstate and national data collection and exchange,* Second edition.

Entries taken from that work are indicated by the symbol ☆ appearing in the left margin. It is hoped that the inclusion of this material will contribute to standardization in usage and greater accuracy in the compilation of statistical data.

While there may be regional differences in pronunciation, a simple guide to acceptable pronunciation has been provided for all foreign language terms as well as for terms which may offer difficulty in pronunciation beyond that of words in general usage.

The assistance of the following persons is acknowledged, with appreciation:

James E. Foran, while enrolled in his final year at St. John's University Law School, assisted, patiently and with dedication, in the laborious work of research and editing.

Susan E. Metz, a magna cum laude graduate of Barnard College with a masters degree in reading from Rutgers University, is now a freelance editorial consultant. Ms. Metz developed the pronunciation guide and meticulously proofread the entire work.

This dictionary is dedicated in affectionate memory to my parents, Bessie and Isidor Shapiro.

I.S.

St. John's University
Jamaica, New York

GUIDE TO PRONUNCIATION

Pronunciations are given for words and phrases of foreign origin and those that are generally unfamiliar or difficult to pronounce. In many cases there may be more than one correct pronunciation in legal usage. To minimize confusion, only one pronunciation is given here.

Pronunciations are indicated in square brackets. Translations and alternate spellings are indicated in parentheses.

ABBREVIATIONS

adj.	-	adjective	pl.	-	plural
adv.	-	adverb	pref.	-	prefix
n.	-	noun	v.	-	verb

PRONUNCIATION KEY

a	fat	o	box
ah	father	oh	boat
ahy	fight	oo	boot
aw	fought	ou	bout
b	baby	oy	boy
ch	chair	p	paper
d	dog	r	ring
e	bet	s	some
ee	beet	sh	shoe
f	full	t	table
g	good	th	thing
h	hot	th	this
i	it	u	pup
j	jump	uh	put
k	kite	v	very
l	like	w	well
m	mother	y	young
n	new	z	zipper
ng	singer	zh	pleasure

Stressed syllables are indicated by capital letters.

☆ This symbol, in the left margin, indicates entries taken from the U.S. Bureau of Justice Statistics, *Dictionary of Criminal Justice Data Terminology: Terms and definitions proposed for interstate and national data collection and exchange,* Second Edition.

Other books by Irving Shapiro:

Shapiro's Explanatory Quizzer for
NYS Civil Practice Law and Rules

Shapiro's Explanatory Quizzer for
NYS Criminal Procedure Law

Shapiro's Explanatory Quizzer for
NYS Penal Law

A

abandon To desert in spite of duty or responsibility, to surrender rights, property or status, to forsake entirely, to yield without restraint.

abandonment Voluntary surrender of rights, property or status; voluntary desertion, as of a family.

abate To terminate, remove, reduce.

abatement Act of termination or reduction, as, abatement of a nuisance.

abdication Renunciation or relinquishment of a status, as, abdication by a sovereign of his throne.

abduction Act of unlawfully taking away a person by fraud, persuasion, or violence, usually defined by statute.

abet To encourage or aid another, usually in relation to commission of a crime.

abettor One who aids or encourages another, as in commission of a crime.

ab initio [ab i NI shee oh] From the beginning, at the outset.

abjuration [ab juh RAY shuhn] Renunciation, disclaimer, abandonment under oath.

abjure [ab JOOR] To renounce, disclaim, abandon under oath.

abnegate To deny, renounce, relinquish.

abnegation Denial, renunciation, relinquishment.

abode The place where one resides; ordinarily means domicile.

abolish To destroy, annul, do away with.

abolition Destruction, annulment, as, abolition of capital punishment.

abort To terminate prematurely.

abortifacient [u bawr ti FAY shuhnt] Drug or other means for producing abortion.

abortion The destruction or bringing forth prematurely of a human fetus before time for natural birth.

abortionist One who induces criminal abortion.

abridge To reduce, shorten, diminish.

abridgement Abstract or digest, that which has been reduced and condensed.

abrogate [A bruh gayt] To repeal, annul, abolish.

abscond To hide in order to avoid legal process, to leave a jurisdiction secretly.

☆ **abscond (corrections)** *recommended statistical terminology* To depart without authorization from a geographical area or jurisdiction, in violation of the conditions of probation or parole.

☆ **abscond (court)** To intentionally absent or conceal oneself unlawfully in order to avoid a legal process.

absolute (1) Unconditional, without relation to or dependence on other things or persons, complete, final; (2) having supreme jurisdiction.

absque hoc [AB skway hok] Without this.

absque injuria [AB skway in JOO ree uh] Without injury.

abstain To forbear, refrain, withhold.

abstract -adj. (1) Theoretical, intangible, detached;-n. (2) summary, precis; -v. (3) to summarize; (4) to remove, detach, separate.

abstract of record Brief history of a legal action as found in its record.

abstract of title Brief history of ownership of real property.

abut (1) To touch along or at a boundary; (2) to terminate at a meeting point.

abutment (1) Parts of a structure which carry its weight; (2) meeting point of two parcels of real estate.

abutting owner Owner of land which touches or is contiguous to a given parcel.

access (1) Approach, passage; (2) ability or right to pass from one place to another without obstruction.

accession (1) Coming into a right or office; (2) act of agreeing; (3) that which has been added.

accessory One who counsels, induces, procures or commands another to commit a crime, but is absent at the time the crime is committed; one who, after commission of a crime by another, knowingly harbors or conceals the offender.

accessory after the fact One who, knowing that a crime has been committed, conceals it and harbors, assists or protects the offender.

☆ **accessory after the fact** Person who, after a crime has been committed, knowingly assists the offender to avoid arrest, trial, conviction or punishment.

accessory before the fact One who, although absent at the time a crime is committed, assists, procures, counsels, induces, encourages, or commands another to commit it.

☆ **accessory before the fact** Accomplice who solicits or knowingly assists another person to commit a crime, often only one who is not present at its commission.

accident Unforeseen event, chance happening.

accommodation Arrangement made for convenience of another.

accommodation indorser One who signs a negotiable instrument to convey title, acting as a guarantor of prior indorsers and without benefit to himself and for the benefit of another.

accomplice One who acts in concert with another, usually in commission of a crime.

accord Agreement between persons, one of whom has a cause of action against the other.

accordance Agreement, harmony, conformity.

accord and satisfaction (1) Settlement of a cause of action; (2) agreement by which a contract or disputed claim is discharged.

accouchment [u KOOSH muhnt] Act of giving birth to a child.

account Detailed statement of debits and credits between parties.

account book Record in which the transactions of a business are entered.

accrual (1) Vesting of a right; (2) accumulation of a sum of money for a specific purpose.

accrual basis Accounting procedure by which income and expenses are recorded as they occur, without regard to actual receipt or payment.

accrue To increase, add; to vest as a legal right.

accrued Due and payable.

accumulated surplus Funds which a company has in excess of its capital and liabilities.

accumulative Additional, increasing, amassing.

accusation Charge against a person that he is guilty of some offense; allegation of wrongdoing or delinquency.

acknowledge To admit, agree, recognize as genuine.

acknowledgment (1) Declaration made before an officer duly qualified to take oaths, that one's execution of an instrument is one's own free act, and certification by the officer to this effect; (2) act of recognizing or admitting something as valid.

acquired rights Rights which one does not naturally enjoy.

acquisition Act of gaining or procuring; thing gained or procured.

acquit (1) To release, discharge; (2) absolve from a criminal charge.

acquittal (1) Act by which one is released or absolved of a criminal charge; (2) discharge from liability.

☆ **acquittal** *recommended statistical terminology* The judgment of a court, based on the verdict of a jury or a judicial officer, that the defendant is not guilty of the offense(s) for which he or she has been tried.

act -n. (1) Something done; (2) legislative enactment, statute; -v. (3) to perform, do, execute.

acting (1) Doing something for another; (2) holding a temporary rank or position.

action (1) Formal proceeding in a court by which one seeks to enforce a right, redress a wrong, or obtain punishment for an offense; (2) conduct, behavior, performance.

actionable Furnishing legal ground for an action, as, words which are claimed to be libelous or slanderous are actionable.

action in personam [AK shuhn in puhr SOH nuhm] Lawsuit against the person.

action in rem [AK shuhn in rem] Lawsuit directed against property, as a suit to reach and dispose of tangible property or some interest therein.

action quasi in rem [AK shuhn KWAY zahy in rem] Action brought against persons to subject only certain property of theirs to the asserted claim, and where judgment therein is conclusive only between the parties and their privies.

act of God Accident attributable to natural causes without human intervention, and which could neither be expected nor prevented.

actual Real, substantial, existing.

actual cash value Fair or reasonable cash price for which property can be sold in the market, not at forced sale.

actual market value Price at which merchandise is freely offered for sale to all purchasers.

actuarial Pertaining to expectancy, as mathematically determined for insurance purposes.

actuary Person using mathematics and statistics in compilation of expectancy and probability data for insurance purposes.

ad [ad] At, to, until, upon, with relation to.

ad absurdum [ad uhb SUHR duhm] To the point of absurdity.

adapted Made suitable for use.

ad damnum [ad DAM nuhm] (to the damage) Clause of a pleading alleging amount of loss or injury.

addict One whose repeated use of a drug has led to emotional or physical dependence on its use.

addiction Compulsive and uncontrolled use of drugs with emotional or physical dependence thereon.

addition Something added, an increase, augmentation.

additional Increased, augmented, further.

address -n. (1) Geographical designation of a place (as a residence or a place of business) where a person or organization may be found or communicated with; (2) formal speech or communication; -v. (3) to speak; (4) to direct.

adduce [u DOOS] (1) To bring forward, as, to adduce testimony at a trial; (2) to present, to offer.

ademption [u DEMP shuhn] Revocation or withdrawal of property transfer, as by testator's withdrawal of legacy, grantor's sale, or destruction of subject matter.

adequate Sufficient, equal to what is required, suitable, satisfactory.

adequate care Care proportionate to the risk involved so as to avoid accident.

adequate cause Motivation or reason sufficient for the purpose.

adequate consideration Value which is equal or reasonably proportioned to the value of that for which it is given.

ad hoc [ad hok] As to this, for this purpose.

ad infinitum [ad in fi NAHY tuhm] Without limit, to an infinite extent, indefinitely.

ad interim [ad IN tuh rim] In the meantime.

adjacent (1) Nearby, close; (2) adjoining, touching.

adjective law Rules of legal procedure concerned with pleading and evidence.

adjoin To lie next to, abut upon, be in contact.

adjoining Touching, contiguous, adjacent.

adjourn To delay, defer.

adjournment Delay until another time.

adjudge To pass on judicially, decide, settle, decree.

adjudicate To decide, rule upon, as in a judicial procedure.

adjudication Ruling, judgment or decision of a court.

☆ **adjudication** The process by which a court arrives at a decision regarding a case; also, the resultant decision.

☆ **adjudication withheld** *recommended statistical terminology* In criminal justice usage, a court decision at any point after filing of a criminal complaint, to continue court jurisdiction but stop short of pronouncing judgment.

☆ **adjudicatory hearing** *recommended statistical terminology* In juvenile justice usage, the fact-finding process wherein the juvenile court determines whether or not there is sufficient evidence to sustain the allegations in a petition.

adjunct -adj. (1) Additional; (2) added as a related component; -n. (3) something added; (4) person associated with or assisting another.

adjuration [a juh RAY shuhn] (1) Solemn charging or binding upon oath; (2) earnest or solemn urging.

adjure [uh JOOR] (1) To charge solemnly on oath; (2) to urge earnestly.

adjust To settle, arrange, free from differences.

ad lib [ad lib] (ad libitum) At pleasure, without restraint, improvised.

ad litem [ad LAHY tuhm] For the litigation.

administer (1) To manage or conduct; (2) to manage and distribute the estate of a decedent; (3) to give or cause to be taken, as an oath; (4) to apply, as a medicine, or to cause to be consumed or used.

administration (1) Management, as, management of a business; (2) management and distribution of assets of estate of a decedent; (3) process of causing to be taken, as, the administration of an oath, or of a medicine consumed by a person; (4) control of government by a political party or person, as, a Democratic administration.

administrative (1) Pertaining to administration, as in managing or superintending the conduct of a business or other endeavor; (2) having the character of executive or ministerial acts, as distinguished from such as are judicial.

administrative agency Governmental body charged with management and supervision of some particular subject, as, National Labor Relations Board.

administrative board Group of persons presiding over and having responsibility for conduct of an administrative agency, including holding hearings, making investigations, promulgating regulations and generally acting in an administrative or quasi-judicial capacity.

administrative discretion Latitude in its operation and rules accorded to an administrative agency by act of Legislature.

☆ **administrative judge** A judicial officer who supervises administrative functions and performs administrative tasks for a given court, sometimes in addition to performing regular judicial functions.

administrative law Branch of law relating to conduct of administrative agencies, and legal practice before such agencies by persons having business with them.

administrative remedy One that is non-judicial, but is provided by a commission or board, as in workers' compensation statutes.

administrator (1) One appointed by a court to act for a decedent who left no will; (2) one managing the affairs of another.

administrator cum testamento annexo [ad MIN uh stray tuhr kuhm tes tuh MEN toh u NEK soh] (administrator with the will annexed) One appointed by a court to act for a decedent, where the designated executor for some reason cannot serve, although the testator's directions are otherwise effective.

administrator de bonis non [ad MIN uh stray tuhr day BOH nis nohn] Person appointed by a court to administer a decedent's effects which have not been included in a former administration.

administrator with will annexed Person appointed by a court to act for a decedent, where the designated executor cannot serve, although the testator's directions are otherwise effective.

administratrix [ad min uh STRAY triks] Female administrator.

admiralty Branch of law having reference to maritime matters.

admission (1) Voluntary acknowledgment of certain facts; (2) statement tending to prove guilt.

☆ **admission (corrections)** In correctional usage, the entry of an offender into the legal jurisdiction of a corrections agency and/or physical custody of a correctional facility.

admit (1) To allow, permit, acknowledge, give entrance; (2) to acknowledge certain facts voluntarily.

admit to bail To fix an amount adequate as security for defendant's appearance in court.

admit to probate To give legal effect and recognition to a will.

admonish To warn or advise against a wrong practice, express disapproval.

admonition Advice, warning or reprimand given as to a person's conduct, as, an admonition given by a court to jurors not to discuss a case until directed to do so.

Admr. Administrator.

Admx. Administratrix.

adolescence Period of life following puberty and preceding maturity, terminating legally at age of majority.

adopt (1) To take up or accept a practice or idea evolved by another; (2) to take by one's choice into a new relationship, as, to adopt a child; (3) to endorse and assume responsibility for, as, to adopt a report of a committee.

adoption (1) Acceptance of a practice or idea evolved by another; (2) act of taking into a new relationship, as, the adoption of a child; (3) the endorsement or assumption of, as, the adoption of a committee report.

ad prosequendum [ad pro suh KWEN duhm] To prosecute, or for purpose of prosecution.

adult One who has attained specified age, generally 18.

☆ **adult** *recommended statistical terminology* In criminal justice usage, a person who is within the original jurisdiction of a criminal, rather than a juvenile, court because his or her age at the time of an alleged criminal act was above a statutorily specified limit.

adulteration (1) Act or process of mixing a false or inferior product with a genuine or superior one of the same general kind, as in adulteration of an article of food; (2) artificially concealing defects in products offered for sale.

adultery Sexual intercourse between two persons, either of whom is married to a third person.

☆ **adultery** Generally, unlawful sexual intercourse between a married person and a person other than that person's spouse.

ad valorem [ad vuh LAW ruhm] According to value, as a tax or duty imposed at a specific rate.

advance -v. (1) To move forward, progress; (2) to lend, to furnish something before receiving its equivalent; -n. (3) payment or giving over of money, as in a loan, or before one is legally obligated to do so; (4) forward movement.

advance sheets Most recently reported opinions of a court, issued under the volume and page numbers by which they may later be found in bound volumes.

adventitious incidental, fortuitous, without previous expectation or design.

adventure A bold undertaking with attendant risk.

adversary An opponent.

adversary proceeding Legal action with opposing sides, each contesting the other.

adverse Hostile, contrary, opposed.

adverse interest Legal position or right opposed and hostile to another.

adverse party An opponent, as in a legal action.

adverse possession Open, notorious, exclusive, continuous and hostile occupancy of land, under claim of right, for a period (usually must continue for a specific number of years), resulting in right of ownership by the possessor, by operation of law.

adverse use Use under a claim of right without the owner's authority.

advice (1) Recommendation as to action; (2) formal notice as to a business transaction.

advise (1) To counsel or recommend a plan or course of action; (2) to give notice, to inform.

advisory That which counsels or suggests without requiring use of the advice by the receiver.

advocate -v. To urge, recommend, persuade or speak in favor of something; -n. one who gives legal assistance to or acts as attorney for another.

☆ **ADW (assault with a deadly weapon)** Unlawful intentional inflicting, or attempted or threatened inflicting, of injury or death with the use of a deadly weapon.

affect To act upon, influence, impress.

affiant [u FAHY uhnt] One who swears to an affidavit, deponent.

affidavit [a fi DAY vit] Written statement made under oath.

affidavit of merits [a fi DAY vit uv ME rits] Written statement, made under oath, by party to an action, that his asserted claim or defense is not dilatory or false but is made in good faith on substantial grounds.

affiliate - n. (1) Person or group that is allied, connected or linked, as a member or branch of an organization; -v. (2) to attach or join, as a member or branch; (3) to connect or associate oneself.

affiliation (1) Process of determination of one as the father of a child; (2) alliance with an organization and its objectives, association.

affinity Close agreement, relationship, kinship.

affirm (1) To make firm, establish, validate; (2) to ratify or confirm the judgment of a lower court; (3) to ratify or confirm a voidable contract; (4) to make a solemn declaration, without oath, that a statement is true.

affirmance Confirmation or ratification of a previous judgment, contract or act.

affirmation Solemn and formal declaration under penalties of perjury that a statement is true, without oath.

affirmative -adj. That which declares positively, agrees, establishes; -n. expression of agreement.

affirmative defense In legal pleading, new matter which constitutes justification for the act complained of.

affirmative proof Evidence establishing truth of matters asserted.

affirmed Ratified, confirmed, upheld.

affirmed without opinion Action by an appellate court upholding the conclusion of a lower court and accepting its reasoning.

affix To attach or fasten.

aforesaid Previously referred to.

aforethought Premeditated, deliberate, planned.

a fortiori [o fawr shee AW ree] All the more, with stronger reason.

after Subsequent to.

after-acquired Acquired after a given date or event.

after-born Born subsequent to a given date or event.

after-discovered Discovered after a given date or event.

agency (1) Relationship by which one party, called the agent, is authorized to act for another party, called the principal. Agency may include that of master and servant, employer and employee or independent contractor; (2) place where an agent transacts business on behalf of a principal.

agency coupled with interest Relationship in contract where one authorized as agent to act for another has a financial interest in the exercise of his authority as agent, as means of reimbursement to him from his principal.

agenda Program or list of matters to be considered at a discussion or meeting.

agent One authorized to represent and act for another.

aggravate (1) To increase the circumstances of an act; (2) to intensify, increase, add weight to; (3) to provoke or annoy.

☆ **aggravated assault** *Uniform Crime Reports usage* Unlawful intentional causing of serious bodily injury with or without a deadly weapon, or unlawful intentional attempting or threatening of serious bodily injury or death with a deadly or dangerous weapon.

☆ **aggravating circumstances** Circumstances relating to the commission of a crime which cause its gravity to be greater than that of the average instance of the given type of offense.

☆ **aggregate maximum release date** Calendar date on which a given offender should be fully discharged on all sentences currently in effect in that jurisdiction.

aggressor One who takes unprovoked hostile action.

aggrieved Injured, wronged, as, an aggrieved party to an action.

agree To concur, consent, settle upon one arrangement satisfactory to both sides.

agreed statement of facts Mutually satisfactory statement by parties to an action as to the facts therein, so that ruling by the court may be solely on the law.

agreement (1) A contract; (2) harmonious meeting of minds on a given subject.

aid -n. Assistance, support, help; -v. to help, assist, strengthen, support.

aid and abet In criminal law, to help knowingly or facilitate the planning or commission of a crime.

☆ **aider or abettor** Accomplice who solicits or knowingly assists another person to commit a crime, often only one who is actually or constructively present at the commission of the crime.

☆ **AKA** Abbreviation for "also known as."

aleatory contract [A lee u taw ree KON trakt] Agreement by which the obligation of one or both parties is conditional upon some uncertain event or contingency.

alia [o lee u] Other things, others, as in et alia (and others).

alias [AY lee uhs] Name not one's true name.

☆ **alias** Any name used for an official purpose that is different from a person's legal name.

alibi [A luh bahy] (1) Defense to a criminal action that one was elsewhere than at the scene of a crime at the time of its commission; (2) plausible excuse for failure of performance or negligent performance.

alien -adj. Foreign, strange, hostile; -n. foreigner, one born in another country, one owing allegiance to another country; -v. to transfer, as property or ownership.

alienate (1) To transfer title to real property; (2) to convey or transfer, generally, as, to alienate one's affection for another.

alienation Act of transferring or diverting from one to another, as in alienation of title to real property or alienation of affection.

alienist Psychiatrist, a doctor qualified in the study of mental diseases.

alimony Allowance paid by a divorced or separated spouse, under court order, for support of the other; in a broad sense, additionally, payment for support of children of the marriage.

alimony pendente lite [A li moh nee pen DEN tay LEE tay] Temporary alimony paid while suit for divorce or separation is pending.

aliunde [o lee UHN day] From another source.

allegation (1) Statement by a party in a pleading setting forth that which he expects to prove; (2) assertion.

allege To state, assert, charge, as, to allege in a legal pleading.

allocution [a loh KYOO shuhn] (1) Invitation to a defendant, before imposition of sentence, to address the court, in mitigation of punishment or for arrest of judgment; (2) act of addressing or exhorting.

allonge [u LONJ] Piece of paper attached to a negotiable instrument to provide space for further endorsements, when no space remains on the instrument itself.

allot To distribute or apportion.

allotment Share, portion, something set apart for a purpose.

allow To approve, accept as true, admit, concede; to grant something as a deduction or addition, to permit, sanction, tolerate.

allowance Deduction, portion assigned.

alter To make a change in, modify, vary in some degree.

alteration Change or variation, as in alteration of a document.

alter ego [AWL tuhr EE goh] (another self) A trusted friend.

alternative Choice between two or more.

amanuensis [u man yoo EN sis] One who writes for another that which is dictated to him.

ambassador In international law, a representative of the head of one country, sent to act in another country.

ambiguity Doubtfulness due to uncertainty or duplicity of meaning.

ambiguous Not clear; having two meanings.

ambit (1) Circumference; (2) sphere of action or influence, as, to go beyond the ambit of one's position.

ambivalence (1) Holding of contradictory emotions toward a particular person or object; (2) uncertainty, fluctuation.

ameliorate To improve, to make better.

ameliorating waste Act of a lessee, resulting in improvement of the property but technically constituting waste.

amenable (1) Subject to answer to the law, accountable, liable to punishment; (2) tractable, governable.

amend To change.

amendment Change, as, amendment of a statute or constitution.

amends Satisfaction given for a wrong, as, to make amends.

a mensa et thoro [o MEN suh et THAW roh] (from table and bed) Describing separation of husband and wife, without further change of their marital status.

amercement [u MUHRS muhnt] Monetary penalty imposed by a court.

amicus curiae [u MEE kuhs KYOO ree ahy] (friend of the court) One who is not a party to an action but is permitted by the court to intervene and present his views.

amnesia Loss of memory.

amnesty Act of pardon for past acts, granted by a government to persons who have been guilty of a crime or political offense.

☆ **amnesty** A kind of pardon granted by a sovereign authority, often before any indictment, trial or conviction, to a group of persons who have committed offenses against the government, which not only frees them from punishment, but has the effect of removing all legal recognition that the offenses occurred.

amortization Gradual reduction of the principal of a debt, as, amortization of a loan by payments on a mortgage.

amount Total sum.

analogous Similar, like.

analogy Logical similarity.

anarchist One who advocates the doctrine of anarchy, that is, absence of established government.

anarchy Lawlessness, absence of all political government, society in which persons have complete freedom of action.

ancestor One from whom a person has descended.

ancillary That which is subordinate or auxiliary to a principal matter.

animo [A nuh moh] With intention or design.

animo furandi [A nuh moh fyuh RON dee] With intent to steal.

animus [A nuh muhs] Mind, intent, design.

animus furandi [A nuh muhs fyuh RON dee] With intent to steal.

animus revocandi [A nuh muhs re voh KON dee] With intent to revoke.

animus testandi [A nuh muhs tes TON dee] With intent to make a will.

annex -n. Supplementary item or structure; -v. to attach, unite.

anno domini [A noh DO muh nee] (in the year of the Lord) Indicating time within the Christian era as measured from the birth of Jesus Christ.

annotation Comment, remark, reference or citation, as, an annotation in a book.

annual Happening once a year.

annuitant [u NYOO i tuhnt] One who receives a regular payment of money, usually during his lifetime, from a fund created for such purpose.

annuity [u NYOO i tee] (1) Regular payment of money from a fund, normally for period of one's life; (2) amount of such payment.

annul To cancel, void, abolish.

annulment Act of making something void, as, the judicial annulment of a marriage.

anomalous Irregular, exceptional, abnormal.

answer -n. (1) Pleading by a defendant; (2) reply, response, defense; -v. (3) to reply, respond, defend.

ante [ON tay] (before) Prior.

ante litem motam [ON tay LAHY tuhm MOH tuhm] Before action was brought.

ante mortem [ON tay MAWR tuhm] Before death.

antecedent -adj. Prior in time; -n. predecessor in a series, as an ancestor is an antecedent to a descendant.

antedate To date an instrument earlier than the day of its execution.

anthropometry [an throh PO muh tree] Measurement of dimensions of the human body, for comparison and identification.

anticipatory breach Failure or refusal to perform before a present duty of performance exists, as in anticipatory breach of a contract.

☆ **anticipatory offense** An offense which consists of an action or conduct which is a step to the intended commission of another offense.

aphasia [u FAY zhuh] Inability to speak or understand due to brain disorder.

a posteriori [o puhs tee ree AW ree] Referring to method of reasoning by which principles or propositions are derived from established or observed facts.

apparent Obvious, evident, manifest.

apparent authority (1) Power which an agent appears to possess; (2) power which the principal knowingly permits the agent to assume; (3) power reasonably necessary to carry out the purpose of an agency.

apparent danger Actual and material risk of substantial personal injury.

apparent defect Flaw in a product which may be discovered by simple inspection.

apparent heir [u PA ruhnt ayr] One whose right of inheritance is clear.

☆ **appeal** Generally, the request that a court with appellate jurisdiction review the judgment, decision, or order of a lower court and set it aside (reverse it) or modify it; also, the judicial proceedings or steps in judicial proceedings resulting from such a request.

appeal bond Amount posted by an appellant as security for damages and costs, if he fails to prosecute an appeal.

☆ **appeal case** *recommended statistical terminology* A case filed in a court having incidental or general appellate jurisdiction, to initiate review of a judgment or decision of a trial court, an administrative agency or an intermediate appellate court.

☆ **appeal of right** An appeal which the court having appellate jurisdiction must hear and decide on its merits, at the request of an appellant. In criminal cases, defense appeals of trial court final judgments are most frequently appeals of right; that is, a defendant's right to appeal from a conviction is generally guaranteed by law.

☆ **appeal proceedings** The set of orderly steps by which a court considers the issues and makes a determination in a case before it on appeal.

appear (1) To come formally before a court or similar body; (2) to seem, to be evident, (3) to come into existence.

appearance (1) Formal coming before a court or similar body of a party to an action or proceeding and the submission to the jurisdiction of that body; (2) act or state of being evident; (3) coming into existence or view.

☆ **appearance (court)** The act of coming into a court and submitting to the authority of that court.

☆ **appellant** [u PEL uhnt] The person who contests the correctness of a court order, judgment, or other decision and who seeks review and relief in a court having appellate jurisdiction, or the person in whose behalf this is done.

appellate [u PEL uht] (1) Pertaining to appeals and review; (2) pertaining to authority to affirm, reverse or modify action of a lower body.

☆ **appellate case disposition** *recommended statistical terminology* The final determination made in an appeal case, request to appeal case or application for postconviction relief or sentence review by a court having appellate jurisdiction.

appellate court [u PEL uht kawrt] Judicial tribunal having jurisdiction of appeal, as distinguished from a trial court.

☆ **appellate court** [u PEL uht kawrt] *recommended statistical terminology* A court of which the primary function is to review the judgments of other courts and of administrative agencies.

☆ **appellate court case** *recommended statistical terminology* A case which has been filed in an intermediate appellate court or court of last resort, including appeal cases, requests to appeal, original proceedings cases, and sentence review cases.

☆ **appellate judge** A judge in a court of appellate jurisdiction who primarily hears appellate cases, and also conducts disciplinary or impeachment proceedings.

☆ **appellate jurisdiction** [u PEL uht joo ris DIK shuhn] The lawful authority of a court to review a decision made by a lower court; the lawful authority of a court to hear an appeal from a judgment of a lower court.

appellee [u pe LEE] (1) One who opposes an appellant; (2) one against whom an appeal is taken; (3) respondent to an appeal.

appendage Something added as an accessory or subordinate part.

appendant Associated with, annexed to or belonging to something else.

appendix Supplement, as, an appendix to a book, containing lists, tables or other specialized data.

appertain To belong to, to relate to.

applicable Suitable, pertinent, appropriate.

applicant One seeking some benefit, as, an applicant for employment.

application (1) A formalized request, as, an application for a position; (2) relationship, use, or connection, as, the application of a doctrine or principle.

apply (1) To make a request, as, to apply for a loan; (2) to use as appropriate.

appoint To designate, assign, establish for a position or purpose.

appointee One designated for a particular purpose, as, an appointee to an office.

appointment (1) Designation of a person to hold a particular office or responsibility; (2) exercise of a legal right to name persons to have an interest in specified property; (3) time and place set for parties to meet.

apportion To divide and distribute in some ratio.

apportionment Division, distribution or partition of a subject matter in parts according to a formula.

apposite [A puh zit] Pertinent, appropriate, relevant.

appraisal Estimate of value, particularly one made by a qualified person.

appraise (1) To estimate price or value; (2) to analyze and determine the merit or status of something.

appraiser Expert in determination of value, as, a real-estate appraiser.

appreciable (1) Capable of being observed or recognized; (2) substantially tangible.

appreciate (1) To increase in value; (2) to be grateful for; (3) to know or understand.

apprehend (1) To arrest, take hold of, take into custody; (2) to fear.

apprehension (1) Seizure, taking or arrest of a person on a criminal charge; (2) premonition, fear.

apprentice Person engaged to render service in order to learn a trade.

appropriate -adj. (1) Fit, suitable, proper; -v. (2) to take as one's own without permission; (3) to designate moneys for some particular purpose.

appropriation (1) Act of setting apart for a specific purpose; (2) designation of moneys for a particular purpose, as, appropriation made by Congress; (3) act of taking as one's own.

approval Act of consenting, confirming or ratifying an act or thing done by another, as, to give one's approval.

approve To be satisfied, agree, consent, ratify, think well of.

approximate -adj. (1) Close or near in amount, quality or distance; -v. (2) to judge, estimate by rough calculation, (3) to bring or come near to; (4) (medical) to bring together.

approximation An estimate, rough calculation.

appurtenance That which is an incidental part of something else, as, a garage is an appurtenance to a dwelling.

appurtenant Belonging to, accessory to, incident to.

a priori [o pree AW ree] (from the former) Deductive, from what goes before.

arbiter (1) One who decides a dispute; (2) person having absolute authority to decide something in controversy.

arbitrage [AHR buh truhj] Transactions by which securities or bills of exchange are simultaneously bought in one market and sold in another, in order to obtain a profit from difference of price.

arbitrary Without reason, absolute, despotic.

arbitration Determination of differences between contending parties by arbitrators or referees chosen by the parties.

arbitrator Person chosen by agreement of parties to a dispute, to hear their contentions and give judgment between them.

archetype [AHR kuh tahyp] The original, from which a copy is made.

archives [AHR kahyvz] (1) Place where records or documents are kept (usually of matters having historical value); (2) documents or records themselves.

archivist [AHR kuh vist] Custodian of records or documents.

arguendo [ahr gyoo EN doh] By way of argument, for the purpose of argument.

argument (1) Effort to establish belief by application of reason; (2) inference drawn from indisputable or highly probable premises; (3) coherent series of reasons, statements or facts intended to support or establish a point of view.

argumentative (1) Containing a process of reasoning; (2) given to or fond of argument.

aristocracy (1) Government by a small privileged class of people, without a monarch, and exclusive of the common people; (2) highest privileged class of a society.

armed Furnished or equipped with weapons.

☆ **armed robbery** Unlawful taking of property in the immediate possession of another by use or threatened use of a deadly or dangerous weapon, or attempting the above act.

armistice Temporary suspension or cessation of hostilities.

arraign [u RAYN] To bring a defendant before a court to be advised of and to answer a criminal charge made against him.

arraignment [u RAYN muhnt] Procedure by which a defendant is brought before a court to be advised of, and to answer to, a criminal charge against him.

☆ **arraignment.** I. Strictly, the hearing before a court having jurisdiction in a criminal case, in which the identity of the defendant is established, the defendant is informed of the charge(s) and of his or her rights, and the defendant is required to enter a plea. II. In some usages, any appearance in court prior to trial in criminal proceedings.

array (1) Entire panel of jurors, (2) display.

arrest -n. (1) (criminal) The taking of a person into custody that he may be held to answer to a crime; (2) (civil) seizure of a person by lawful authority to answer a demand against him in a civil action; (3) any restriction of a person's liberty without that person's consent; -v. (4) to apprehend or restrain a person by the execution of legal process; (5) to stay, to delay temporarily.

☆ **arrest** *recommended statistical terminology* Taking an adult or juvenile into physical custody by authority of law, for the purpose of charging the person with a criminal offense or a delinquent act or status offense, terminating with the recording of a specific offense.

arrest of judgment Act of staying judgment in a criminal case for some matter appearing on the face of the record, which would render judgment, if given, erroneous or reversible.

☆ **arrest register** The document containing a chronological record of all arrests made by members of a given law enforcement agency, containing at a minimum the identity of the arrestee, the charges at time of arrest, and the date and time of arrest.

☆ **arrest report** The document prepared by the arresting officer describing an arrested person and the events and circumstances leading to the arrest.

☆ **arrest warrant** *recommended statistical terminology* A document issued by a judicial officer which directs a law enforcement officer to arrest an identified person who has been accused of a specific offense.

☆ **arrestee dispositions** The class of law enforcement or prosecutorial actions which terminate or provisionally suspend proceedings against an arrested person before a charge(s) has been filed in court.

☆ **arrests** In Uniform Crime Reports terminology, all separate instances where a person is taken into physical custody or notified or cited by a law enforcement officer or agency, except those relating to minor traffic violations.

☆ **arson** *tentatively recommended national category for prosecution, courts and corrections statistics* The intentional damaging or destruction or attempted damaging or destruction, by means of fire or explosion of the property of another without the consent of the owner, or of one's own property or that of another with intent to defraud.

☆ **arson** In Uniform Crime Reports terminology, the burning or attempted burning of property with or without intent to defraud.

art (1) Craft, specialized skill; (2) creative expression of beauty or aesthetic perception.

art, words of Words having a technical meaning because of special context in which they are used.

articles (1) Subdivisions of a statute, code or document; (2) connected series of propositions, system of rules established by competent authority, as, articles of war; (3) a form of contract or agreement, as, articles of partnership.

articles of agreement Written memorandum of an agreement, sometimes describing the rules of a voluntary association, by which its membership is governed.

articles of impeachment Formal specification of grounds for impeachment, comparable to an indictment in a criminal proceeding.

articles of incorporation Instrument governing conduct and operation of a private corporation.

articles of partnership Written agreement setting forth the terms and conditions agreed to by partners.

articles of war Written code promulgated for legal regulation of a military force.

artifice Trickery, deception.

artificial False, contrived, unnatural.

artificial person Person or entity such as a corporation, created by operation of law, as distinguished from a natural person.

as is In its present state. Use of the term indicates that a purchaser of property so identified has thereby been given notice of any defects, so as to bar a claim by him as to defect or damage.

as of course As a routine matter, in the ordinary course of business.

asportation [as puhr TAY shuhn] Removal, carrying away, as in a felonious asportation of goods.

assassination (1) Murder for hire; (2) murder committed by stealth, treachery, or lying in wait.

assault -n. (1) Intentional injury to the person of another; (2) attempted violence upon another, or threat of violence accompanied by menacing act; -v. (3) to attack, assail.

☆ **assault** *recommended statistical terminology* Unlawful intentional inflicting, or attempted or threatened inflicting, of injury upon the person of another.

assault and battery In some jurisdictions, assault is the threat of physical injury, and battery is the actual imposition of physical injury.

☆ **assault on a law enforcement officer** A simple or aggravated assault, where the victim is a law enforcement officer engaged in the performance of his duties.

assay [u SAY] Proof or testing of precious metals for purity.

assembly (1) Meeting of persons at a given place; (2) body of a state legislature (usually, in bicameral legislatures, the body having the more numerous membership) based upon a population ratio.

assembly, unlawful In criminal law, as defined by statute, the meeting together of a specified number of persons to do some unlawful act or in pursuance of a common scheme to disturb public peace.

assent Agreement, approval.

assert (1) To state as true, declare; (2) to urge against contradiction.

assess (1) To determine or fix the value, quality, or extent of, as, to assess damages, to assess real property for tax purposes; (2) (sometimes) to levy or collect a tax; (3) to distribute the amount of a tax equitably among several liable for its payment.

assessed valuation Monetary determination of taxable value of real property, on which tax rate is payable.

assessment (1) Charge levied against real property, as, an assessment for new sewers; (2) valuation of property; (3) act of apportioning an amount to be paid, as, an assessment on members of an organization to secure necessary funds; (4) an appraisal or evaluation.

asset (1) Article of value; (2) condition affording advantage or benefit.

asseveration [u sev uh RAY shuhn] Affirmation, solemn declaration.

assign (1) To transfer to another, as, to assign property; (2) to point out, as, to assign errors in presenting an argument on appeal.

assignation [a sig NAY shuhn] (1) Act of transferring title; (2) appointment made for illicit sexual relations; (3) attribution.

☆ **assigned counsel** A defense attorney assigned by the court on a case-by-case basis to represent in court indigent defendants and offenders, sometimes compensated from public funds but sometimes not compensated at all.

assigned risk Plan whereby an insurance carrier accepts an insured who does not meet its underwriting standards, providing coverage in its turn as one of a group of insurers, usually in automobile liability coverage.

assignee [u sahy NEE] Grantee, one to whom an assignment is made.

assignee for benefit of creditors [u sahy NEE fawr BE nuh fit uv CRE duh tuhrz] One to whom the property of a debtor is transferred, to be administered by him as a trustee for the benefit of the creditors.

assignment Act of transferring a property interest or cause of action to another.

assignment of error Specification of errors upon which an appellant relies.

assignor [u SAHY nuhr] One who transfers a property interest or cause of action to another; grantor.

assist To help, aid, give encouragement to, participate with others in a particular purpose or endeavor.

assistance Act of helping or participating with others in some purpose or endeavor.

assize [u SAHYZ] An ancient form of court.

associate -n. Co-worker, colleague; an attorney who acts with another attorney for a case or several cases; -v. to join, connect.

association (1) Body of persons joined together for a particular purpose; (2) an unincorporated society.

assumpsit [u SUMP sit] (he undertook) A form of action at common law to secure damages for breach of agreement.

assumption (1) Act of taking something for granted; (2) act of taking on a debt or obligation; (3) acceptance of a postulate as a basis for discussion or argument.

assumption of indebtedness Act by which a person obligates himself to pay another's financial obligations.

assumption of risk (1) Acceptance of responsibility for a hazard incidental to one's employment; (2) a concept that one who subjects himself to a known danger or hazard may not thereafter seek redress for injury arising from that situation.

assured -n. Person insured by an insurance company against specified loss or hazard; -adj. unquestionable, confident, convinced.

assurer Insurer, underwriter, one who indemnifies loss upon the happening of a contingency.

asylum (1) Shelter, refuge, protection; (2) institution for the protection and relief of mentally, physically, or socially disabled persons.

asylum state State of refuge for one evading criminal prosecution in another state.

at arm's length (1) Beyond personal influence or control; (2) without trusting or accepting the honesty of another, in a cautious manner.

at bar Before the court.

at issue In controversy.

at large (1) Not limited to any particular area; (2) in an extended form, in detail; (3) not apprehended, as, a criminal is at large.

at law According to law; in law, as distinguished from in equity.

attach (1) To take or apprehend by commandment of a writ or precept; (2) to fasten or connect.

attaché [a ta SHAY] Person connected with an office, such as an embassy, legation or court.

attachment (1) Seizure or taking into custody of persons or property by virtue of a legal process; (2) writ or precept commanding such seizure; (3) removable part which can be affixed to a machine, implement or instrument to increase its utility.

attain To arrive at, reach.

attainder [u TAYN duhr] Extinction of one's civil rights by reason of imposition of death sentence or judgment of outlawry.

attempt -n. (l) Act done with intent to achieve an objective, and which tends to achieve the objective; -v. (2) to try.

☆ **attempt** The intentional performance of an overt act directed toward the commission of a crime, with intent to commit the crime and ability to do so, but without completion of it.

attenuation Diminution, weakening.

attest To certify, authenticate, bear witness to.

attestation (1) Act of bearing witness; (2) official written authentication; (3) affirmation of truth or genuineness.

attestation clause (1) Certificate, usually referring to a will, setting forth facts and circumstances attending its execution; (2) clause wherein witnesses certify that an instrument was executed in their presence, and setting forth the manner of such execution.

attorn [u TURN] To turn over, transfer to another.

attorney [u TUR nee] Generically, agent, one authorized to act for another; usually lawyer, one licensed to practice law.

☆ **attorney** [u TUR nee] A person trained in the law, admitted to practice before the bar of a given jurisdiction, and authorized to advise, represent, and act for other persons in legal proceedings.

attorney at law [u TUR nee at law] Lawyer, one licensed to practice law.

attorney-general [u TUR nee JEN ruhl] (1) Member of President's cabinet as head of Department of Justice; (2) highest ranking legal officer of a state.

attorney general opinions Interpretations of law issued by an Attorney General for the guidance of government agencies. Although these opinions are not binding on courts, they are generally considered persuasive.

attorney in fact [u TUR nee in fakt] Agent duly authorized to act for another in respect to specified matters.

attractive nuisance Instrument or condition likely to attract children in play; one who maintains this may be liable to a child injured thereby under the attractive nuisance doctrine.

auction Public sale of property to the highest bidder.

auctioneer One who conducts auction sales.

audit -n. Examination of accounts, vouchers, and entries in financial record books; -v. to examine financial accounts and records for accuracy.

auditor One who examines financial accounts, records and vouchers, and verifies their accuracy.

augment To increase, add to.

authentic Genuine, true.

authenticate To establish as true, genuine, or having authority.

authentication Establishment of authority, truth or genuineness.

authorities (1) References to and citations of supportive sources (such as statutes, precedents, textbooks, judicial opinions); also, the sources so cited; (2) persons having jurisdiction or command, as, police authorities.

authority (1) Citation supporting one's position, justification for conduct; (2) power, superiority, jurisdiction, right to expect obedience; (3) individual whose expert opinion is widely accepted; (4) public administrative body controlling a public enterprise, such as the Port of New York Authority.

authority coupled with an interest Authority given to an agent for a valuable consideration.

authorization Sanction, grant of power to act.

authorize To empower, give the right to act, permit.

autocracy Government by the unlimited will of one man.

automatism [aw TOM uh tiz uhm] Medical condition in which action or conduct occurs in a person without his will, purpose or intention.

autonomy Power of self-government, independence.

autopsy Dissection to determine cause of death.

autoptic proference [aw TOP tik PROF ruhns] The offering in open court of articles for inspection or observation by the court.

autre [OH truh] Another.

autrefois [oh truh FWO] At another time, heretofore.

auxiliary Aiding, ancillary, attendant on.

available Usable, effectual, obtainable.

avails Proceeds, profits.

aver [u VUHR] To declare, assert, allege.

average -adj. Of ordinary or usual type; -n. the mean point between two quantities.

averment [u VUHR muhnt] Positive statement of facts.

a vinculo matrimonii [o VEENG kyoo loh ma truh MOH nee ee] From the bond of marriage.

avocation Diversion from one's ordinary or principal occupation; hobby.

avoid (1) To evade or escape; (2) to cancel, make void, annul.

avow (1) To acknowledge and justify an act done; (2) to assert.

award -n. (1) Decision of arbitrators; (2) something conferred, as, award of a medal; -v. (3) to grant, concede, confer; (4) to give by judicial determination.

axiom A self-evident truth.

B

☆ **backlog (court)** The number of cases awaiting disposition in a court which exceed the court's capacity for disposing of them within the period of time considered appropriate.

bad debt Loan which is not collectible.

bad faith (1) Design to mislead or deceive another; (2) neglect or refusal with interested or sinister intent to fulfill an obligation, as distinguished from honest error, as, the seller, acting in bad faith, concealed from the buyer the defective condition of the merchandise sold.

bail -n. Security given to a court for one's appearance therein as required, in order to obtain release from custody, as, the man is out of prison on bail; -v. to release from custody on an undertaking that the person released will appear in court or forfeit property as in the undertaking.

☆ **bail** I. To effect the release of an accused person from custody, in return for a promise that he or she will appear at a place and time specified and submit to the jurisdiction and judgment of the court, guaranteed by a pledge to pay to the court a specified sum of money or property if the person does not appear. II. The money or property pledged to the court or actually deposited with the court to effect the release of a person from legal custody.

bailable Capable of being bailed, entitled to bail, as, a misdemeanor is usually bailable.

bail bond Obligation signed by sureties for the person named as principal to appear as may be required by a court.

☆ **bail bondsman** A person, usually licensed, whose business it is to effect releases on bail for persons charged with offenses and held in custody, by pledging to pay a sum of money if a defendant fails to appear in court as required.

bailee (1) Person to whom goods are given in trust for a specific purpose; (2) person who receives goods under a contract of bailment.

☆ **bail forfeiture** The court decision that the defendant or surety has lost the right to the money or property pledged to guarantee court appearance or the fulfillment of another obligation, or has lost the right to the sum deposited as security for the pledge, and that the court will retain it.

bailiff [BAY lif] (1) Court officer; (2) sheriff's deputy; (3) one to whom some authority or jurisdiction is given, such as an overseer or manager of property for another.

☆ **bailiff** [BAY lif] The court officer whose duties are to keep order in the courtroom and to maintain physical custody of the jury.

bailment (1) The giving of property to a bailee, in trust, for a specific purpose; (2) delivery and subsequent return of personal property by one person (bailor) to another (bailee) in trust for the execution of a specific purpose or object.

bailor One who gives his property to a bailee in a contract of bailment.

☆ **bail revocation** The court decision withdrawing the status of release on bail previously conferred upon a defendant.

☆ **balance of sentence suspended** *recommended statistical terminology* A type of sentencing disposition consisting of a sentence to prison or jail, which credits the defendant for time already spent in confinement awaiting adjudication and sentencing, suspends the execution of the time remaining to be served, and results in the release from confinement of the defendant.

ballistics Study of motion of power-propelled projectiles.

ballot -n. Paper upon which a voter designates his choice of candidate for an office or upon some proposition; -v. to vote or decide.

ban -n. Prohibition, censure, as, a ban on alcoholic beverages in some states; -v. to prohibit by social or legal means.

banc [bahngk] -adj. With the judicial authority of the full court, as, en banc or in banc; -n. bench on which a judge sits.

bandit (1) Outlaw, brigand, gangster; (2) person put under a ban.

banishment (1) Punishment of exclusion or dismissal compelling one to leave a group or area for some period; (2) legal expulsion from a country.

banking game Gambling operation in which bets must be laid against a gambling house.

banking hours Period of day during which one may present a note for payment to the bank on which it is drawn.

bankrupt -adj. Insolvent' impoverished' destitute; -n. one who because of inability to pay his creditors has been adjudged insolvent so that creditors may have his estate administered, according to law, for their benefit.

bankruptcy (1) State of being bankrupt, state of depletion; (2) insolvency declared by judicial decree.

bar (1) Restriction, exclusion, prohibition, as, a bar to prosecution of an action; (2) railing in a courtroom to separate judge, jury, counsel and parties from the public; (3) body of members of the legal profession; (4) "at bar", meaning before the court.

bargain -n. (1) Agreement between parties; (2) advantageous purchase; -v. (3) to sell for cash or on agreed terms; (4) to discuss terms of agreement, negotiate.

bargainee (1) In a bargain, the vendee; (2) party to a bargain who receives the property which is the subject matter of the bargain.

bargainor (bargainer) (1) Person who makes a bargain; (2) party to a bargain who is to receive the consideration and deliver the subject matter of the bargain.

barratry [BAR uh tree] Exciting or stirring up lawsuits or quarrels.

barred Obstructed, forbidden, prevented, as, a claim that is barred by the Statute of Limitations.

barrister [BAR i stuhr] (1) Lawyer, attorney; (2) legal counsel who conducts trial proceedings, as distinguished from solicitor, who drafts legal papers and prepares case for trial.

barter -n. Agreement for exchange of goods for other goods; -v. to trade or exchange goods for other goods.

base -adj. Unworthy; -v. to make or use as a foundation.

based upon Grounded on, as, the lawyer's argument was based upon the Bill of Rights of the United States Constitution.

basis Foundation, support, footing.

bastard -adj. Of inferior or questionable origin; -n. illegitimate child.

bastardy (1) Condition of being an illegitimate child; (2) offense of begetting an illegitimate child.

bastardy proceeding Method provided by statute for proceeding against a putative father to secure maintenance for an illegitimate child.

battery (1) Unlawful physical force upon a person, unlawful touching of another; (2) arrangement, use or connection of similar items, as, a battery of weapons.

☆ **battery** Intentional unlawful inflicting of physical violence or constraint upon the person of another.

bawdy house House of prostitution, brothel.

bear -n. (1) One who wishes or expects a fall in stock prices; -v. (2) to support or carry, as the right to bear arms; (3) to tolerate; (4) to give rise to, bring forth.

bear arms To carry and use weapons.

bear interest To yield interest, produce interest at a specified rate.

bearer bond Instrument issued as evidence of debt, transferable by delivery from one holder to another, without registration of ownership.

before (1) Prior to, in advance of, preceding; (2) in the presence of, as, appearance before a court.

behavior Conduct, manners, deportment, reaction to stimulation.

behoof Use, benefit, profit, advantage.

belief Faith, trust, acceptance, credence.

belligerent -adj. Warlike, pugnacious, combative; -n. party to a war.

belong To be a part or the property of.

belongings Property' possessions.

below Lower than, beneath, as, the court below reached a different conclusion.

bench -n. (1) Seat occupied by a judge in court; (2) judgeship, office of a judge; (3) the judge himself, as, the attorney addressed the bench.

bench warrant Writ issued by a court "from the bench" for the arrest of a person, as in case of contempt or where an indictment has been found.

☆   **bench warrant** *recommended statistical terminology* A document issued by a court directing that a law enforcement officer bring the person named therein before the court, usually one who has failed to obey a court order or a notice to appear.

beneficial Profitable, advantageous, tending to one's advantage, as, the beneficial terms of an agreement.

beneficial enjoyment Enjoyment of another's estate in one's own right and for one's own benefit.

beneficial estate Future right of possession given to a devisee for his own use and benefit.

beneficial interest Benefit or advantage accorded to one from some transaction in which he is not a party.

beneficial power Authority given to a person to perform an act which will benefit himself.

beneficial use Right given by an owner to another to enjoy owner's property, including any profit deriving therefrom.

beneficiary One designated to receive something, as, a beneficiary of a trust or insurance policy.

benefit -n. (1) Advantage, good, help; (2) payment, gift; (3) social event to raise funds for a cause; -v. (4) to aid, advance, improve.

benefit of clergy Ministration of a church, as, to live together as man and woman without benefit of clergy.

benevolent Kind, generous, charitable.

benign (1) Gentle, mild, kind; (2) not adversely affecting health, as opposed to malignant.

bequeath To give or leave property by will.

bequest Property given by will.

Bertillon system [bayr tee YOHN SIS tuhm] Method of identifying persons based upon size and other physical data; named for Alphonse Bertillon, a French criminologist (1835–1914).

best -n. Excelling all others; -v. to get the better of, outdo.

best evidence Rule of evidence which holds that a copy shall not be received when the original can be obtained.

bestial (1) Relating to animals; (2) brutish, barbarous,depraved.

bestow To apply, give, confer.

bet -n. (1) Wager on the outcome of an event; (2) possibility on which a wager is made; -v. (3) to wager on the outcome of an event.

beyond Past, outside, far from.

bias (1) Inclination of temperament or outlook; (2) prejudice, tendency, trend.

bicameral [bahy KAM ruhl] Having two chambers, as, the United States Congress is bicameral; that is, composed of the Senate and the House of Representatives.

bid -n. (1) Offer, statement of what one will do, as, a bid at an action to buy at the bid price; (2) invitation, as, a bid to join an organization; (3) attempt to win, achieve, attract; -v. (4) to invite, ask for, beseech, offer.

biennial Occurring every two years.

bifurcated trial [BAHY fuhr kay tuhd TRAHY uhl] A split trial, tried in two separate stages, so that a jury first might consider the question of liability or responsibility and then, if indicated, a separate proceeding would be conducted to determine damages.

☆ **bifurcated trial** In criminal proceedings, a special two-part trial proceeding in which the issue of guilt is tried in the first step, and if a conviction results, the appropriate sentence or applicable sentencing statute is determined in the second step.

bigamy The offense of one who, having a husband or wife living, marries another person.

☆ **bigamy** Unlawful contracting of marriage by a person who, at the time of the marriage, knows himself or herself already to be legally married.

bilateral Having two sides.

bill (1) Itemized statement of goods sold or services rendered, with charges; (2) draft of a proposed law as presented to a legislative body; (3) paper money, as, a ten-dollar bill; (4) formal written declaration, as, a bill of particulars; (5) written advertisement of an exhibition or performance; (6) commercial note, as, a bill payable.

bill of attainder [bil uv u TAYN duhr] Law pronouncing a person guilty without trial.

bill of costs Itemized account of costs incurred by successful party in a legal action.

bill of exceptions Written statement of exceptions to rulings of a trial court arising during progress of the trial, made for the purpose of appeal.

bill of exchange Unconditional written order requiring the person addressed to pay amount specified to bearer or to order, on signature of its maker; usually used in foreign transactions.

bill of health Satisfactory report about some condition or situation, as, the investigator gave the house a clean bill of health.

bill of lading [bil uv LAY deeng] Written account of goods shipped, made by the carrier, acknowledging receipt of the goods and setting forth terms of contract for their delivery.

bill of particulars Detailed statement of the facts on which an action or counterclaim is based.

bill of sale Formal instrument used to convey title to goods.

binder (1) Temporary agreement pending execution of a more formal instrument, as in real estate or insurance matters; (2) detachable cover for holding together sheets of paper.

binding (1) Imposing duty or responsibility; (2) requiring conformity or obedience.

binding over Act by which a court holds a person, as by setting bail, for later appearance as a defendant or witness.

☆ **bind over** 1. To require by judicial authority that a person promise to appear for. trial, appear in court as a witness, or keep the peace. II. *recommended statistical terminology* The decision by a court of limited jurisdiction requiring that a person charged with a felony appear for trial on that charge in a court of general jurisdiction, as the result of a finding of probable cause at a preliminary hearing held in the limited jurisdiction court.

bipartite Being in two parts.

birth (1) Act of coming forth, beginning; (2) period during which fetus of a mammal becomes detached and independent from its mother: (3) lineage, descent, as, a person of noble birth.

blacklist List of persons or groups disapproved or discriminated against.

☆ **blackmail** The popular name for the kind of extortion where the threat is not physical but relates to exposing some secret or true or alleged fact which would do harm to the personal circumstances of a person, or damage his or her reputation.

blank -adj. (1) Devoid of interest or change, as, a blank expression on her face; (2) free from writing or mark, as, a blank piece of paper; (3) plain or unbroken, as, a blank wall or a key blank; -n. (4) empty space left on a paper, as, a blank for signature.

blank endorsement Endorsement of commercial paper such as checks and promissory notes made by signature of the payee on back of the paper, thereby making the instrument payable to bearer.

blanket policy Insurance coverage which includes various classes of property, as, a blanket policy on clothing.

blockade Isolation of a strategic area by a belligerent; restrictive measures employed as an obstacle to passage.

blood Relationship through common ancestry.

bludgeon -n. Club heavier at one end than at the other; -v. to overbear, bully.

Blue Book The generally used term for "A Uniform System of Citation," a manual published and distributed by the Harvard Law Review Association for standardized use of citations and abbreviations in court papers.

blue chip (1) Valuable asset; (2) stock issue of a corporation having substantial assets and wide public acceptance.

blue law Rigid law regulating work, commerce or entertainment on Sunday.

blue sky law Law intended to regulate and supervise sale of securities in such concerns as visionary oil wells or gold mines.

board -n. (1) Group of persons meeting together for a common public or private purpose, as, a board of directors, examining board, or a board of appeals; (2) place for posting of information, as, a listing of stock-market quotations; (3) furnishing of daily meals; -v. (4) to enter a train, plane or ship; (5) to provide with regular meals and lodging; (6) to cover, as, to board the windows of a building.

boarder One provided with regular meals, or regular meals and lodging.

board of directors Governing body of a corporation or organization.

bodily (1) Having a physical form; (2) relating to the body.

body (1) Physical organism, material part; (2) main or principal part, as of a building; (3) enclosed part of a vehicle, as an automobile; (4) mass or portion of matter; (5) group of persons united for some purpose.

body execution Court order commanding arrest and commitment of a person.

bona fide [BOH nuh fahyd] In good faith, legally valid.

bond -n. (1) Contract to pay a certain sum of money, usually conditioned upon the performance or failure of a specified act, as, a performance bond given by a contractor; (2) uniting or binding force, as, a bond of friendship; (3) interest-bearing document, issued as proof of debt; (4) state of goods until taxes are paid, as, tobacco in bond; -v. (5) to bind together or connect; (6) to place under conditions of a bond by providing security for performance or appearance, as, to bond an employee.

bonded debt That part of indebtedness of an organization for which bonds have been issued.

bondsman (1) One who bails another by putting up a bond; (2) person licensed to act in bail-bonding business.

bonus Something given or received in excess of expectation.

book (1) Collection of printed pages bound between a cover; (2) record of bets accepted by a bookmaker.

☆ **booking** A law enforcement or correctional administrative process officially recording an entry into detention after arrest, and identifying the person, the place, time, and reason for the arrest, and the arresting authority.

bookmaking Business of determining odds, receiving bets and paying winners.

☆ **bookmaking** An organized, continuous operation for the unlawful receiving and paying off of wagers on uncertain events.

book of account Continuous and permanent record of business affairs.

book value (1) Value of capital stock as shown by excess of assets over liabilities; (2) value according to books of account; (3) value of an automobile as found in trade publication showing current values.

bootleg (1) To manufacture or sell illegally, as, to bootleg liquor; (2) to produce or obtain for sale without required inspection, permission or approval.

booty Plunder, spoils, reward, gain.

born (1) Brought into existence; (2) natural, innate, as, a born leader.

borrow To secure temporarily from another for one's own use.

borrower One who borrows.

borrowing power (1) Statutory or constitutional limitation of indebtedness that may be incurred by a public body; (2) ability to acquire funds by loan.

bound -adj. Intending to go, as, homeward bound; -n. limiting line of an object or area; -v. to set limits to, circumscribe, enclose.

boundary (1) Separating line; (2) that which indicates a limit.

bounty (1) Goodness, kindness, liberality, generosity; (2) yield, as of a crop; (3) reward.

bourse [boors] Market, exchange.

bowie knife [BOO wee nahyf] Large hunting knife adapted for fighting.

boycott Combination to prevent social or business intercourse, as an expression of disapproval or to apply economic pressure.

branch -n. (l) Something that extends from a main body or source, as, a branch of a river; (2) section of an organization; -v. (3) to diverge, extend activities.

brass knuckles Set of four linked metal finger rings worn as a weapon for fighting.

brawl Noisy quarrel.

breach Breaking, violation, infraction, infringement.

breach of contract Failure to comply with terms of a contract.

breach of promise Violation of a promise, usually a promise to marry.

breach of the peace Disturbing the public peace, as by disorder, violence, force or noise.

breach of trust Violation by a trustee of terms of his trust.

breach of warranty Failure or non-performance of a promise, representation, undertaking or stipulation constituting basis of a transaction.

break -n. (1) Interruption, hiatus, interval; -v. (2) to split into pieces, maim, mutilate, cut, rupture, shatter; (3) to violate or transgress; (4) to force entry into; (5) to escape from; (6) to defeat, abolish, dismiss, discontinue, end a relationship.

breakage (1) Quantity of articles broken; (2) allowance for things broken; (3) in pari-mutuel betting, amount retained by the house in excess of some designated multiple.

break and enter Physical entry into a premises, accompanied by any movement of any part of the premises, as, to break and enter a building accomplished even by slight movement or turning knob of an unlocked door.

breaking Act of demolishing or injuring.

bribe (1) Reward or favor given or promised to pervert justice or corrupt one's conduct; (2) something given as an inducement to desired conduct.

bribery Act of giving or taking a bribe.

☆ **bribery** The giving or offering of anything of value with intent to unlawfully influence a person in the discharge of his duties, and the receiving or asking of anything of value with intent to be unlawfully influenced.

brief -adj. (1) Concise, curt, abrupt; -n. (2) summary, concise article; (3) statement of a legal case, setting forth one's arguments; -v. (4) to abstract, abridge; (5) to give final precise instructions.

bring To convey from one place to another, deliver, lead.

bring suit To institute a legal action.

bring up (1) To rear, educate; (2) to stop suddenly; (3) to introduce.

broad General, widely applicable, not limited or restricted.

broker Negotiator, intermediary, agent acting for a fee, as, a real estate broker.

brokerage (1) Business of a broker; (2) fee paid to a broker for his services.

brothel Establishment for the conduct of prostitution.

brother Male person having same father and mother as another.

bucket shop (1) Place where people place wagers under pretense of buying and selling stocks on an exchange; (2) dishonest brokerage house in securities, that does not execute customers' margin orders but relies upon profit from fluctuations adverse to their customers' interest.

budget -n. Detailed estimate of receipts and expenditures for a specific period; -v. to provide, allow, plan, as, to budget one's time.

bug -v. To overhear or record conversation intentionally, without consent of at least one of the parties, by some mechanical means; -n. a device for this purpose.

buggery Unnatural sexual intercourse.

building -n. Enclosed edifice constructed upon land; -v. act of making or establishing.

building and loan association Banking organization whose funds for loans are accumulated by member's stock subscriptions and savings deposits.

building permit Governmental authorization to construct or alter a building.

building restriction Covenant in the nature of an easement which limits nature of a building that may be erected on a site.

bulk (1) Volume, magnitude, mass; (2) main or greater part, majority; (3) "in bulk", not divided into parts.

bulk sales act Statute regulating sale of goods in bulk, for protection of creditors.

bulletin Brief statement or announcement.

bullion [BUHL yuhn] Gold or silver in mass, uncoined precious metals.

bull pen (1) Enclosure used as a temporary place of confinement; (2) large detention cell, as in a courthouse or police station house.

bunco game (1) Any trick or cunning calculated to win confidence and deceive, whether by conversation, conduct, or suggestion; (2) swindling by misrepresentation.

burden Obligation, encumbrance, restriction.

burden of proof Obligation of affirmatively proving a fact in issue between the parties, as, in a criminal case the burden of proof is on the prosecution.

bureau Specialized administrative unit or agency, as, the Bureau of the Budget.

bureaucracy [byuh ROK ruh see] Administrative system usually considered as revealing indifference to needs, showing lack of initiative and a tendency to defer decisions.

burgess [BUHR jes] (1) Magistrate or member of governing body of a borough or town; (2) representative in colonial legislatures of Maryland and Virginia.

burglar One who commits burglary by unlawfully entering or remaining in a building with intent to commit a crime therein.

burglarious [buhr GLE ree uhs] Of or resembling burglary.

burglary Act of unlawfully entering or remaining in a building with intent to commit a crime therein, as defined by statute.

☆ **burglary** I. By the narrowest and oldest definition, trespassory breaking and entering of the dwelling house of another in the night-time with the intent to commit a felony. II *recommended statistical terminology; Uniform Crime Reports usage* Unlawful entry of any fixed structure, vehicle or vessel used for regular residence, industry or business, with or without force, with intent to commit a felony or larceny.

bursar [BUHR suhr] Administrative officer in charge of funds.

business (1) Trade, commerce; (2) one's concern or responsibility; (3) role, function, duty, work.

buttress Support, sustain, strengthen, as, to buttress an argument.

buy -n. (1) A thing purchased; (2) a purchase at a favorable price; -v. (3) to obtain by purchase.

buy in (1) To buy for one's self that which one has offered for sale at auction; (2) to obtain an interest by purchase.

buy long To purchase commodities or securities with the expectation of their future resale at a profit.

buy short To agree to sell for future delivery commodities or securities which one does not presently own, with the expectation that the seller can purchase them at a lower price and thereby realize a profit.

by color of office By reason of supposed official status which may not in fact provide authority for the act done.

by-law Regulation made by a corporation or society for conduct of its affairs.

by operation of law Effected by statute or legal principle.
bystander One present but not taking part.
by virtue of By reason of, by authority of.

C

cabal [kuh BOL] An association for intrigue.

Cabaret [ka buh RAY] Restaurant providing liquor and entertainment.

cabinet (1) Advisory board of an executive or sovereign; (2) advisory council of a president, composed of heads of executive departments of the government.

cadaver [kuh DA vuhr] Dead body.

calamity Disaster, major misfortune, loss.

calculate (1) To compute mathematically; (2) to intend, plan, figure out, believe.

calculated Intended, adapted, ascertained, planned.

call (1) To make a demand, as for payment; (2) to make a request or appeal.

callable Capable of being redeemed on notice, as, a callable bond may be redeemed by the obligor on call.

calling Business, trade or profession.

calumny [KAL uhm nee] Slander, false accusation.

camera [KAM ruh] Chamber, room, as, in camera (referring to a judge's chambers).

campaign Organized effort to secure a desired result, as, an election campaign.

cancel To revoke, recall, expunge, erase.

cancelable (cancellable) Able to be revoked or recalled.

cancellation Act of deleting, nullifying, invalidating.

candidate (1) Nominee; (2) one seeking an office, position, or right.

canon [KAN uhn] Basic general principle or rule, as, the canons of ethics of the bar.

canvass Act of tallying votes or determining opinions.

capable Competent, qualified, possessing legal qualification.

capacity Ability, qualification, stature.

☆ **capacity** In criminal justice usage, the legal ability of a person to commit a criminal act; the mental and physical ability to act with purpose and to be aware of the certain, probable or possible results of one's conduct.

capias [KAP ee uhs] (that you take) An order to arrest.

capital (1) Property or estate; (2) gain or loss from sale of property; (3) source of income or interest; (4) fixed assets used in conduct of business; (5) seat of government.

capital crime Crime punishable by death.

☆ **capital offense** I. A criminal offense punishable by death. II. In some penal codes, an offense which may be punishable by death or by imprisonment for life.

capitalize (1) To profit by, as, to capitalize on an idea; (2) to compute, appraise or estimate the present value of an income extended over a period of time; (3) to supply capital, as, to capitalize a business; (4) to determine amount of capital stock to be authorized or issued.

capitation tax Poll tax, tax upon the person.

capitulation Surrender, yielding.

capricious Changeable, erratic, based upon whim.

caption (1) That part of a legal instrument showing names of parties, name of court and court docket number; (2) heading or title of a document or article.

capture Taking or seizing of person or property.

carbon copy Reproduction of an original by means of carbon impressed upon the copy as the original is being made.

cardinal (1) Central, basic, or critical, as, a cardinal element in a plan; (2) dignitary of Catholic Church, next in rank to the Pope.

care Serious attention, charge, custody, management, prudence, safekeeping, regard.

☆ **career criminal** In prosecutorial and law enforcement usage, a person having a past record of multiple arrests or convictions for serious crimes, or an unusually large number of arrests or convictions for crimes of varying degrees of seriousness.

careless Negligent, unconcerned, heedless.

carnal (1) Relating to crude bodily satisfaction; (2) sexual, sensual.

carnal abuse (1) Sex act not amounting to penetration; (2) sexual contact between a male and a female minor, with or without penetration.

carnal knowledge Sexual intercourse.

carrier (1) Transporter for hire of persons or property, as, a common carrier; (2) insurance company bound on a risk.

carry To bear, transport, have upon one's person.

carry arms To wear or have weapons upon one's person for offensive or defensive action.

carry on a business To conduct or continue a mercantile operation.

carte blanche [kahrt blahnsh] Unlimited authority; literally, a white sheet of paper, as a signed instrument of authority given to an agent to be filled in as the agent may see fit.

cartel [kahr TEL] Voluntary combination of businesses of common interests to control production, distribution and price of their products.

case Action, controversy, condition, special set of circumstances.

☆ **case** At the level of police or prosecutorial investigation, a set of circumstances under investigation involving one or more persons; at subsequent steps in criminal proceedings, a charging document alleging the commission of one or more crimes, or a single defendant charged with one or more crimes; in juvenile or correctional proceedings, a person who is the object of agency action.

case at bar The particular legal action under consideration.

case in point A judicial opinion dealing with issues similar to one being researched.

case law Aggregate of reported cases comprising the law on a given subject, as distinguished from statutory law.

☆ **caseload (corrections)** The total number of clients registered with a correctional agency or agent on a given date or during a specified time period, often divided into active supervisory cases and inactive cases, thus distinguishing between clients with whom contact is regular, and those with whom it is not.

☆ **caseload (court)** The number of cases requiring judicial action at a certain time, or the number of cases acted upon in a given court during a given time period.

case system Method of teaching law by study of leading cases.

cashier Officer of a bank or other organization entrusted with receipt and payment of its funds.

cash surrender value Reserve value of a life insurance policy available to its owner, representing excess of premiums paid over mortality costs and overhead charges.

cash value (1) Value of an article at market price, with payment on delivery of the article; (2) usual selling price, fair market price.

cast (1) To deposit formally, as, to cast a ballot; (2) to discard, as, to cast off restraint; (3) to impel with force, throw.

castigate To punish, severely criticize.

casual Haphazard, occasional, uncertain, precarious, random.

casual employment Occasional, irregular, incidental, unexpected employment.

casualty Serious accident, disaster, victim, as, a casualty loss by fire.

casus belli [KAY suhs BEL ahy] Cause of war.

caucus Conference of leaders or members of a group to select candidates or plan strategy.

causa [KOU zuh] Cause, reason, motive, inducement.

causa mortis [KOU zuh MAWR tis] In contemplation of imminent death.

causa proxima [KOU zuh PROK si muh] Immediate, producing cause.

cause -n. (1) That which produces an effect or result; (2) ground of legal action; (3) reason, motive; -v. (4) to serve as occasion of; bring into existence.

cause célébre [kawz say LEB ruh] Sensational, widely-known case, episode or situation.

cause of action Ground on which a legal action may be brought.

causeway A raised roadbed through low land.

caution -n. Warning, precaution; -v. to admonish, put on guard.

cautious Careful, prudent.

caveat [KO vay ot] (let him beware) Caution.

caveat emptor [KO vay ot EMP tawr] (let the buyer beware) Warning maxim applicable in trading.

cease To stop, discontinue, terminate.

cease and desist order Order by an administrative agency to refrain from a practice found by the agency to be unfair.

cede [seed] To yield, grant, assign, transfer.

celebrate (1) To engage in joyful ceremony, as, to celebrate an anniversary; (2) to perform or solemnize a sacrament, as, to celebrate a marriage; (3) to extol, glorify; (4) to observe a holiday, perform a religious ceremony or take part in a festival.

celibacy (1) Condition of an unmarried person; (2) abstention from sexual intercourse.

censor One who reviews written matter as in a letter, book or play, and removes therefrom material deemed objectionable.

censorship Review of written matter for removal of material deemed objectionable, as in censorship of mail, books, and movies.

censure -n. Admonition for improper conduct; -v. to criticize adversely, disapprove.

census Official enumeration of persons or items in a given area.

centralization Unification of control and management in one organization or person.

certain (1) Precise, clearly known, definite, fixed, settled, as, a sum certain; (2) some among others; (3) sure, dependable, inevitable.

certainty Absence of doubt, quality of being certain.

cert. den. [suhrt duh NAHYD] **(certiorari denied)** [SUHR shee uh rah ree duh NAHYD] Determination by a superior court (such as the United States Supreme Court) by which it refuses to review the proceedings of an inferior court.

certificate Formal documentary testimonial or representation of some fact.

certificate of deposit Written acknowledgment by a bank of an interest bearing time deposit.

certificate of incorporation Instrument filed in a designated public office, by which a corporation is created.

certificate of occupancy Written acknowledgment by appropriate authority that premises comply with zoning and building regulations.

certificate of reasonable doubt Formal statement issued by trial or appellate court stating that it is reasonable to believe a criminal conviction may be reversed on appeal, so that defendant may be admitted to bail pending outcome of the appeal.

certificate of stock Written instrument stating ownership of designated number of shares of stock in a corporation.

certification Act of giving written acknowledgment.

certified check Negotiable instrument directing payment of money, on which acknowledgment has been made by a proper officer of the bank on which it was drawn that the maker's signature is genuine, that funds are allocated for its payments, and that the bank will pay it on presentation.

certified copy Copy of a document signed and certified as a true copy by the officer having custody of the original or by other authorized person.

certified public accountant One licensed and authorized by a state to examine books of account and make reports thereon.

certify To testify in writing, confirm, assure, license.

☆ **certiorari** [SUHR shee uh rah ree] A writ issued from an appellate court for the purpose of obtaining from a lower court the record of its proceedings in a particular case.

cession [SE shuhn] Surrender, act of yielding; in international law, transfer of territory by one sovereign state to another.

cestui que trust [SET ee kuh trust] Person who possesses the equitable and beneficial right to property where the legal estate is in a trustee.

cf. (confer) Compare.

chain of title Consecutive history of conveyances affecting a parcel of real property.

chairman Presiding officer of a group, such as chairman of a convention, organization or board of directors.

challenge -n. Act of accusing, objecting, protesting or taking objection, as, a challenge to a juror; -v. to call into question, stimulate, dare.

chambers Private rooms or office of a judge.

champerty and maintenance [CHAM puhr tee and MAYN tuh nens] Illegal agreement by which a party's right of action is maintained and paid for by a person having no interest in the subject matter, in return for a share of the proceeds.

champion -n. One who engages in a contest or speaks in behalf of another; -v. to defend, uphold, advocate, as, to champion an unpopular cause.

chance -adj. Unexpected, unforeseen, as, a chance encounter; -n. result of uncertain conditions, hazard, as, there is a chance of rain tomorrow; -v. to risk, accept hazard.

chancellor [CHAN suh luhr] Judge of a court of equity; official head of a university.

chancery [CHAN suh ree] Equity, jurisdiction in equity as distinguished from jurisdiction in law.

change -n. Alteration, modification, substitution; -v. to alter, exchange, modify.

change of beneficiary Designation of a beneficial interest in one person, in place of such interest formerly in another, as, change of beneficiary in a life insurance policy.

change of grade Elevation or depression of the surface of a street by order of competent authority.

☆ **change of venue** [chaynj uv VEN yoo] The movement of a case from the jurisdiction of one court to that of another court which has the same subject matter jurisdictional authority but is in a different geographic location.

channel Customary path, groove, as, the channel of a river.

chapter (1) Main division of a book; (2) local branch or unit of an organization, as, a chapter of a national organization.

character (1) Person's distinguishing attributes, essential nature; (2) complex of mental and moral qualities and habitual ethical traits; (3) mark, sign, distinctive quality, personality.

character evidence Testimony concerning a person's reputation in the community (more properly termed reputation evidence).

charge (1) Complaint, information or indictment; (2) burden, obligation, duty, liability, care, supervision; (3) instruction by court to jury prior to their deliberation in a case.

☆ **charge** In criminal justice usage, an allegation that a specified person(s) has committed a specific offense, recorded in a functional document such as a record of an arrest, a complaint, information or indictment, or a judgment of conviction.

chargeable Subject or liable to be charged, accused, held responsible.

☆ **charging document** *recommended statistical terminology* A formal written accusation submitted to a court, alleging that a specified person(s) has committed a specific offense(s).

charitable (1) Benevolent, kindly, as, a person of charitable views toward his associates; (2) having the character of charity, love and good will for others.

charitable bequest Devise to a religious, educational or social welfare organization for conduct of its work.

charitable corporation One devoted to advancement of a charitable purpose, such as a religious or social welfare corporation.

charitable trust Fiduciary relationship created for furtherance of a specified charitable purpose.

charity (1) Plan or effort to better condition of society; (2) benevolence, philanthropy, good will; (3) kindly or sympathetic disposition to aid needy or suffering persons.

charlatan [SHAHR luh tuhn] (1) Quack, fraud; (2) pretender to medical knowledge.

charter (1) Instrument from an authorized body in the nature of a grant, franchise or privilege; (2) act of legislature creating a corporation; (3) written instrument from constituted authorities of an order or society creating a branch or local unit and defining its powers.

chaste (1) Pure, innocent, abstaining from all sexual relations or from unlawful sexual relations; (2) restrained, subdued, modest.

chastity (1) Abstention from all sexual intercourse, or from unlawful sexual intercourse; (2) decency, modesty, purity in act and will.

chattel [CHA tuhl] Article of personal property.

chattel mortgage [CHA tuhl MAWR guhj]] Mortgage on personal property.

chattel real [CHA tuhl reel] A form of interest in real property which descends under law of personal property.

cheat -n. Deception, fraud, pretender, deceiver; -v. to deceive, defraud.

check -n. (1) Draft upon a bank for payment of money; -v. (2) to control, restrain, stop; (3) to examine and verify another's work; (4) to compare with a source, as, to check a copy against an original.

☆ **check fraud** The issuance or passing of a check, draft, or money order that is legal as a formal document, signed by the legal account holder but with the foreknowledge that the bank or depository will refuse to honor it because of insufficient funds or closed account.

check-off Authorized deduction made by employer from wages due employee, for a designated purpose, as, a check-off for payment of union dues.

chief -adj. Principal, leading, superior in authority, power or influence; -n. head, as, a head of state is its chief.

child (1) One under age of majority specified by statute; (2) a direct descendant of a parent.

☆ **child abuse** The standard name in the behavioral sciences for a pattern of parental behavior that includes physical abuse of a child.

☆ **child neglect** Situations where a child lacks proper care, including those where he suffers psychological or physical damage for any reason.

Ch. J. Chief Judge or Chief Justice.

chose [shohz] Thing, item of personal property.

chose in action [shohz in AK shuhn] Personal right that may be recovered by lawsuit.

circa [SUHR kuh] About, around, as, the house was built circa 1850.

circuit (1) Geographical division, as, the country is divided into circuits for the administration of judicial business; (2) circumference, area, scope.

circuit court (1) One that sits at two or more places; (2) in Federal practice the intermediate appellate court next in jurisdiction below the United States Supreme Court.

circuitous Indirect, roundabout.

circuity of action Roundabout, indirect course of legal proceeding.

circumstance Fact, occurrence, surrounding event, specific part, phase or attribute.

circumstantial evidence Evidence inferred from the existence of established facts, as, wet streets may indicate circumstantially that rain has occurred.

circumvent To encircle, defeat, anticipate.

cit. Citation.

citation (1) Reference to authorities in support of an argument; (2) summons to appear.

☆ **citation (appear)** *recommended statistical terminology* A written order issued by a law enforcement officer directing an alleged offender to appear in a specific court at a specified time in order to answer a criminal charge, and not permitting forfeit of bail as an alternative to court appearance.

☆ **citation (forfeit)** The name for those written orders where payment of money is expected to be forfeited as an alternative to the requirement of a court appearance.

cite (1) To summon; (2) to command one's presence; (3) to refer to authorities in support of an argument or proposition.

citizen Native or naturalized person who owes allegiance to a government and is entitled to its protection and its rights and privileges.

☆ **civil commitment.** I. In general usage, the action of a judicial officer or administrative body ordering a person to be placed in an institution or program for custody, treatment or protection, usually one administered by a health service. II. *recommended criminal justice statistical terminology* A non-penal commitment to a treatment facility resulting from findings made during criminal proceedings, either before or after a judgment.

civil contempt Violation of a legal mandate arising out of a dispute between two litigants, such as failure to pay alimony or obey a subpoena in a civil proceeding.

☆ **civil contempt** An offense against the party in whose behalf the mandate of the court was issued. A penalty of fine or confinement can be imposed. The purpose of the penalty is to enforce the court's original order, and the penalty can be avoided by compliance with that order.

civil remedy Redress which an injured party has in a civil court against the party committing the injury.

civil rights Basic rights granted to citizens by Constitution.

claimant One who asserts a right or title.

class action Legal proceeding brought by a representative party in behalf of all members of a group having the same cause of action.

☆ **clearance** In Uniform Crime Reports terminology, the event where a known occurrence of a Part I offense is followed by an arrest or other decision which indicates a solved crime at the police level of reporting.

☆ **clemency** In criminal justice usage the name for the type of executive or legislative action where the severity of punishment of a single person or a group of persons is reduced or the punishment stopped, or a person is exempted from prosecution for certain actions.

codicil A supplement to or modification of a will.

cohabitation (1) Living together as man and wife; (2) sexual intercourse.

☆ **cohort** In statistics, the group of individuals having one or more statistical factors in common in a demographic study.

coinage (1) Process of manufacture of metal money; (2) invention of new words.

coinsurance (1) Sharing of risk by two or more insurance underwriters; (2) insurance system by which an insured who fails to maintain adequate coverage to a stipulated percentage suffers damage in the event of loss in proportion to the deficiency.

coitus [KOH i tuhs] Completed act of sexual intercourse.

collateral (1) Supplementary, ancillary, subsidiary; (2) security to assure performance, as, a deposit of stocks with a lender as collateral to secure repayment of a loan.

collateral attack Attempt to avoid or defeat a judicial proceeding by argument directed to an incidental issue, not related to the main issue raised by the pleadings.

collateral estoppel [kuh LAT uh ruhl e STOP uhl] Defeat of a legal issue by reason of some relevant prior and subsidiary determination.

collateral fact Actual circumstances not directly or immediately connected with the principal issue in dispute.

collateral impeachment Attempt to defeat a judicial proceeding by assertion of an issue not relevant to the main issue.

collateral line Succession to an inherited estate by a line of descent connecting persons having a common ancestor, as, descent from brother to brother.

collective bargaining Negotiation between employer and representatives of organized employees in respect to terms and conditions of employment.

collide To strike against, meet in direct opposition.

collision Violent encounter, sudden impact between two objects, disagreement.

colloquy [KOL uh kwee] Conversation, serious discussion.

collusion Deceitful or secret arrangement between persons with intent to defraud another.

collusive Deceitfully joined, fraudulent.

color (1) Appearance, semblance, aspect; (2) apparent right, appearance of authenticity.

colorable (1) That which is seemingly valid and genuine, plausible; (2) counter feit, not authentic, feigned.

color of law Appearance of legal right.

color of office Pretense or appearance of authority by virtue of an office, which office lacks the authority claimed.

color of title Apparent but invalid title.

combination in restraint of trade Association of two or more persons or organizations to restrict trade, regulate competition, maintain prices or otherwise interfere with free competition.

comity [KOM i tee] Courtesy, respect, mutual consideration, as, comity between states to assist in enforcing each other's laws.

command -n. Imperative direction, order, mandate; -v. to order, enjoin, control, govern.

comment -n. (1) Expression of judgment or interpretation; (2) statement intended to explain, illustrate or criticize; -v. (3) to remark, observe, discuss, criticize.

commercial paper Negotiable instruments, such as checks, bills of exchange and promissory notes.

commingle To join together in one, mingle, mix together.

commission (1) Rank or authority conferred; (2) authority to do some act, as, a commission to take depositions; (3) body of persons presiding in a governmental function, with powers appropriate to their duties; (4) act of perpetrating an offense; (5) percentage compensation for broker's services, as, a real estate broker's commission.

commissioner (1) Person charged with administration of law in some particular subject matter, as, commissioner of police; (2) member of a commission.

commission merchant One who sells goods for another and receives compensation from the owner in proportion to the sale price of the goods.

commit (1) To perpetrate, perform, as, to commit a crime; (2) to deliver into custody, as, to commit a person to prison.

commitment (1) Written instrument directing imprisonment; (2) act of doing or performing something; (3) obligation to carry out some action or policy.

☆ **commitment** *recommended statistical terminology* The action of a judicial officer ordering that a person subject to judicial proceedings be placed in a particular kind of confinement or residential facility, for a specific reason authorized by law; also, the result of the action, the admission to the facility.

committee Person or group having jurisdiction to consider, determine, investigate or manage some particular matter, as, a committee to manage the affairs of an incompetent person.

committing magistrate Judicial officer authorized to hold preliminary examination of one charged with crime, and to discharge person, hold him in custody or fix bail pending further prosecution of the charge.

common (1) General; pertaining to all or to a number; (2) usual, ordinary, familiar, prevalent; (3) shared or owned by several, jointly.

common knowledge Matter of such general application that court may take judicial knowledge of it, without necessity of proof.

common law Body of law as developed in England, based on customs, usage, and decisions, changed and adapted in the light of different circumstances and new situations; in United States, law as it existed in England at time of the American Revolution or other time fixed by statute.

common-law contempt Criminal form of contempt, as distinguished from civil form.

common-law copyright Exclusive right of an author to his unpublished literary creations, giving him control over first publication of his work or right to prevent its publication, and continuing until the work is published.

common-law crime One punishable at common law, as distinguished from statutory crime enacted by legislative body and not known at common law.

common-law larceny Taking and carrying away personal property of another, with intent to deprive the owner of his property, and convert it to use of the taker.

common-law marriage Agreement by man and woman to live together as husband and wife, and cohabitation without religious or civil ceremony or contract (illegal in many jurisdictions, including New York).

common-law wife (1) Female party to a common-law marriage; (2) female who asserts claim as wife after death of alleged husband, based upon claim of common-law marriage.

common nuisance Danger or annoyance to general public or persons in a particular locality.

common stock Capital invested in a corporation, not entitled to preference as compared with other securities of the corporation.

commonwealth (1) Corporate entity of a government, as, the Commonwealth of Massachusetts; (2) group of persons united by common consent and interest.

communism System of social and economic organization espoused by Communist Party, as in Union of Soviet Socialist Republics, whereby means of production are owned by the state, and private property does not exist.

communist (1) One who belongs to the Communist Party; (2) one who believes in and supports communism.

community (1) Neighborhood, vicinity, locality; (2) group having common interests.

community of interest Participation by persons in a joint endeavor directed to their mutual interest.

community property Property owned in common by husband and wife, acquired during or as an incident of their marriage.

commutation (1) Change, substitution; (2) substitution of a lesser punishment for a greater; reduction of punishment.

☆ **commutation (of sentence)** An executive act changing a punishment from a greater to a lesser penalty; in correctional usage, a reduction of the term of confinement resulting in immediate release or reduction of remaining time to be served; also, the change from a sentence of death to a term of imprisonment.

commute (1) To change punishment to one less severe; (2) to change, substitute, alter.

commuted value Amount required to provide for future payments of an annuity.

compact -adj. Closely united or arranged, brief; -n. agreement, contract, as, an interstate compact.

company General term referring to group of persons united in purpose.

comparable Similar, substantially equal, equivalent.

comparative Based on comparison or relative evaluation with another.

comparative negligence Doctrine permitting recovery by plaintiff where his negligence was less than that of the defendant, the damages being divided between the parties in proportion to the fault of each.

compatibility Agreement, coordination, congruity, as, compatibility of husband and wife.

compel To force, drive, require.

compensable That for which payment or compensation should be made, as, a compensable injury.

compensation (1) Payment of damages, making good; (2) remuneration or equivalent given for property taken, value received or services rendered; (3) something that equalizes or neutralizes.

compensatory Equivalent, making up for loss.

compensatory damages Reimbursement for actual loss or injury, as distinguished from exemplary or punitive damages.

competence (1) Sanity, mental capacity, functional adequacy; (2) qualification, ability, adequacy, capability.

competent Legally qualified, mentally and physically capable, satisfactory, adequate.

competent authority One having jurisdiction and power with respect to the subject matter.

competent court One having legal jurisdiction of the subject matter.

competent evidence That which is legally admissible in a lawsuit.

competent witness One legally qualified to give testimony.

competition Rivalry.

compilation Methodical assembly from various sources, as, a compilation of references on some subject matter.

compile To gather together, collect and assemble, gather as an original work, as, to compile a dictionary.

complainant Person on whose allegation a legal proceeding is founded, as, the complainant in a criminal prosecution.

☆ **complaining witness** In criminal proceedings, the person who originally causes the case to be prosecuted, or who initiates the complaint against the defendant, usually the victim.

complaint (1) First pleading by a plaintiff in a civil action; (2) sworn allegation before a magistrate charging one with crime; (3) expression of protest, grief, injustice; (4) formal allegation of some wrong, as, a complaint to a health department concerning an unsanitary condition.

☆ **complaint** I. In general criminal justice usage, any accusation that a person(s) has committed an offense(s), received by or originating from a law enforcement or prosecutorial agency, or received by a court. II. In judicial process usage, a formal document submitted to the court by a prosecutor, law enforcement officer, or other person, alleging that a specified person(s) has committed a specified offense(s) and requesting prosecution.

complicated Hard to understand, involved, intricate.

☆ **complicity** Any conduct on the part of a person other than the chief actor in the commission of a crime, in which the person intentionally or knowingly serves to further the intent to commit the crime, aids in the commission of the crime, or assists the person who has committed the crime to avoid prosecution or to escape from justice.

comply To act in conformity with, yield, assent.

composition (1) Agreement or settlement whereby differences are resolved; (2) agreement by which creditors agree to accept proportion of their debts from the debtor in satisfaction of the whole sum; (3) arrangement or combination of parts.

composition in bankruptcy Arrangement by which a bankrupt is permitted to retain his assets, upon condition that he will make payments to total a liquidated sum.

compos mentis [KOM puhs MEN tis] Sound of mind.

compound a crime (1) To agree not to prosecute one charged with a crime, on condition of reparation, reward or a bribe; (2) to conceal a crime, delay prosecution therefor, withhold evidence or abstain from prosecution.

☆ **compounding a criminal offense** Unlawful agreement by a person to forebear or cease prosecution, or assistance in prosecution, in return for reparation or any other payment of money or thing of value.

compound interest Interest earned upon combined sum of interest previously earned and added to principal.

compromise -n. (1) Agreement to settle differences or a cause of action by mutual concessions; -v. (2) to abate demands in order to achieve agreement; (3) to embarrass, humiliate or shame, as, to compromise one's integrity by falsehood.

compromise verdict Verdict of a jury based upon reconciliation or adjustment of conflicting views, as distinguished from verdict based upon conscientious beliefs.

compulsion (1) Force used to bring about a result; (2) coercion, duress; (3) irresistible impulse, as, a compulsion to steal or commit arson.

compulsory Involuntary, coerced, enforced.

compulsory arbitration Determination of a controversy by an arbitrator whose findings are enforceable against the parties.

☆ **computer crime** A popular name for crimes committed by use of a computer or crimes involving misuse or destruction of computer equipment or computerized information, sometimes specifically theft committed by means of manipulation of a computerized financial transaction system, or the use of computer services with intent to avoid payment.

concede To yield, admit, allow, acknowledge, as, to concede a point in an argument.

conception (1) Idea, notion, concept; (2) commencement of pregnancy.

concert Unity, concord, agreement, as, to act in concert.

concession Voluntary grant, yielding of a claim, rebate, abatement, admission, as, a concession of one month's rent on the signing of a lease.

conciliation (1) Process by which a third party endeavors to cause agreement between opposing parties, as, conciliation of a labor dispute by a conciliator mediator; (2) effort to establish harmony.

conclusion of fact Logical determination based on established facts or valid inference.

conclusion of law Legal determination arrived at by application of legal rules.

conclusive evidence That which overcomes and determines all doubt.

conclusory statement One which makes a determination, without establishing the basis on which the determination was made.

concordat [kon KAWR dot] Compact or formal agreement between two bodies, as, a concordat between a national government and a religious group.

concubinage [kon KYOO buh nuhj] Cohabitation of man and woman without marriage.

concubine [KON kyoo bahn] Woman who cohabits with a man as his wife although not married to him.

concur To agree, act together, consent, approve, agree.

concurrence Agreement, cooperation, union.

concurrent Running together, contemporaneous, operating simultaneously.

concurrent sentence Term of imprisonment to be served at the same time as another sentence of imprisonment is being served.

☆ **concurrent sentence** *recommended statistical terminology* A sentence that is one of two or more sentences imposed at the same time after conviction for more than one offense and to be served at the same time; or, a new sentence imposed upon a person already under sentence(s) for a previous offense(s), to be served at the same time as one or more of the previous sentences.

☆ **concurring opinion** An opinion which states the reasons and reasoning of one or more judges who agree with the majority decision, but on different grounds.

concussion Injury to one's person without laceration of tissue, caused by a fall, blow or other external injury.

condemn (1) To pronounce as wrong or evil; (2) to appropriate private property for public use under right of eminent domain.

condemnation (1) Process of taking private property for public use and making payment therefor; (2) censure, blame.

condition (1) Mode or state of being, essential quality; (2) agreement in regard to some uncertain future event.

conditional That which is founded upon a condition; that is, founded upon an uncertain future event or supposition.

conditional bill of sale Instrument whereby seller retains title to property sold although possession is delivered to buyer, until some condition is performed, usually payment of the purchase price.

☆ **conditionally suspended sentence** *recommended statistical terminology* A court disposition of a convicted person specifying a penalty of a fine or commitment to confinement but holding execution of the penalty in abeyance upon good behavior.

☆ **conditional pardon** An executive act releasing a person from punishment, contingent upon his or her performance or non-performance of specified acts.

☆ **conditional release** *recommended statistical terminology* The release by executive decision from a federal or state correctional facility, of a prisoner who has not served his or her full sentence and whose freedom is contingent upon obeying specified rules of behavior.

conditional sale One in which vesting of title depends upon performance of conditions made a part of the sale.

conditional sale contract Formal agreement by which possession of subject matter is delivered to buyer with title remaining in seller until specified conditions are performed, usually payment of the purchase price.

condominium Estate in real property by which the several owners of units in a building containing more than one unit have an absolute undivided interest in their respective units, which interest is alienable, mortgageable, devisable and inheritable.

condonation (1) Pardoning of a conjugal offense (usually adultery) by a party to the marriage; (2) voluntary overlooking or forgiveness of an offense.

condone To pardon, forgive.

conduct -n. Behavior, mode of action, management; -v. to guide, escort, manage, control.

confederacy (1) Association of two or more persons to commit an unlawful act; (2) compact between two or more persons for mutual action.

confederate Ally, one of parties to a confederacy.

confess To admit the truth of a charge, concede, acknowledge.

confession (1) Voluntary admission of guilt; (2) substantial acknowledgement of guilt.

confession and avoidance In pleading, a defense which admits the facts alleged but avoids or neutralizes their legal effect by allegations of new matter.

confidence Trust, reliance.

confidence game Swindle.

☆ **confidence game** A popular name for false representation to obtain money or any other thing of value, where deception is accomplished through the trust placed by the victim in the character of the offender.

confidential Intended to be kept secret, private.

confidential communication Information passing between persons in a confidential or fiduciary relationship to each other and privileged against disclosure, as a communication between husband and wife, attorney and client, physician and patient, priest and penitent.

confinement Physical restraint.

☆ **confinement** In correctional terminology, physical restriction of a person to a clearly defined area from which he or she is lawfully forbidden to depart and from which departure is usually constrained by architectural barriers and/or guards or other custodians.

confirm To ratify, make firm, give new assurance, corroborate, verify, validate.

confiscate (1) To seize and condemn private property for public use; (2) to deprive of property by seizure.

conflict of laws Branch of jurisprudence relating to diversity or inconsistency of several legal jurisdictions over same subject matter.

conformity Agreement, harmony, compliance.

confrontation In criminal law, procedure whereby defendant may observe (confront) witness against him, face to face, and is afforded opportunity to cross-examine the witness.

confute [kuhn FYOOT] To prove false, overcome by argument.

congregate To come together assemble.

congregation Assembly of persons.

conjecture -n. Surmise, guess, supposition; -v. to indulge in, surmise, to suppose.

conjugal [KON juh guhl] Matrimonial.

conjunctive Connecting, united.

connect To join, meet, unite.

connection (1) State of being joined, act of connecting, union; (2) context, reference; (3) sexual intercourse.

connivance (1) Permission or consent given by one to wrongdoing by another; (2) intentional failure to prevent wrongdoing by another.

connive (1) To pretend ignorance of wrongdoing; (2) to fail intentionally to prevent wrongdoing by another; (3) to give permission or consent to wrongdoing by another.

consanguinity [kon sang GWIN uh tee] Blood relationship, descent from a common ancestor.

conscience Sense of moral right and wrong.

conscientious objector One who refuses military service on religious or moral grounds.

conscientious scruple Objection based upon one's moral views, as, a conscientious scruple against imposition of death penalty in a capital case.

conscription Compulsory military service.

consecutive Successive, one after the other.

☆ **consecutive sentence** *recommended statistical terminology* A sentence that is one of two or more sentences imposed at the same time, after conviction for more than one offense, and which is served in sequence with the other sentences; or, a new sentence for a new conviction, imposed upon a person already under sentence(s) for a previous offense(s), which is added to a previous sentence(s), thus increasing the maximum time the offender may be confined or under supervision.

consensual contract One based solely upon consent of the parties without any formal act.

consensual marriage One based solely upon consent of competent parties without any formal act.

consensus Agreement, meeting of minds, harmony, accord.

consent Agreement, acquiescence, compliance.

consent decree Binding judgment entered in a court on consent of the parties, following an equity suit.

consequential damages Damages flowing incidentally from an act rather than from the act itself.

conservator [kuhn SUHR vuh tawr] Guardian, preserver, protector.

conserve To preserve, save from loss.

consider To examine, deliberate, reflect.

consideration (1) Price paid or inducement for a contract; (2) motive, reason, contemplation.

consign To send, deliver or transfer property to an agent for his act in behalf of the sender.

consignee One to whom goods are sent, for sale, without transfer of title.

consignment (1) Act of consigning goods; (2) goods sent from consignor to consignee.

consignor One who sends goods in a consignment.

consistent Harmonious, compliant, unchanging.

consolidate (1) To unite into one mass; (2) to make solid, compress.

consolidated laws Compilation of all laws of a state, usually by subject matter.

☆ **consolidated trial** A trial in which two or more defendants named in separate charging documents are tried together, or where a given defendant is tried on charges contained in two or more charging documents.

consolidation Union of several into one.

consort -n. Companion, spouse; -v. to associate, harmonize.

consortium [kuhn SAWR shee uhm] (1) In marriage, right of husband and wife to companionship, aid and affection of each other; (2) in commerce, international business agreement or combination.

conspicuous Prominent, manifest.

conspiracy Agreement by two or more persons to engage in an unlawful act.

☆ **conspiracy** An agreement by two or more persons to commit or to effect the commission of an unlawful act, or to use unlawful means to accomplish an act which is not in itself unlawful, plus some overt act in furtherance of the agreement.

conspirator One of two or more persons associated in a conspiracy.

conspire To engage in conspiracy, to plan an unlawful act with another.

constable Local law enforcement officer.

constant Fixed, invariable, steady.

constituted authority Public official or body duly chosen.

constitution Fundamental law of a state, nation or organization.

constitutional Authorized by constitution.

constitutional law Branch of law concerned with correct construction and interpretation of a constitution, and the nature, power and organization of government.

constitutional right Fundamental right provided by constitution and not amenable to change by legislation.

constraint Restraint, compulsion.

construct To build, erect.

construction (1) Process of interpretation of a statute, written instrument or oral agreement; (2) creation of something new, as, construction of a building.

constructive Implied by law, though not actual in fact.

constructive eviction Act by landlord which so deprives or materially impairs enjoyment by tenant of his interest in leased premises as to be legally equivalent to actual eviction.

constructive force Latent or implied force which produces effect comparable to use of actual force.

constructive notice Information or knowledge of a fact, implied by law as having been given to a person although not given in fact.

construe To ascertain meaning, as, to construe the terms of a contract.

consul [KON suhl] Representative of a country in a foreign jurisdiction.

consular [KON suh luhr] Pertaining to function of a consul.

consulate [KON suh luht] Office of a consul.

consumer fraud Deceptive or misleading practice by merchant or salesman.

☆ **consumer fraud** Deception of the public with respect to the cost, quality, purity, safety, durability, performance, effectiveness, dependability, availability and adequacy of choice relating to goods or services offered or furnished, and with respect to credit or other matters relating to terms of sales.

consummate -adj. Completed, perfect, extreme; -v. to finish, fulfill, achieve, complete.

consummation (1) Completion of a thing, the end; (2) sexual intercourse following marriage.

contemner [kuhn TEM nuhr] One who has committed contempt of court.

contemplate (1) To consider with continued attention; (2) to intend, plan, meditate, consider.

contemplation (1) Continued attention of the mind to a particular subject; (2) act of looking forward to an event, expectation.

contemplation of death Apprehension, expectation, thought of death, arising from some presently existing condition or danger.

contempt Wilful disregard, disobedience, disrespect of the authority of a court or legislative body.

contempt of court (1) Act which embarrasses or obstructs the court in its administration of Justice; (2) wilful disobedience to lawful mandate of a court. (See also **civil contempt** and **criminal contempt**).

☆ **contempt of court** Intentionally obstructing a court in the administration of justice, or acting in a way calculated to lessen its authority or dignity, or failing to obey its lawful orders.

contentious Contested, litigated, argumentative.

contest -n. Struggle, action, dispute between opponents; -v. to oppose, resist, dispute.

context Parts of a written or spoken passage preceding and following a particular portion,as, to read matter in context so that its proper meaning may be determined from that which precedes and follows it.

contiguous (1) Touching or connected (customary meaning in real estate transactions); (2) nearby, adjoining; (3) next in time or sequence; (4) near in time or sequence.

continent -adj. Exercising restraint of sexual desire, temperate, moderate; -n. great geographical division of land area of the earth.

contingency An event that may or may not happen.

contingent Conditional, dependent upon the possible happening of some event.

contingent claim One not yet accrued and dependent on a future and uncertain event.

contingent fee Compensation for services, to be paid in the event of success, as, a lawyer accepting as a contingent fee an agreed percentage of amount obtained for his client.

contingent fund Allocation of moneys for undetermined but anticipated expenses.

contingent liability Obligation dependent on a future and uncertain event.

continuance (1) Postponement of a pending action to a later date; (2) making current a report prepared as of an earlier date, as, a continuance of title search in transfer of title to real property.

continuous Without interruption.

contra [KON truh] Against, on the contrary, opposite to.

contraband Goods or materials which are prohibited or illegal.

contract Agreement between competent parties, for a consideration, which creates an obligation on the parties to do or refrain from doing some act.

contractor One who agrees with another for a specified compensation to render a service, furnish materials or both.

contradict To disprove, dispute, take issue with.

contrary -adj. Against, opposed, in conflict with; -n. the opposite.

contravene To oppose, dispute disregard, deny.

contravention Violation, infraction, transgression, breach.

contribute (1) To lend assistance, share in a common purpose or act; (2) to submit articles for publication.

☆ **contributing to the delinquency of a minor** The offense committed by an adult who in any manner causes, encourages or aids a juvenile to commit a crime or status offense.

contribution (1) Participation by each of two or more persons in an act; (2) something voluntarily given, as, a charitable contribution; (3) payment of one individual's share in a loss for which several are jointly liable.

contributory Lending assistance to desired result.

contributory negligence Lack of prudent care by an injured party, which, in combination with negligence of the defendant, is the proximate cause of the injury complained of.

control Power, restraint, authority in management, regulation or conduct.

controvert To dispute, deny, oppose.

contumacious [kon too MAY shuhs] Stubbornly disobedient, rebellious, insubordinate, as, a contumacious witness.

contumacy [kon TOO muh see] Stubborn resistance to authority, wilful contempt of court.

contumely [kon TOO muh lee] Scornful insolence, disdain, insult, humiliation.

contusion [kuhn TOO zhuhn] A bruise or injury to an external part of the body caused by a fall or blow, with or without breaking of the skin.

convene (1) To meet, come together, as, the court will convene at 10:00 a.m.; (2) to summon or cause persons to appear before some body having authority.

convenience and necessity Basis upon which common carrier is given a franchise by public regulatory body.

convenient Suitable, proper, appropriate.

convention (1) Custom, usage, practice; (2) meeting, assembly of persons for some purpose, as, a political convention; (3) agreement between persons or parties.

conventional Customary, traditional, usual, ordinary.

conversion (1) Unlawful appropriation of another's property; (2) change from one status to another, as, a conversion of American dollars into English pounds.

convey (1) To pass or transfer title to property to another (usually real property); (2) to lead, conduct, transport, carry.

conveyance (1) Transfer of ownership of real property; (2) act by which title to property is transferred; (3) means of transportation.

convict -n. One whose guilt has been determined in a judicial proceeding; -v. to find one guilty of some crime.

convicted Found guilty by legal process.

conviction (1) Act of finding and adjudging a person guilty of a crime; (2) strong persuasion or belief.

☆ **conviction** *recommended statistical terminology* The judgment of a court, based on the verdict of a jury or judicial officer, or on the guilty plea or nolo contendere plea of the defendant, that the defendant is guilty of the offense(s) with which he or she has been charged.

convince To secure agreement, overcome by argument.

convincing proof Quantity of proof sufficient to establish a question beyond a reasonable doubt.

convocation General assembly.

convoy -n. A force organized for safe passage, as, a convoy of ships; -v. to provide safe passage, accompany, escort.

cooperate To act jointly with others in a common goal.

cooperation Combined effort of several toward a common goal.

cooperative -adj. Helpful, contributing towards a common goal; -n. association of persons joined in a mutual enterprise, as, membership in a housing cooperative.

coordinate -adj. Equal, of the same rank, as, a court of coordinate jurisdiction; -v. to adjust, bring in harmony, as, to coordinate a plan.

coordinate jurisdiction Equal, concurrent, equivalent authority.

copartner Member of a partnership.

copartnership Business association of two or more individuals acting as one.

copy -n. Reproduction, imitation of an original; -v. to duplicate, reproduce.

copyright Exclusive privilege given by law to an author or originator to reproduce, publish and sell his original work.

coram [KAW ruhm] Before, in the presence of.

☆ **coram nobis** [KAW ruhm NOH bis] A writ issued by a court for the purpose of correcting a judgment entered in the same court, on the ground of error of fact. This writ is sought where the error which is alleged to have occurred does not appear on the record of court proceedings. The petitioner asks the court to go beyond the official record to examine the relevant facts If the petitioner's allegations are sustained, the writ is issued to correct the judgment.

coram non judice [KAW ruhm nohn JOO di see] Before a judge or court not having jurisdiction or not being properly constituted.

co-respondent In an action for divorce based on adultery, the person with whom the marriage partner is claimed to have had sexual relations.

corner -n. ;Combination of traders who buy up available supply of a commodity in order to advance its price.

corollary Deduction, practical consequence, result.

coroner Public official having duty to hold an inquest into the cause of violent or unusual death.

coroner's inquest Examination before a coroner and jury as to cause of unnatural death.

corporal Bodily, material.

corporal punishment Physical bodily chastisement of any degree of severity.

corporate body Private corporation.

corporate bond Written obligation, under seal, of a corporation to repay a loan with interest.

corporate franchise Formal right given by government to a corporation to conduct its business.

corporate purpose Aim relevant to the object for which the corporation was founded.

corporation Artificial entity created under legislative sanction to engage in business or other specified activities.

corporeal [kawr PAW ree uhl] Tangible, material, having a body.

corporeal hereditaments [kawr PAW ree uhl he ruh DIT uh muhnts] Substantial permanent objects which may be inherited.

corpus [KAWR puhs] Body, person, whole, as, the corpus of a crime.

corpus delicti [KAWR puhs duh LIK tahy] Body of a crime, the crime itself material upon which crime has been committed.

corpus juris [KAWR puhs JOO ris] Body of law, comprehensive collection of law of a given jurisdiction.

☆ **correctional agency** *recommended statistical terminology* A federal, state, or local criminal or juvenile justice agency, under a single administrative authority, of which the principal functions are the intake screening supervision, custody, confinement, treatment, or pre-sentencing or pre-disposition investigation of alleged or adjudicated adult offenders, youthful offenders, delinquents, or status offenders.

☆ **correctional day program** *recommended statistical terminology* A publicly financed and operated nonresidential educational or treatment program for persons required by a judicial officer to participate.

☆ **correctional facility (adult)** *recommended statistical terminology* A building or part thereof, set of buildings, or area enclosing a set of buildings or structures, operated by a government agency for the physical custody, or custody and treatment, of sentenced persons or persons subject to criminal proceedings.

☆ **corrections** A generic term which includes all government agencies, facilities, programs, procedures, personnel, and techniques concerned with the intake, custody, confinement, supervision, or treatment, or pre-sentencing or predisposition investigation of alleged or adjudicated adult offenders, delinquents, or status offenders.

correlative Having a mutual relation, corresponding so that one necessarily implies existence of the other, as, in a democratic society, rights and duties of citizens are correlative.

corroborate To strengthen, give added credibility by additional or confirming data, confirm.

corroborating evidence Evidence supplementary to that already given and tending to strengthen or confirm it; additional evidence to the same point.

corroboration Act of strengthening, giving additional weight and credence to that already established.

corrupt -adj. Spoiled, tainted, debased, depraved, evil; -v. to spoil, taint, bribe.

corruption Illegality; that forbidden by law; depravity.

corruption of blood Result of attainder, in that the person attained can neither inherit nor transmit property by descent.

corruptly Illegally, with unlawful design to gain advantage.

costs (1) Expenses, such as fees and charges incurred by a party in pursuing a legal action; (2) generally, amount fixed by statute which may be awarded to party in whose favor a judgment is entered.

council Advisory or legislative body.

counsel -n. (1) One who gives advice, usually legal; (2) opinion, advice, direction; -v. (3) to advise, recommend, consult.

☆ **counsel** A person trained in the law, admitted to practice before the bar of a given jurisdiction, and authorized to advise, represent, and act for other persons in legal proceedings.

counselor (counsellor) (1) Adviser; (2) diplomatic official at an embassy or legation, ranking just below ambassador or minister.

counselor at law Attorney.

☆ **count** Each of the allegations of an offense in the charging document entered in the record of a court to initiate criminal proceedings.

counter -adj. Adverse, contrary, opposing; -v. to argue against, contend with, check, offset.

counterclaim Claim presented by a defendant as a cause of action to offset claim by the plaintiff.

counterfeit -adj. Spurious, fake, forged; -v. to forge, copy, imitate, disguise.

☆ **counterfeiting** The manufacture or attempted manufacture of a copy or imitation of a negotiable instrument with value set by law or convention, or the possession of such a copy without authorization, with the intent to defraud by claiming the genuineness of the copy.

countermand Change or revocation of orders, authority or instructions previously given.

counterpart (1) In conveyancing, a corresponding copy of the original instrument, as an indenture; (2) something remarkably similar to another.

countersign -n. Military secret signal; -v. to attest the authenticity on an instrument of a first signature by affixing a second.

☆ **count (prisoner)** I. In published summary data, usually the number of inmates present in a given facility or facility system on a regular, specified day of the year, quarter or month. II. In management usage, the daily, weekly, or other periodic tally of inmates present in a particular facility.

county Geographical division of a country or state, for administrative, judicial and political purposes.

coupled with an interest In the law of agency, the vesting in an agent of a monetary interest in the subject matter of the agency.

course of employment Activity arising out of and in the course of employment, or naturally flowing from and directly connected therewith.

court (1) That organ of government charged with the administration of justice; (2) judge presiding.

☆ **court** *recommended statistical terminology* An agency or unit of the judicial branch of government, authorized or established by statute or constitution, and consisting of one or more judicial officers, which has the authority to decide upon cases, controversies in law, and disputed matters of fact brought before it.

☆ **court administrator** The official responsible for supervising and performing administrative tasks for a given court(s).

☆ **court calendar** The court schedule; the list of events comprising the daily or weekly work of a court, including the assignment of the time and place for each hearing or other item of business, or the list of matters which will be taken up in a given court term.

☆ **court clerk** An elected or appointed court officer responsible for maintaining the written records of the court and for supervising or performing the clerical tasks necessary for conducting judicial business; also, any employee of a court whose principal duties are to assist the court clerk in performing the clerical tasks necessary for conducting judicial business.

☆ **court decision** In popular usage, any official determination made by a judicial officer; in special judicial usages, any of several specific kinds of determinations made by particular courts.

☆ **court disposition** For statistical reporting purposes, generally, the judicial decision terminating proceedings in a case before judgment is reached, or the judgment; the data items representing the outcome of judicial proceedings and the manner in which the outcome was arrived at.

☆ **courtesy supervision** Supervision by the correctional agency of one jurisdiction, of a person placed on probation by a court or on parole by a paroling authority in another jurisdiction, by informal agreement between agencies.

court martial Military court having jurisdiction over offenses relating to the military establishment and its personnel.

court of chancery [kawrt uv CHAN suh ree] Court having general equity powers.

court of claims Court having jurisdiction of claims against a government.

court of common pleas Court having original jurisdiction of matters according to common law principles.

court of first instance Court having original jurisdiction of a case.

☆ **court of general jurisdiction** *recommended statistical terminology* A trial court having original jurisdiction over all subject matter not specifically assigned to a court of limited jurisdiction.

court of inquiry Court, usually military, authorized to investigate a matter and render a report.

☆ **court of last resort** *recommended statistical terminology* An appellate court having final jurisdiction over appeals within a given state.

☆ **court of limited jurisdiction** *recommended statistical terminology* A trial court having original jurisdiction over only that subject matter specifically assigned to it by law.

court of oyer and terminer [kawrt uv OY uhr and TUHR mi nuhr] In American law, a state court for trial of felonies, usually a court having full criminal jurisdiction.

court of probate Court having jurisdiction over estates of decedents, minors and incompetents.

☆ **court of record** A court in which a complete and permanent record of all proceedings or specified types of proceedings is kept.

☆ **court order** A mandate, command or direction issued by a judicial officer in the exercise of his judicial authority.

☆ **court ordered release from prison** *recommended statistical terminology*
A provisional exit by judicial authority from a prison facility system of a
prisoner who has not served his or her full sentence, whose freedom is conditioned upon an appeal, a special writ, or other special legal proceedings.

☆ **court probation** *recommended statistical terminology* A criminal court
requirement that a defendant or offender fulfill specified conditions of behavior
in lieu of a sentence to confinement, but without assignment to a probation
agency's supervisory caseload.

☆ **court reporter** A person present during judicial proceedings, who records all
testimony and other oral statements made during the proceedings.

covenant -n. An agreement or stipulation made with some formality, as in a
deed; -v. to promise solemnly, pledge in formal agreement, stipulate.

cover (1) In insurance, to insure a risk pending issuance of a formal policy of
insurance; (2) doctrine under the Uniform Commercial Code where a
buyer, after breach of contract by seller may "in good faith and without
unreasonable delay, make any reasonable purchase of or contract to
purchase goods in substitution for those due from the seller."

coverture [KUV uhr chuhr] Legal status of a married woman.

C.P.A. Certified Public Accountant.

credentials Instruments which establish one's authority to act in given
circumstances.

credibility Believability, worthiness of belief.

credible Worthy of belief.

Credit (1) Ability to obtain goods or money on promise of future payment;
(2) balance in a person's favor in an account; (3) deduction from an
amount, otherwise due, as, a credit for returned merchandise; (4) faith,
trust, belief.

☆ **credit card fraud** The use or attempted use of a credit card in order to obtain
goods or services with the intent to avoid payment.

creditor One who gives credit; one to whom money is due.

creed (1) System of religious belief; (2) religious sect; (3) formulation of
principles and precepts.

cretinism [KREE tin i zuhm] Physical condition characterized by mental
deficiency and lack of physical and mental development.

crier Officer of a court who proclaims its orders and directions.

crime Act or omission of act prohibited by law and defined as either a felony
or-misdemeanor or which is punishable upon conviction in a
proceeding brought by the state.

☆ **crime** *recommended statistical terminology* An act committed or omitted in
violation of a law forbidding or commanding it for which the possible penalties
for an adult upon conviction include incarceration, for which a corporation can
be penalized by fine or forfeit, or for which a juvenile can be adjudged
delinquent or transferred to criminal court for prosecution.

☆ **Crime Index** In Uniform Crime Reports terminology, a set of numbers indicating
the volume, fluctuation and distribution of crimes reported to local law
enforcement agencies, for the United States as a whole and for its
geographical subdivisions, based on counts of reported occurrences of UCR
Index Crimes.

crimen falsi [KRAHY muhn FAWL see] Crime involving deceit or falsification, as
forgery or perjury.

☆ **crime rate** In national UCR reports, the number of Crime Index offenses known to police, per 100,000 population.

☆ **crime score** A number assigned from an established scale, signifying the seriousness of a given offense with respect to personal injury or damage to property.

criminal action Process by which one is accused of crime and brought to trial and punishment.

☆ **criminal case** *recommended statistical terminology* A case initiated in a court by the filing of a single charging document containing one or more criminal accusations against one or more identified persons.

criminal contempt Conduct in presence of court or judge or so near as to interfere with proceedings, which tends to degrade or obstruct justice; wilful disobedience of lawful order of a court.

☆ **criminal contempt** An offense against the court. A fine or confinement can be imposed for the purpose of punishment.

criminal conversation (1) Unlawful intercourse with a married person; (2) adultery.

☆ **criminal incident** In National Crime Survey terminology, a criminal event involving one or more victims and one or more offenders.

criminal information Complaint, sworn allegation charging a person with commission of designated crime.

criminal intent Unlawful design to commit a crime; malice.

criminal jurisdiction Authority for trial and punishment of criminal offenses.

☆ **criminal justice** In the strictest sense, the criminal (penal) law, the law of criminal procedure, and that array of procedures and activities having to do with the enforcement of this body of law.

☆ **criminal justice agency** *model definition* Any court with criminal jurisdiction and any government agency or identifiable subunit which defends indigents, or which has as its principal duty(s) the performance of criminal justice functions (prevention, detection, and investigation of crime; the apprehension, detention and prosecution of alleged offenders; the confinement or official correctional supervision of accused or convicted persons, or the administrative or technical support of these functions) as authorized and required by statute or executive order.

criminal law Branch of law concerned with violations of penal law and their punishment.

criminal libel Malicious defamation of a person by writing, punishable criminally.

☆ **criminal mischief** Intentionally destroying or damaging, or attempting to destroy or damage, the property of another without his consent, usually by a means other than burning.

criminal motive Inducement of the mind to intend and commit a crime.

criminal negligence Conduct by a person who fails to perceive a substantial and unjustifiable risk of a specified result or circumstance, where the risk is of such nature and degree that the failure to perceive it constitutes a gross deviation from the standard of care that a reasonable person would observe in the situation.

☆ **criminal offense** *recommended statistical terminology* An act committed or omitted in violation of a law forbidding or commanding it for which the possible penalties for an adult upon conviction include incarceration, for which a corporation can be penalized by fine or forfeit, or for which a juvenile can be adjudged delinquent or transferred to criminal court for prosecution.

☆ **criminal proceedings** The regular and orderly steps, as directed or authorized by statute or a court of law, taken to determine whether an adult accused of a crime is guilty or not guilty.

criminal syndicalism Crime of violence or advocacy of violence or other unlawful means of bringing about political change.

cross-action Legal action brought by defendant against plaintiff arising out of the same matter in controversy.

cross-claim Claim made by a defendant against a plaintiff or against a codefendant, concerning matters in controversy in the original proceeding.

cross-examination Examination of one's witness by the opposing party.

C. T. A. Cum testamento annexo (with the will annexed).

culpa [KUL puh] Fault, neglect, negligence.

culpability Fault, guilt.

☆ **culpability** 1. Blameworthiness; responsibility in some sense for an event or situation deserving of moral blame. II. In Model Penal Code (MPC) usage, a state of mind on the part of one who is committing an act, which makes him or her potentially subject to prosecution for that act.

culpable Guilty, criminal, meriting condemnation or censure.

culpable negligence Failure to exercise that degree of care which one of ordinary prudence would have used in same circumstances.

cum [kuhm] With.

cum animo criminale [kuhm 0 ni moh krim i N0 lee] With criminal intent.

cum grano salis [kuhm GR0 noh S0 lis] (with a grain of salt) With allowance for disbelief.

cum testamento annexo [kuhm tes tuh MEN toh u NEK soh] With the will annexed.

cumulative Additional, increasing, added together, as, the sentences of the court were cumulative.

cumulative evidence Additional or corroborative evidence to that already received.

cumulative sentence Sentence separately imposed to be served after expiration of a previous sentence.

cumulative voting Plan for electing directors of a corporation whereby stock-holders have voting power equal to their number of shares multiplied by number of directors to be chosen, which votes they may cast in any manner they desire.

cunnilingus [kun i LEENG guhs] Sexual contact of mouth and female sexual organ.

curative Tending to cure.

curator Guardian, manager, person appointed to take care of something for another, as, the curator of a museum.

☆ **curfew and loitering laws (juveniles)** In Uniform Crime Reports terminology, the name of the UCR offense category used to record and report arrests made for violations of curfew and loitering laws regulating the behavior of juveniles.

☆ **curfew violation** The offense of being found in a public place after a specified hour of the evening, usually established in a local ordinance applying only to persons under a specified age.

cursory Superficial, hasty, readily observable, as, a cursory examination.

curtail To shorten, abridge, reduce, diminish.

curtesy [KUHR tuh see] The potential interest which a husband has in his wife's estate after her death.

curtilage [KUHR ti luhj] Yard, ground and buildings surrounding a dwelling.

custodia legis [kuh STOH dee uh LEG is] In the custody of the law.

custodian Guardian, monitor; building superintendent.

custody Restraint, detention, safe keeping, guardianship.

☆ **custody** Legal or physical control of a person or thing; legal, supervisory or physical responsibility for a person or thing.

custom Practice established by long usage.

customary Ordinary, commonly practiced, according to custom or usage.

customer's man Employee of a securities brokerage firm who represents firm in its transactions with customers by receiving and executing their orders.

customs Taxes payable upon goods imported or exported.

cwt. Hundred-weight.

cy pres [see pray] (as near as) An equitable doctrine that in carrying out the charitable wishes of a testator, one should give effect as nearly as possible to the testator's intentions.

D

damage Loss due to harm, injury or deterioration.

damages Monetary compensation or indemnity for wrong or injury caused by the violation of a legal right.

damnify To cause damage or loss to.

damnum absque injuria [DAM nuhm AB skway in JOO ree uh] Damage which does not give rise to an action for damages against the person causing the loss.

danger Exposure to harm, injury or peril.

dangerous Hazardous, perilous, extremely unsafe.

☆ **dangerous person** In law enforcement usage, a person who, when at large, is believed likely to cause serious harm to himself or herself or to others.

dangerous weapon Any instrument which may produce a fatal injury.

date Point or fixation of time.

daughter An immediate female descendant of a parent.

day certain A specified day.

day in court Time and opportunity given for judicial determination of one's rights, as, to afford plaintiff his day in court.

days of grace Additional period allowed after the time limited for some action has expired.

D. B. N. (de bonis non) Of the goods not administered, as, an administrator de bonis non is appointed to succeed another who has left an estate partially unsettled.

deadly weapon One likely to produce death or serious bodily injury.

☆ **deadly weapon** An instrument designed to inflict serious bodily injury or death, or capable of being used for such a purpose.

dead storage Storage without use, as of an automobile remaining uninterruptedly in a garage.

deal -n. (1) Act of buying and selling; -v. (2) to transact business, to negotiate; (3) to divide, apportion.

dealer One who carries on a business of selling goods and commodities.

death (1) Cessation of life, total stoppage of bodily functions; (2) status of one who has lost all his civil rights and is considered legally dead.

death trap Structure or situation presenting imminent danger or risk to life.

debase (1) To lower in esteem; (2) to lower the quality or character of; (3) to depreciate the intrinsic value of.

debauch [duh BAWCH] To corrupt with lewdness, seduce.

debauchery [duh BAWCH uh ree] Sexual corruption, excessive indulgence of sexual desire.

debenture [duh BEN chuhr] An instrument under seal issued by a company as security for a loan.

debit (1) A sum charged to an account; (2) something disadvantageous.

de bonis asportatis [day BOH nis a spawr TO tis] Common law action to recover damages for taking away or damaging property.

de bonis non [day BOH nis nohn] Of the goods not administered, referring to that part of an estate not settled by an administrator.

de bonis non administratis [day BOH nis nohn ad min i STRO tis] Of the goods not administered (frequently abbreviated to de bonis non or d.b.n.).

debt Obligation, something due from one to another by agreement.

debtor One who owes a debt.

decease -n. Death; -v. to die.

deceased Dead person.

decedent [duh SEE duhnt] Deceased person.

deceit Fraudulent misrepresentation, trick.

deception Act of deceiving, intentional misleading by use of falsehood, fraud.

decide To evaluate reasons and make a choice.

decision (1) Judgment or decree of a court upon a question before it; (2) determination of a judicial nature; (3) finding by a court upon a question of law or fact; (4) act of deciding.

declarant [duh KLA ruhnt] One who makes a declaration.

declaration (1) Generally, a statement made out of court; (2) act of proclaiming or announcing publicly.

declaration against interest Statement which, when made, conflicts with financial interest of person making it. Such declarations may be received as evidence of the facts so declared.

declaratory Explanatory, that which establishes or fixes the meaning.

declaratory judgment One fixing rights of parties without ordering anything to be done.

declare To make known, publish, solemnly assert, announce.

decline -n. Downward tendency; -v. to refuse.

decree (1) Order of a court in an equity, admiralty or probate matter; (2) authoritative decision.

☆ **decree** The sentence or order of the court in civil proceedings making a determination about the issues of fact and law in a case and stating the relative duties and rights of the concerned parties, also called a "judgement" in some usages.

decree nisi [duh KREE NI see] Conditional decree of divorce which becomes absolute unless cause to the contrary is shown within a fixed time.

decrepit Disabled or incompetent by reason of age, physical or mental defect, or other cause.

decretal [duh KREE tuhl] (1) Granting or denying of the remedy sought; (2) relating to, containing or having the binding effect of a decree.

decry To express strong disapproval of, denounce, disparage.

dedicate (1) To set apart, as, to dedicate private property to public use; (2) to inscribe or name by way of compliment or honor.

dedication (1) In real property, giving of land by its owner to public use; (2) zeal, faithfulness, enthusiasm.

deduct To subtract, take away.

deductible That which may be taken away or subtracted, as, a deductible expense in the computation of income tax.

deduction (1) That which has been taken away or subtracted; (2) conclusion derived by reasoning.

deed Written instrument by which one conveys title to realty to another.

deem To consider, treat as if, as, to deem an exhibit marked in evidence although no mark is affixed.

de facto [duh FAK toh] In fact, actually, but without legal status.

defalcation [dee fal KAY shuhn] Misappropriation of trust funds or money held in a fiduciary capacity.

defamation [def uh MAY shuhn] Offense of injuring another's reputation by false statements.

☆ **defamation** [def uh MAY shuhn] Intentional causing or attempting to cause damage to the reputation of another, by communicating false or distorted information about his actions, motives, or character.

defamatory [duh FAM uh taw ree] Injurious to reputation, libelous, slanderous.

default Omission, failure, absence of that which is required to be done.

defeasible [duh FEE zi buhl] Subject to be defeated, annulled or revoked upon some condition or the happening of an event; usually refers to estates and interests in land.

defeat -n. Loss, frustration, destruction; -v. to prevent, frustrate, overcome.

defect Deficiency, imperfection, irregularity, fault.

defective Incomplete, insufficient, faulty.

defective title (1) In negotiable instruments, title to an instrument obtained by fraud, force, illegal consideration or other unlawful means; (2) in real property, title whose validity is impaired by some legal omission or impairment in chain of title.

defect of form Imperfection in style or arrangement of a legal instrument, not affecting its substance.

defect of substance Imperfection in a legal instrument, in omission or inaccuracy of some essential matter.

defend (1) To contest a claim or charge; (2) uphold by force or argument; (3) to prevent, prohibit, resist.

defendant One called upon to defend, deny or answer a legal action.

☆ **defendant** *recommended statistical terminology* In criminal justice usage, a person formally accused of an offense(s) by the filing in court of a charging document.

☆ **defendant dispositions** *recommended statistical terminology* The class of prosecutorial or judicial actions which terminate or provisionally halt proceedings regarding a given defendant in a criminal case after charges have been filed in court.

defense (1) Answer made by defendant to plaintiff's actions; (2) denial of truth or validity of plaintiff's or prosecutor's case; (3) conduct of defendant's case on a trial.

defer To delay, postpone, suspend.

deferred sentence Sentence whose pronouncement is withheld.

defiance Challenge, act of opposition.

deficiency Shortage, insufficiency, inadequacy.

deficiency bill Legislation appropriating funds for which insufficient provision was previously made.

deficiency judgment (1) In a foreclosure proceeding, a personal right of action against the mortgagor for the amount still due to the mortgagee after sale; (2) generally, judgment for unpaid balance remaining after proceeds of security have been applied to payment of a debt.

deficit Deficiency, loss.

defile To dishonor, corrupt, debase, dirty.

define To determine precise meaning, limit, make clear, describe, distinguish.

definite Fixed, determined, bounded, limited.

definition (1) Description or explanation of a word or phrase by use of other words; (2) prescribed or official standard for a commercial product; (3) action of making distinct.

definitive That which completely settles a controversy, most authoritative, definite, complete.

deflect To turn aside, bend.

defloration Sexual act by which female loses virginity.

defraud To deprive of property by fraud or deceit.

defunct Deceased, extinct.

degrade (1) To lower in public estimation, rank or status; (2) to debase, corrupt.

dehors [duh AWR] Out of, without, foreign to.

de jure [day JOO ray] Of right, lawful.

delay -n. Obstruction, postponement; -v. to retard, defer. postpone.

delegate -n. One authorized to act for another; -v. to entrust to another, transfer.

delegation (1) A body of delegates; (2) act of investing with authority to act for another, as, a delegation of power from an executive to an assistant.

delete To strike out, destroy.

deleterious Harmful, unwholesome.

deliberate -adj. Carefully considered, well advised, slow and unhurried; with awareness; -v. to weigh, discuss, consider before forming a decision.

deliberately Intentionally, with premeditation.

deliberation Act of weighing and examining the reasons for and against a contemplated act or course of conduct, prolonged premeditation.

delictum [duh LIK tum] Wrong, injury, tort, offense.

delimit To fix limits, demarcate, bound.

delinquency Failure or violation of duty, transgression of law.

☆ **delinquency** In the broadest usage, juvenile actions or conduct in violation of criminal law, juvenile status offenses, and other juvenile misbehavior.

delinquent -adj. Guilty of violation of law, failing in duty, in arrears in payment of debt; -n. one who is grossly negligent, a transgressor against law or duty.

☆ **delinquent** *recommended statistical terminology* A juvenile who has been adjudged by a judicial officer of a juvenile court to have committed a delinquent act.

☆ **delinquent act** *recommended statistical terminology* An act committed by a juvenile for which an adult could be prosecuted in a criminal court, but for which a juvenile can be adjudicated in a juvenile court, or prosecuted in a court having criminal jurisdiction if the juvenile court transfers jurisdiction; generally, a "felony or misdemeanor level offense" in states employing those terms.

delirium (1) Transient mental disturbance in which the mind acts without volition; (2) frenzied excitement, wild enthusiasm.

deliverance (1) Public expression of opinion or decision; (2) rescue, release, delivery.

delivery (1) Act of transferring possession; (2) rescue, release, liberation.

delusion Unreasoning belief in the existence of facts which are impossible or false.

demand -n. Request to pay money or to do something, assertion of a legal right; -v. to require, ask, claim.

demand note Note in which no time for payment is expressed, but which is payable on presentation.

demeanor Physical appearance, external attributes observable by others, bearing, conduct.

demented Deranged, of unsound mind.

dementia [duh MEN shuh] Insanity, madness.

de minimis non curat lex [day MIN i mis nohn KYOO rot leks] The law is not concerned about trifles; sometimes shortened to "**de minimis**" and also spelled "**de minimus.**"

demise [duh MAHYZ] -n. (1) Death; (2) conveyance of an estate, usually a lease; -v. (3) to create or convey a specified estate; (4) to die.

democracy Form of government in which sovereign power rests in its citizens, who themselves or by elected representatives take part in conduct of their government.

demolish To destroy, ruin, tear down.

demonstrate (1) To illustrate by operation and exhibition of samples; (2) to prove by logical sequence of reasoning; (3) to indicate, show clearly.

demonstration (1) Act of pointing out, exhibiting; (2) public display of group feeling; (3) logical proof by which a conclusion is reached from established premises.

demonstrative evidence Evidence consisting of objects which may be examined, without testimony.

demur [duh MUHR] (1) To object to a pleading on the ground that while the facts alleged may be true, no legal consequence follows; (2) to take exception, balk.

demurrage [duh MUHR uhj] Charge made by the owners of a ship or railroad car for its detention for unloading or loading beyond the period agreed upon.

demurrer [duh MUHR uhr] (1) Pleading that assumes the truth of the matter alleged but claims that the matter is insufficient in law, or contains other legal defect; (2) objection or exception.

denial Refusal, rejection, repudiation.

denominational Sectarian, as, a denominational church.

de novo [day NOH voh] Anew, from the beginning.

deny To refuse, negate, contradict, traverse.

depart To leave, withdraw, go away.

department Territorial or administrative division of a country, area or organization, as, in New York there are four Appellate Departments of the Supreme Court, Appellate Division.

dependable Trustworthy, reliable.

dependence (1) State of being sustained, supported or maintained by something or someone else; (2) reliance, trust.

dependency (1) Territory under the jurisdiction of a country, and subject to its laws and control; (2) status of one who is sustained, supported or maintained by something or someone else.

☆ **dependency** The state of being dependent for proper care upon the community instead of one's family or guardians.

dependent One who is sustained, supported or maintained by something or someone else.

☆ **dependent** *recommended statistical terminology* A juvenile over whom a juvenile court has assumed jurisdiction and legal control because his or her care by parent, guardian or custodian has not met a legal standard of proper care.

☆ **dependent and neglected** *recommended statistical terminology* A juvenile over whom a juvenile court has assumed jurisdiction and legal control because his or her care by parent, guardian or custodian has not met a legal standard of proper care.

deplete To lessen, empty, drain, exhaust.

depletion Act of reducing, lessening or exhausting, as, the depletion of a coal mine.

deponent [duh POH nuhnt] One who gives information on oath or on affirmation, usually in writing.

deportation Removal of an alien from a country where he is considered to be an enemy or otherwise undesirable.

deposit -n. (1) Money or other property pledged by a person as security to complete a transaction or repay a loan; (2) delivery of money to a bank for credit to a designated account; -v. (3) to place or entrust for safekeeping or to guarantee performance.

depositary Person or organization receiving funds or other items in a bailee capacity, for safekeeping or convenience.

deposition (1) Testimony of a witness upon interrogatories taken in pursuance of a commission to take testimony, issued by a court, and reduced to writing, duly authenticated, and intended to be used upon the trial of an action in court, where the witness is unable to appear in person; (2) deprivation of authority, as, the deposition of a sovereign from his throne; (3) declaration, testimony, allegation.

depositor Party making a deposit.

depository Physical place where funds or other items are kept by a person or organization in a bailee capacity, for safekeeping or convenience.

deprave To defame, vilify, malign.

depraved mind One deficient of moral values and having no regard for life and safety.

depreciation Loss of value due to age, decay or obsolescence.

depression (1) Period of low general economic activity; (2) a hole, area lower than its surroundings; (3) an unhealthy emotional or mental state charac-terized by chronic sadness, feelings of inadequacy and guilt, self-depreciation and often suicidal tendencies.

deprivation Taking away, confiscation, removal.

deprive To take away, confiscate, destroy, divest.

deputize To appoint one to act as a deputy or substitute in another's place.

deputy Substitute; one authorized to act for another, usually in a public office, as, a deputy sheriff.

derelict -adj. Forsaken, abandoned, run-down, neglectful; -n. person or thing abandoned or forgotten.

dereliction Intentional or conscious neglect; deviation from conventional conduct.

derivation Source from which something is derived; origin.

derivative -adj. (1) Coming from another; (2) lacking originality; -n. (3) something that grows out of or results from an earlier condition.

derivative action Legal proceeding by a stockholder to enforce a corporate cause of action based upon an asserted right of the corporation.

derive To receive, obtain, acquire, as, to derive income from an investment of capital.

derogate To lessen, impair, disparage, lower in esteem, detract.

derogation Lessening, detriment, detraction, impairing of efficiency or force, as, a statute in derogation of the common law is strictly construed.

descend (1) To pass down from one generation to another, derive; (2) to go or come down, move downward.

descendant (1) One to whom an estate passes from a deceased intestate; (2) one descended from another or from a common stock; (3) an offshoot from an antecedent practice or idea.

descent (1) Vesting of title to real property from an ancestor to his heirs, by operation of law; (2) process of descending from a higher to a lower level; (3) extraction, lineage; (4) inclination downward.

describe To explain, define, communicate from personal observation, distinguish from others.

description (1) Act of identification by enumeration of characteristics; (2) individualizing or identifying designation; (3) specification of boundaries of real property with sufficient particularity for legal purposes.

descriptive Tending or serving to explain, describe or represent.

desecrate To profane, violate sanctity of, contaminate, defile.

desert To abandon, leave permanently, withdraw from, betray.

deserter One who leaves without authority, intending not to return, such as a deserter from a military force.

desertion (1) Act of abandoning a status or duty with evasive intent, as, desertion from marriage; (2) defection.

deserving Worthy, meritorious.

design -n. Plan, scheme, intent, form, purpose, pattern; -v. to intend, plan, conceive.

designate To set apart for a purpose, specify, nominate, indicate, delegate, appoint.

designation (1) Appointment to an office; (2) act of describing, identifying or distinguishing, as, the designation of a trade name.

designed Made or done for a particular purpose.

designedly Intentionally, deliberately.

desire -n. Request, wish, craving, urge, passion; -v. to long for, covet, ask, request, want, wish.

de son tort [duh sohn tawrt] (of his own wrong) An executor de son tort is one not properly appointed, who acts in such capacity at his own risk.

desperate Hopeless, worthless, crucial, overpowering, outrageous.

despoil (1) To deprive of property by violence or stealth; (2) to plunder, denude, ravage.

despot [DES puht] Tyrant, autocrat, ruler with virtually absolute power.

despotism [DES puh tiz uhm] Tyranny, arbitrary exercise of power, absolutism.

destitute (1) Lacking the necessities of life; (2) subject to a lack or deficiency.

destroy (1) To render unfit or ineffective; (2) to ruin, raze, demolish, wreck.

destruction Process of demolition, cancellation, annihilation, elimination.

detail -n. Individual item, particular circumstance; selection of some from a group for a task, as, a military detail assigned to some purpose; -v. to enumerate, specify.

detain To restrain from proceeding, stop, hold in, delay.

☆ **detainee** Usually, a person held in local, very short term confinement while awaiting consideration for pretrial release or first appearance for arraignment.

detainer Act or instrument by which a person or property is held in custody.

☆ **detainer (corrections)** An official notice from a government agency to a correctional agency requesting that an identified person wanted by the first agency, but subject to the correctional agency's jurisdiction, not be released or discharged without notification to the first agency and opportunity to respond.

detection Observation of that which was hidden.

detective One engaged, in civilian attire, in investigation usually of crime and the apprehension of criminals.

detention (1) Act of withholding a person or thing; (2) restraint, enforced delay.

☆ **detention** The legally authorized confinement of a person subject to criminal or juvenile court proceedings, until the point of commitment to a correctional facility or until release.

☆ **detention hearing** *recommended statistical terminology* In juvenile justice usage, a hearing by a judicial officer of a juvenile court to determine whether a juvenile is to be detained, continue to be detained, or be released, while juvenile proceedings in the case are pending.

deter To discourage, prevent from acting by providing impediments, inhibit.

deterioration Gradual impairment by degeneration of substance, as, deterioration caused by decay or lack of refrigeration.

determinate [duh TUHR min uht] Known, fixed, definite, established.

☆ **determinate sentence** A type of sentence to imprisonment where the commitment is for a specified single time quantity, such as three years.

determination (1) Ending of a controversy; (2) decision based upon evaluation of facts and reasoning rather than arithmetical computation; (3) conclusion, resolution.

determine (1) To bring to an end; (2) to decide, resolve.

detinue [DET in yoo] Form of common law action to recover personal property or its value, which has been legally obtained but wrongfully detained.

☆ **detoxification center** A public or private facility for the short-term medical treatment of acutely intoxicated persons, or drug or alcohol abusers, often functioning as an alternative to jail for persons who have been taken into custody.

detract To disparage, belittle, derogate.

detriment Damage or harm incurred.

devastation Act of laying waste, desolation.

develop To progress, continue, promote, expound, explain, mature.

devest (divest) (1) To take away from one an estate, interest or status which he presently has; (2) to deprive, take away, withdraw, discard, alienate.

deviant -adj. Departing from an accepted norm; -n. person or quality markedly different from that which is considered normal or acceptable, as, a sexual deviant.

deviation Divergence, change of direction, deflection.

device (1) Invention, plan, project, contrivance; (2) trick, scheme, artifice, stratagem.

devise -n. (1) Real property given by will; -v. (2) to contrive, intent, plan; (3) to give real property by will.

devisee One to whom real property is given by a will.

devisor One who gives real property by will.

devolution Transfer to a successor or descendant of a person's right, title, office or ownership of property.

devolve To pass, transfer from one to another, accrue to one as the successor of another, descend.

☆ **diagnosis or classification center** *recommended statistical terminology*
A functional unit within a correctional or medical facility, or a separate facility, which contains persons held in custody for the purpose of determining whether criminal proceedings should continue or the appropriate sentencing or treatment disposition, or which correctional facility or program is appropriate for a committed offender.

☆ **diagnostic commitment** *recommended statistical terminology* The action of a court ordering a person subject to criminal or juvenile proceedings to be temporarily placed in a confinement facility, for study and evaluation of his or her personal history and characteristics, usually as a preliminary to a sentencing disposition, juvenile court disposition, or other disposition of the case.

dialectic (1) Branch of logic which teaches methods of reasoning; (2) argument by critical examination of logical consequences.

dicta [DIK tuh] (pl. of **dictum**) Judicial observations not embodying an actual determination of an issue; judicial opinions on points not necessarily involved in a case under consideration.

dictator One who rules with supreme authority.

dictum [DIK tuhm] The expression by a judge of an opinion not necessary for the decision of the matter before him; sometimes called obiter dictum.

die -n. (1) Mold; (2) one of a pair of dice; -v. (3) to cease to live, expire perish.

diffuse adj. Widespread, scattered; -v. to disperse, scatter over wide area, spread freely.

digest -n. Classified and consolidated compilation of legal work, as, a digest of cases on a particular topic; -v. to arrange systematically, classify, codify compress, comprehend.

dilapidation Status of neglect or decay.

dilatory [DIL uh taw ree] Causing delay, tardy, slow.

dilatory defense [DI L uh taw ree duh FENS] One which delays progress of an action without bearing upon merits.

dilatory tactics [DIL uh taw ree TAK tiks] Those which seek to defeat a matter by evasive maneuvers designed to prevent a final decision or trial on the merits.

diligence (1) Care, prudence, caution; (2) painstaking and devoted effort.

diligent Persistent, untiring, energetic, as, a diligent employee.

diminution Decrease, reduction, depreciation.

diplomacy (1) Tact; (2) conduct of relations between countries.

dipsomania [dip soh MAY nee uh] Uncontrollable desire for alcoholic beverages.

direct -adj. In a natural line, proximate, by the shortest route, by immediate connection, straightforward; -v. to guide, assign, focus, conduct, devote, administer.

direct cause Active, effective, producing cause.

direct evidence Means of proof which tends to show the existence of a fact without intervention of any other fact.

direct examination Process of eliciting testimony from a witness by the party calling the witness to testify.

☆ **directed verdict** A not guilty verdict (1) returned by the jury at the direction of the court, or (2) entered on the record by the court after dismissal of the jury, when the judicial officer decides that the case presented against the defendant obviously falls short of that required to establish guilt.

direction (1) Act of management, guidance, supervision; (2) instruction given by court to a jury; (3) an order, command; (4) purpose, objective.

directory -adj. Instructional, advisory, having no mandatory or obligatory effect, as, a directory provision of a legal instrument; -n. compilation, as of names, addresses and telephone numbers of residents of a locality.

disability (1) Incapacity to do a legal act as in the case of infants or incompetents; (2) deprivation, disadvantage, physical handicap.

disable To incapacitate, render ineffective, disqualify.

disaffirm To repudiate, contradict prior approval, annul, reverse.

disaffirmance Repudiation, annulment, reversal, negation, denial.

disagreement (1) Failure of jury to agree upon verdict; (2) difference of opinion.

disallow To deny the validity of or reject, as, to disallow a claim for an insured loss.

disapprove To refuse consent, condemn, reject.

disaster Sudden and extensive misfortune, calamity, catastrophe.

disavow To repudiate acts of an agent, deny authority of another to act in one's behalf.

disbar To rescind an attorney's license to practice law, exclude, disqualify.

disbursements Sums paid out, as, disbursements by an attorney having charge of a pending action.

discharge (1) To set at liberty a person held to answer to a crime; (2) to release a bankrupt from all liability; (3) to relieve a jury from further consideration of a case; (4) to exempt, acquit, exonerate; (5) to shoot, as, to discharge a firearm.

☆ **discharge** In criminal justice usage, to release from confinement or supervision, or to release from a legal status imposing an obligation upon the subject person.

discipline -n. (1) Training to secure obedience to orders; correction, punishment; (2) branch of learning; -v. (3) to impose penalty as training for obedience to orders, train by instruction.

disclaimer Disavowal or formal renunciation of a claim or power.

disclose To reveal, make known, expose to view.

disclosure Revelation, exposure.

discontinuance (1) Failure to proceed in, or voluntary dismissal of, a case by a plaintiff; (2) interruption, shutdown.

discount -n. (1) Interest taken in advance at the time a loan is made; (2) deduction permitted from an amount due; (3) reduction in price; -v. (4) to disregard, depreciate, disbelieve.

discovery (1) Pre-trial process by which a party to an action secures information from his opponent as to facts or documents in the opponent's possession or control; (2) revelation, disclosure, recognition.

discredit -n. Reproach, doubt, disadvantage; -v. to impair credibility, impeach, disbelieve.

discreet Prudent, tactful, unobtrusive.

discrepancy Variance, difference where none should exist, inconsistency.

discretion (1) Use of private and independent judgment, power of decision; (2) prudence, secrecy, delicacy.

☆ **discretionary review** An appeal which the court having appellate jurisdiction may agree or decline to hear, at its own discretion. Procedurally, in these cases, a party wishing to appeal must first make a request to the court for permission to make the appeal, stating the reasons for doing so. The court can grant or deny the request.

discrimination (1) Favoritism, unequal treatment; (2) discernment, identification of differences.

discussion Argument, discourse, consideration of a question in open debate.

disease Sickness, ailment, deviation from healthy or normal condition of a living organism that modifies performance of a vital function.

disfigurement That which impairs appearance, defacement.

disfranchise To deprive of the rights of a citizen, deprive of statutory or constitutional right such as the right to vote.

disgrace -n. Shame, dishonor, ill repute; -v. to revile, reflect discredit upon.

disguise -n. (1) Outfit worn to alter appearance so that wearer will not be recognized; (2) pretense, deception, masquerade; -v. (3) to conceal by dress, obscure identity.

dishonor -n. (1) Disgrace, shame, loss of prestige; (2) non-acceptance of draft or other commercial paper by party on whom it is drawn; -v. (3) to refuse to accept or pay a bill, check or note when duly presented for payment; (4) to disgrace, deprive of honor.

disinherit The act of an owner of an estate to deprive another of any part of the estate he would otherwise take as an heir.

disinter [dis in TUHR] To unbury, exhume, remove from a grave.

disinterested Not concerned, not having any possible gain or loss, free from selfish motive.

disinterested witness One having no interest in the outcome of the proceedings.

disjunctive Not joined, involving alternate choices.

dismiss (1) To discharge from duty or employment; (2) to cease further consideration of, terminate a legal action.

dismissal (1) Order or judgment terminating a legal action; (2) discharge from employment.

☆ **dismissal** I. In judicial proceedings generally, the disposal of an action, suit, motion or the like without trial of the issues; the termination of the adjudication of a case before the case reaches judgment. II. *recommended criminal justice statistical terminology* The decision by a court to terminate; adjudication of all outstanding charges in a criminal case, or all outstanding charges against a given defendant in a criminal case, thus terminating court action in the case and permanently or provisionally terminating court jurisdiction over the defendant in relation to those charges.

☆ **dismissal for want of prosecution** In criminal proceedings, the judicial termination of a case against a defendant, occurring after the filing of a charging document but before the beginning of a trial, on grounds that prosecution has not been continued.

☆ **dismissal in the interest of justice** In criminal proceedings, the judicial termination of a case against a defendant, on the grounds that the ends of justice would not be served by continuing prosecution.

dismissal without prejudice Dismissal not on the merits and which does not bar subsequent action on the same cause.

dismissal with prejudice Dismissal made on the merits of the issue and preventing further or later proceedings on the same subject matter.

☆ **disorderly conduct** In Uniform Crime Reports terminology, the name of the UCR category used to record and report arrests for committing a breach of the peace.

disorderly house Place where people behave so badly as to become a nuisance to the neighborhood (usually refers to a house of prostitution).

disparage To discourage, run down, depreciate.

dispel To drive away, scatter, dissipate.

dispensation (1) Exemption from some law, permission to do something forbidden; (2) favor, exemption.

dispense To distribute, pay out, administer, provide.

☆ **disposition** In criminal justice usage, the action by a criminal or juvenile justice agency which signifies that a portion of the justice process is complete and jurisdiction is terminated or transferred to another agency; or which signifies that a decision has been reached on one aspect of a case and a different aspect comes under consideration, requiring a different kind of decision.

☆ **disposition hearing** *recommended statistical terminology* A hearing in juvenile court, conducted after an adjudicatory hearing and subsequent receipt of the report of any predisposition investigation, to determine the most appropriate form of custody and/or treatment for a juvenile who has been adjudged a delinquent, a status offender, or a dependent.

dispossess -n. Summary proceeding by a landlord to oust the tenant and regain possession of the premises; -v. to oust tenants from land by legal process.

disprove To refute, prove false, controvert.

disqualify To render ineligible or unfit, deprive of a power, right or privilege.

disregard -n. Intentional slight or neglect; -v. to ignore, take no notice of, overlook.

disrepute Low estimation, dishonor.

dissection (1) Act of cutting into separate parts for examination; (2) detailed critical analysis.

dissemble To conceal by presenting a false appearance, hide, overlook.

dissent -n. Opinion disagreeing with that of the majority, nonconcurrence, disagreement, difference of opinion; -v. to object, disagree.

☆ **dissenting opinion** An opinion of one or more judges who disagree with the decision of the majority.

dissolute Unrestrained, loose in conduct and morals, wanton.

dissolution (1) Legal severance, cancellation, abrogation, as, the dissolution of a contract; (2) disintegration, decay.

dissolve To cancel, annul, abrogate, disintegrate, as, to dissolve a corporation.

dissuade To advise one against a course of conduct, divert by persuasion.

distill (1) To vaporize volatile parts and condense the vapor; (2) to find essential quality, as, to distill an argument; (3) to concentrate, purify.

distillery Place where alcoholic liquor is manufactured.

distinct Separate, clear, plain, different.

distinguish To demonstrate an essential difference, differentiate, exercise discrimination.

distort To twist out of regular shape or meaning; deform.

distrain [dis TRAYN] To take and hold personal property in order to obtain payment of a debt or as indemnification.

distress -n. (1) Taking of personal chattels without legal process from the possession of a wrongdoer to enforce payment or obtain reparation; (2) suffering, affliction; pain; -v. (3) to afflict, harass, disturb, oppress.

distribute To divide in shares or in proportion, give out, apportion, allot.

distributee One entitled by law to receive share of estate of a deceased person.

distribution (1) Process of division among legatees or heirs of an intestate of that portion of an estate remaining after paying debts and costs of administration; (2) apportionment, allotment.

distributive That which apportions and divides in shares.

district Geographical division of a country, state, county or other political subdivision for judicial, administrative or other functions.

☆ **district attorney** *recommended statistical terminology* An attorney who is the elected or appointed chief of a prosecution agency, and whose official duty is to conduct criminal proceedings on behalf of the people against persons accused of committing criminal offenses; and any attorney deputized to assist the chief prosecutor.

disturb To throw into disorder, interrupt, agitate.

disturbance Act which annoys, interrupts or interferes with others, commotion, derangement.

☆ **disturbing the peace** *tentatively recommended national category for prosecution, courts and corrections statistics.* Unlawful interruption of the peace, quiet or order of a community, including offenses called "disorderly conduct," "vagrancy," "loitering," "unlawful assembly," and "riot."

diverge To proceed in different directions from a common point, digress.

diverse [dahy VUHRZ] Various, several.

diversion (1) Turning aside, deviation, digression; (2) relaxation, amusement.

☆ **diversion** I. In the broadest usage, any procedure which (a) substitutes non-entry for official entry into the justice process, or (b) substitutes the suspension of criminal or juvenile proceedings for continuation, or (c) substitutes lesser supervision or referral to a non-justice agency or no supervision for conventional supervision, or (d) substitutes any kind of non-confinement status for confinement. II. *Standards and Goals definition* The official suspension of criminal or juvenile proceedings against an alleged offender at any point after a recorded justice system intake but before the entering of a judgment, and referral of that person to a treatment or care program administered by a non-justice or private agency, or no referral.

diversity of citizenship Condition wherein parties to an action are citizens of different states, thus affording jurisdiction to Federal courts under United States Constitution.

divert To turn aside, deviate, deflect.

divest (1) To take away from one an estate, interest or status which he presently has; (2) to deprive, take away, withdraw, discard, alienate.

dividend (1) Proportionate share of profits allotted for payment to stock-holders, as declared by board of directors of a corporation; (2) return, reward.

division of opinion Disagreement among judges considering and deciding an issue.

divorce -n. Legal dissolution of a marriage for some cause arising after the marriage; -v. to separate, disunite.

divulge To reveal, make known.

dock -n. (1) Place in court where prisoner stands or sits; (2) basin between piers or wharves to receive ships (sometimes used to include the piers);
-v. (3) to curtail or reduce, as, to dock an employee for lateness by reducing his pay; (4) to guide a ship to a pier.

docket (1) Abstract or brief entry; (2) book in which of entries proceedings in a court are made.

☆ **docket** A brief record of all the important court actions in a case from its beginning to its conclusion.

doctrine Principle, theory or rule of law.

document -n. Paper or other substance containing, writing, photograph, map, plans or other matter which may be used evidentially to prove a fact; -v. to teach, furnish supporting evidence.

documentary evidence Evidence furnished by written instruments, such as public records, wills, contracts or other writings.

dogma Something held as an established opinion.

doing business Exercise in a state of some function or business activity so as to subject the business to jurisdiction of that state in a legal action.

dole -n. (1) Distribution in portions; (2) ration for the needy; -v. (3) to distribute as a charity.

domain (1) Possessions of a sovereign or country; (2) area of concern, circumscribed sphere of activity.

domestic -adj. (1) Of local origin or creation, as, a domestic wine is one consumed in the country of its origin, as compared with foreign or imported wines; (2) pertaining to a house or family; -n. (3) a servant.

domestic animals Those commonly found in people's homes, living and breeding in a tame condition.

domestic corporation One created by or under the laws of the state where an action is pending.

domestic purposes Those relating to sustenance of human beings, including washing, cleaning, feeding and housing.

domestic servant One who resides in master's house and assists in household chores.

domesticate To convert to domestic use, convert into conformity with home environment.

domicile [DOM uh sahyl] (1) One's permanent residence, place to which one who is absent intends to return; (2) state in which a corporation or business concern is incorporated, principal place of business of a corporation as legally registered.

domiciled [DOM uh sahyld] Established in a given state or jurisdiction for legal purposes.

dominant Commanding, controlling, superior, paramount.

dominant estate One to which an easement or service is due.

dominate To rule, control, hold supremacy over.

dominion Supremacy, sovereignty, control.

donation Gift, voluntary alienation of property.

donee (1) One to whom a gift is made; (2) one given a power to transfer property by will or deed.

donor One who gives a gift.

dope -n. (1) (slang) Narcotic, habit-forming drug; (2) thick substance, such as grease used in lubrication; (3) (slang) stupid person; (4) information, details prediction, comment; -v. (5) to smear or lubricate; (6) to administer a drug; (7) to forecast or guess.

dormant Sleeping, silent, inactive.

dot [doh] Money or dowry which a wife brings to her husband.

dotage [DOH tuhj] Decay of mental faculties due to age.

double entry Bookkeeping system in which two entries are made, one to the receiving and the other to the paying side of a transaction, so that the total credits will always equal the total debits.

double jeopardy Danger of twice being tried, convicted and punished for the same offense.

doubt -n. Uncertainty of mind, absence of settled opinion or conviction; -v. to be uncertain or undecided.

doubtful title Ownership as to whose validity there is some question of fact or law, so as to invite or expose the holder to litigation.

dowager [DOU uh juhr] (1) A widow endowed with title or property from her husband; (2) in England, title for a widow of a king, prince, duke, earl or other nobleman, as distinguished from the wife of an heir, who has a right to the title formerly held by the widow; (3) elderly woman of imposing appearance or assured position in society.

dower [DOU uhr] Common law life estate possessed by a widow in one-third of her husband's real property.

dowry [DOU ree] Property or money which the wife brings to the husband; in marriage.

draft -n. (1) An order in writing by one party drawn on another party to pay money to a third party or to bearer; (2) a preliminary or rough copy of a document, plan or other work; (3) selection of persons for compulsory military service; -v. (4) to select for some purpose; (5) to prepare a preliminary plan or outline.

draftsman (1) One who prepares a legal instrument; (2) one who prepares construction and engineering drawings.

draw (1) To attract, entice, allure; (2) to make a written demand for payment of money, as, to draw on funds in a bank; (3) to select persons by lot,as,to draw a jury; (4) to compose a legal instrument; (5) to remove a weapon from one's person in preparation for immediate use; sometimes, to point a weapon intentionally.

drawee A person or organization to whom a bill of exchange is addressed and who is requested to pay the amount of money mentioned.

drawer Person issuing a bill of exchange; maker of a promissory note.

drift (1) In mining law, an underground passage driven horizontally along the course of a mineralized vein; (2) deviation, observable course or direction towards an effect; (3) meaning, import; (4) gradual shift in attitude, opinion or position.

☆ **driving under the influence** *recommended statistical terminology* Unlawful operation of any motor vehicle while under the influence of alcohol or a controlled substance(s) or drug.

☆ **driving under the influence** In Uniform Crime Reports terminology, the name of the UCR category used to record and report arrests for offenses of driving or operating any vehicle or common carrier while drunk or under the influence of liquor or drugs.

droit [dwo] Law, right.

drop shipment In a transaction between buyer and seller, delivery of the merchandise directly to the buyer from its source.

drug (1) Any substance used as a medicine; (2) a substance other than food which affects the structure or function of the body of a person or animal; (3) term commonly used to refer to a controlled substance illegally used.

☆ **drug abuse violations** In Uniform Crime Reports terminology, the name of the UCR category used to record and report arrests for offenses relating to growing, manufacturing, making, possessing, using, selling, or distributing narcotic and dangerous non-narcotic drugs.

☆ **drug law violation** *recommended statistical terminology* The unlawful sale, purchase, distribution, manufacture, cultivation, transport, possession, or use of a controlled or prohibited drug, or attempt to commit these acts.

drunkard One who is habitually intoxicated.

dual nationality Status wherein two countries claim allegiance of one person at the same time.

duces tecum [DOO suhs TAY kuhm] (that you bring with you) Form of legal process requiring one to appear as a witness, and bring with him specified books and records in his possession. (see **subpoena duces tecum**).

due (1) Just, proper, reasonable, lawful; (2) remaining unpaid.

due care That standard of caution which would be exercised by a reasonably prudent man.

due consideration Such weight or deliberation as appears justified in the premises.

due course Regular, ordinary sequence.

due diligence Vigilant activity proportionate to the subject matter.

due notice Such notice as is proper under all the circumstances.

due process of law Law in its regular course of administration through courts of justice according to rules and forms established for protection of private rights.

☆ **due process of law** A right guaranteed by the Fifth, Sixth, and Fourteenth Amendments of the U.S. Constitution, and generally understood, in legal contexts, to mean the due course of legal proceedings according to the rules and forms which have been established for the protection of private rights.

due proof Adequate evidence.

due to Owing to, because of.

duel Formal combat between two or more persons using deadly weapons.

dues Fee or charge for membership in an organization.

duly (1) According to legal requirements; (2) in proper form, time and degree.

duly qualified Having all qualifications required by law.

dummy One who although seeming to act for himself is in reality acting for another.

dummy director Director who is a figurehead and exercises no independent action or judgment.

dun To demand or urge payment repeatedly.

dunnage [DUN uhj] Pieces of wood used in a ship, truck or railway car to protect the cargo from shifting or leakage of water.

duplicate -adj. Corresponding or identical; -n. that which resembles
something else, so that the two are substantially alike; -v. to make double.

duplicity (1) Duplication, use of two when one would be sufficient; (2) double
dealing, deception, bad faith.

durable Lasting, enduring.

duress [duh RES] Unlawful restraint compelling a person to do some act that he
otherwise would not have done, coercion, compulsion, constraint.

duty (1) Moral obligation, respect, obedient behavior; (2) conforming to an
obligation, obligatory task; (3) obligation of performance resting upon one
acting in an official or fiduciary capacity; (4) tax due to government on
imported or exported goods.

dying declaration Statement of material facts made by one in immediate
prospect of death and having no hope of recovery.

dying without issue Death occurring at a time when no children are living.

dynasty (1) Succession of rulers in the same family line; (2) class of individuals
having power in some activity and able to choose their successors.

E

each -adj. One of two or more; -n. everybody.

earn To acquire by labor, service or performance.

earned income Income derived from personal labor, as wages, salary, fees or commissions, and not merely from ownership of property.

earnest -adj. (1) Serious, intent; -n. (2) pledge or payment to bind a contract; (3) serious, intent mental state.

earnest money Pledge or payment to bind a bargain, deposit on contract.

earning capacity That income which an individual is able to earn by reason of training, experience and business acumen.

earning power Relative ability of an individual or organization to command a reward for performance of services or sale of goods.

easement Right held by one person to use the land of another for a special purpose not inconsistent with general property rights of owner against whom the easement exists, as, an easement to cross land.

eave Lower edge of a roof projecting over the wall of a house.

eavesdropping Listening without authority to private conversations.

ecchymosis [ek i MOH sis] Localized discoloration in and under the skin, a black and blue spot.

ecclesiastic Clergyman, priest.

eclectic Composed of elements drawn from various sources, selected from various sources and doctrines.

economy (1) Frugality; (2) structure of economic life in a country or area.

ecumenical General, universal.

edict Law proclaimed by competent authority.

edition (1) Quantity of a book put forth at one time from a single type setting; (2) one of the forms in which something is issued to the public; (3) a set of copies differing in some way from another set of the same text previously published.

editor One who writes, revises, corrects, selects articles for publication, directs or supervises policies and subject matter of a publication.

effect -n. Result, outcome, accomplishment, fulfillment; -v. to do, perform, execute, accomplish.

effects Movable property.

efficient Causing an effect, satisfactory in use.

efficient cause Producing, originating or immediate agent in production of an effect.

effigy Representation, crude figure of a person.

effort Attempt, endeavor, physical exertion.

e.g. (exempli gratia) For example.

egress [EE gres] Exit, outlet, act of going out.

either One or the other of two.

eject To throw out, expel, dispossess, turn out of possession.

ejection Turning out of possession, expulsion.

ejectment Action to recover possession of land and damages for its wrongful withholding.

ejusdem generis [ay JUHS dem JEN uh ris] Of the same kind, class or nature.

elastic (1) Having property of returning to original form after being disarranged; (2) resilient, flexible, adaptable.

elder -adj. (1) Of earlier birth than another; -n. (2) one who is older; (3) member of governing body, as, an elder of a church.

elect -adj. Exclusive, choice; -n. one or a group chosen or set apart; -v. to choose, pick out, select.

election Act or process of choosing by vote.

elective (1) Chosen by election; (2) optional.

elective franchise Right of voting at public elections.

elector (1) One duly qualified to vote; (2) member of electoral college.

electoral Pertaining to electors or elections.

electoral college Body of state electors chosen to elect president and vice president of the United States.

electrocute To kill by electric current.

eleemosynary [el ee MO suh ne ree] Charitable.

element Material, substance, component, ingredient.

☆ **element of the offense** Any conduct, circumstance, condition, or state of mind which in combination with other conduct, circumstances, conditions or states of mind constitutes an unlawful act.

elements Rudiments, simplest principles.

eligibility Qualification to be selected, fitness, suitability.

eligible -adj. Fit to be chosen, desirable; -n. one qualified for some status, as, an eligible on a civil service list for appointment to a position.

☆ **eligible for parole** The status of a person committed to the jurisdiction of a federal or state prison system and usually in confinement in an institution, who by a combination of such factors as sentence effective date, statutory provisions concerning length of sentence to be served in confinement, time credit deductions, and individual sentence, can legally be considered for release from confinement in prison to parole status.

eliminate To remove, expel, exclude.

elope To leave one's home secretly for purpose of marriage.

emancipate (1) To set free, liberate; (2) to release a child from parental power.

emancipated minor An individual who is completely self-supporting and has not attained the age of 18.

emancipation (1) Surrender of care and custody, as, the emancipation of a minor child by its parents, which also entails a renunciation of parental duties; (2) liberation.

embargo (1) Prohibition of entry or departure of vessels in port by government order, usually in time of war; (2) legal prohibition of some aspect of commerce.

embassy Physical establishment provided for office and residence of an ambassador.

embezzlement Fraudulent appropriation of property by one to whom it has been entrusted.

☆ **embezzlement** The misappropriation, misapplication, or illegal disposal of legally entrusted property by the person(s) to whom it was entrusted, with intent to defraud the legal owner or intended beneficiary.

☆ **embezzlement** In Uniform Crime Reports terminology, the name of the UCR offense category used to record and report arrests for offenses of "misappropriation or misapplication of money or property entrusted to one's care, custody, or control."

emblement [EM bluh muhnt] Crop unreaped when a lease has ended although the crop has resulted from care and labor of the tenant.

embolism [EM buh liz uhm] Mechanical obstruction of an artery or capillary by some body (embolus) travelling in the blood.

embolus [EM buh luhs] Foreign particle circulating in the blood.

embraceor [em BRAY suhr] One who has committed the offense of embracery.

embracery [em BRAY suh ree] Attempt to influence a jury corruptly by promises, entreaties or other unlawful means.

emendation [em uhn DAY shuhn] Amendment, correction, alteration.

emerge To arise, come to light, come forth.

emergency Sudden unexpected happening, pressing necessity.

emergent (1) Issuing forth; (2) urgent.

emigrant One who leaves his country to settle elsewhere.

emigration Act of removing from one country to another.

eminent domain Right of a government to take private property for public use, on payment of just compensation.

emissary One sent on a mission as an agent of another.

emission Ejection or throwing out of a secretion or other matter.

emit To give forth, issue, discharge, release.

emolument [e MOL yoo ment] Advantage, gain, profit arising from the possession of an office.

empanel (impanel) To enter or enroll as part of a group, as, to empanel a jury.

emperor Sovereign ruler of an empire.

emphasis (1) Forcefulness of expression; (2) prominence or stress given in order to focus attention.

emphatic Made prominent, insistent, forceful.

empire (1) Large territory with great variety of people under one ruler; (2) dominion of an emperor.

empiric Proceeding on experience, disregarding theoretical and philosophic considerations.

employ -n. Hire, business, occupation; -v. to use or engage the services of, make use of.

employee Person employed by another to perform labor or service for wages.

employer One who engages the services of another for wages or salary.

employment (1) Act of hiring; (2) use, as, the employment of a dictionary for reference; (3) labor or services performed by employee and paid for by employer.

enable (1) To give power; (2) to make possible, practical or easy; (3) to allow.

enabling statute Legislative enactment which confers new powers for a particular purpose.

enact To establish by law.

en banc [ahn bahngk] (in full court) A session of a court with all its judges participating.

enceinte [ahn SANT] Pregnant.

enclose To surround, bound, confine.

enclosure (1) Confined area; (2) something sent with a package or letter.

encourage To help, embolden, stimulate.

encroach To trespass, intrude, advance beyond normal limits.

encroachment (1) That which illegally protrudes into or invades the space of another; (2) action of encroaching.

encumber To weigh down, burden, hamper, hinder.

encumbrance (incumbrance) (1) Impediment; (2) burden or charge upon property which does not prevent its transfer.

endeavor -n. Systematic or continuous effort; -v. to exert physical and intellectual strength toward attainment of an object, strive.

endorse (indorse) (1) To place one's signature on the back of a check, bill, note or similar instrument in order to obtain the proceeds or to transfer its possession to another; (2) to show approval or acceptance, as, to endorse a country's foreign policy.

endow To bestow upon, make financial provision for, provide.

endowment (1) Act of creating a fund for support, as, endowment of a charity or college; (2) income derived from a fund created for support.

endowment policy In life insurance, a policy in which the face amount is payable when insured attains a given age, or upon his death if that occurs earlier.

endurance (1) Permanence, duration; (2) fortitude, power of continuing under pain, hardship or distress.

enemy (1) Person or country at war with another; (2) adversary, opponent; (3) something injurious, harmful or deadly.

enforce To give force to, compel, constrain, cause to take effect.

enforceable Performable, capable of being compelled.

enfranchise (1) To set free; (2) to invest with a franchise, such as to enfranchise persons as eligible to vote.

engage (1) To take part in, embark on, participate; (2) to employ, provide occupation for, as, this will engage our efforts for a long time; (3) to enter into contest with, as, to engage an enemy; (4) to promise, pledge, guarantee.

engagement (1) Obligation, contract; (2) involvement, appointment; (3) betrothal; (4) encounter of hostile forces.

engender To cause, excite, call forth, propagate.

engine Combination of mechanical means working together to effect a given end.

en gros [ahn groh] In gross, total.

engross (1) To prepare text of a bill for legislative action; (2) to copy a document in a fair large hand.

engrossed bill Legislative bill in final form ready to be passed into law.

engrossing -v. Buying up large quantities of a commodity with intent to resell at a profit; -adj. absorbing, fascinating.

enhance To increase, improve, elevate, augment.

enjoin (1) To command, require, direct performance; (2) to forbid, prohibit or restrain by judicial order or decree.

enjoy To have, possess and use with satisfaction.

enjoyment (1) Beneficial use of property; (2) pleasurable possession and use of something.

enlarge (1) To make larger, magnify, expand; (2) to extend a time limit.

enlist (1) To enter voluntarily into military service; (2) to secure the support and aid of.

enroll (1) To insert, register, enter, enlist oneself; (2) to write out in legal form.

enrolled bill One passed by legislature, approved by executive authority, and duly filed as required by law.

en route [ahn root] On the way, along the way.

ensue To follow in order of events, result.

entail (1) To settle or limit succession to real property; (2) to impose or require as a necessary result.

enter (1) To form a part of, contribute; (2) to place before a court or upon a record, as, to enter a judgment; (3) to go upon land, make a physical entrance, penetrate; (4) to make a beginning, start.

entering judgment Ministerial act of clerk of court by which formal entry of judgment is made upon court rolls as a permanent record.

enterprise Project, undertaking, venture.

entice To allure, attract, tempt.

enticement (1) Act of tempting one to do something; (2) object that entices.

entire Whole, complete, total, undivided.

entire day 24 hour period beginning at midnight.

entirety Whole, sum, total.

entitle (1) To name, give a right or title; (2) to qualify for.

entity Being, self-contained existence.

entrap (1) To catch, ensnare by artifice; (2) to involve in contradictions or difficulties.

entrapment For purposes of arrest and prosecution, an act by government officers or agents in inducing a person to commit a crime and where such act creates "a substantial risk that the offense would be committed by a person not otherwise disposed to commit it" (§40.05 Penal Law of New York State).

entreat To beg, urge, plead.

entry (1) Act of making or entering a record; (2) passage, hallway, door, gate, vestibule of a structure; (3) in criminal law, unlawful passage of a person into a structure; (4) entrance, ingress, admission; (5) descriptive record in a book.

enumerate List, number specifically, count.

enure (inure) [en YOOR] To take effect, be available, accustom, accrue.

envoy (1) Minister to a foreign government, next in rank to an ambassador; (2) person sent to represent one government in its relations with another.

eo die [AY oh DEE ay] On the same day.

eo instanti [AY oh in STON tee] At the same instant, immediately.

eo nomine [AY oh NOM i nay] Under that name.

epilepsy Chronic nervous disease that involves changes in state of consciousness and motion.

epoch [EP uhk] (1) Era; (2) time marked by an event considered as beginning a distinct period; (3) extended period of time.

equal -adj. Alike, uniform, of the same quantity, equivalent; -n. match; -v. to be identical in value or quantity.

equal protection of the laws Status of protection and security of life, liberty and property afforded to all persons in equal measure and without discrimination.

equality Simultaneous possession by two or more persons of same rights, privileges and immunities, and subjection to same duties.

equalization (1) Process of bringing about conformity to a common standard; (2) process of equalizing real estate assessments or taxes as between various taxing districts, so as to make tax burden in dollars proportionate to value of property being taxed in the various districts.

equalize (1) To cause to correspond or be alike in quantity; (2) to make uniform.

equally divided Method of dividing estate by which all individuals receive the same amount.

equilibrium (1) State of adjustment between opposing forces; (2) poise, balance.

equitable (1) That which exists or can be obtained through equity or a court of equity; (2) just, fair.

equitable action One in which jurisdiction lies in a court of equity.

equitable defense One founded on a distinct ground within the jurisdiction of a court of equity.

equitable election Obligation imposed upon a person to choose between inconsistent rights or benefits, where it was clearly the intention of the donor that only one was to be enjoyed.

equitable estoppel [EK wit uh buhl e STOP uhl] Condition whereby one is precluded by act or silence from asserting rights which might otherwise prevail.

equity (1) Fairness, impartiality; (2) system of jurisprudence first administered by the English courts of chancery to protect and enforce legal rights and obligations; (3) monetary value of an interest in property.

equity jurisdiction Cases and controversies calling for exercise of power of an equity court.

equity of redemption Right of the mortgagor of an estate to redeem it after a forfeiture, upon payment of the debt together with interest and costs.

equivalent (1) Equal in value, force, power or effect; (2) tantamount.

equivocal Ambiguous, having several meanings, inconclusive.

erasure Obliteration of matter from a written instrument by rubbing, scraping or scratching out.

erect -adj. Upright, vertical; -v. to construct, build, raise, establish.

ergo [UHR goh] Therefore, hence.

ermine White fur lining of the state robe of a judge, symbolic of purity, honor, dignity and authority.

erosion (1) Gradual wearing away of soil by operation of currents or tides; (2) progressive impairment or destruction.

erotic Sexual, amatory.

errant Wandering, itinerant, fallible.

erratum [e ROT uhm] Error (pl.: errata).

erroneous Inaccurate, mistaken.

error (1) Mistake, lapse, slip, offense, fault; (2) incorrect application of the law in a case so as to furnish ground for review of the proceedings and reversal of judgment.

error coram nobis [E ruhr KAW ruhm NOH bis] (error before us) Writ of error which seeks to vacate a judgment of conviction in the court where it was rendered.

error of fact One which renders a judgment void or voidable by reason of proceedings based on a fact not known to the court and not apparent on the record.

error of law Erroneous legal conclusion drawn from facts accurately presented.

error, writ of (see **writ of error**) Legal pleading which seeks to vacate a judgment of conviction because of error in the proceedings.

escalation clause Provision in a lease or contract calling for increase in its financial terms upon happening of some event.

escalate (1) To ascend or carry up; (2) to increase in quantity.

escape -n. Evasion, leakage, secret departure of one from custody without authority; -v. to break away, get free, issue from confinement, avoid, elude, evade.

☆ **escape** *tentatively recommended national category for prosecution, courts and corrections statistics* The unlawful departure of a lawfully confined person from official custody.

escrow [ES kroh] Fund or instrument held by a third person conditionally as security for the happening of a contingency or performance of a condition between two parties.

escrowee [es kroh EE] Person holding an escrow in trust.

espouse (1) To marry; (2) to advocate, adopt, defend, support.

Esquire English title of dignity (next above gentleman) used by members of legal profession in the United States as a title of courtesy without precise meaning.

essence That which is an indispensable attribute or necessary element of a thing.

essential Requisite, necessary, basic, fundamental.

establish To make, form, bring into being, found, prepare.

establishment Institution, place of business, settled arrangement.

estate (1) Interest in real property; (2) subject matter of ownership, condition of an owner with respect to his property, both real and personal; (3) that which a man can sell or pass on to another; (4) social or political class or rank.

estate by entirety Co-ownership of property by husband and wife where upon the death of either, the survivor takes undivided estate under the original conveyance.

estate for life (see **life estate**) Interest in property for one's lifetime, and its transfer upon death by operation of law.

estate in common Interest in property wherein two or more persons hold a joint and undivided interest without right of survivorship as between them.

estate in fee simple Absolute property interest clear of any limitation, condition or restriction; the highest estate known to the law.

estate in joint tenancy [es TAYT in joynt TEN uhn see] Property interest held by two or more persons each having the same interest.

estate in severalty [es TAYT in SEV ruhl tee] Property interest held by one person in his own right, without interest therein of any other person.

estate of inheritance Property interest which may descend to heirs.

estate on conditional limitation Property interest held by a grantee subject to a contingent event so that upon the happening or failure of the contingency the estate shall Pass to another.

estate on limitation Property interest created by words denoting duration of time, to revert thereafter to the grantor upon occurrence of the limiting event.

estate pur autre vie [es TAYT poor OH truh vee] (see **pur autre vie**) Property interest to extend during the life of another.

estate tax Excise tax on privilege of transferring property by reason of death. Estate tax is upon the interest which ceases by reason of death; inheritance tax is upon the interest to which the living person succeeds.

estate upon condition Interest in property which depends upon the happening of a specified event to create, enlarge or end the estate.

estimate -n. Judgment, approximation, valuation; -v. to consider, judge, value, appraise.

estop [e STOP] To stop, impede, prevent, preclude, bar, prohibit.

estoppel [e STOP uhl] Legal preclusion or bar by which a person is precluded or prevented from claiming that which he has previously denied, or denying that which he has previously claimed.

estoppel in pais [e STOP uhl in PAY is] Preclusion of one from asserting rights against another who has relied upon the conduct of the first party and been led thereby to change his status to his detriment.

et [et] And.

et al [et ol] (et alii) And others.

etc. [et SET uh ruh] (et cetera) And so forth, and others.

ethical Conforming to moral precepts or professional standards.

ethics (1) Discipline dealing with moral duty and obligation, right and wrong; (2) principles of conduct governing an individual or a profession.

et seq. [et sek] (et sequentes) And the following.

et ux. [et uks] (et uxor) And wife.

et vir [et veer] And husband.

eunuch [YOO nuhk] Castrated male.

euthanasia Act of painlessly killing a person suffering from an incurable disease.

evade To avoid, escape, elude.

evasion (1) Act of avoidance, escape or flight; (2) act of dodging or circumventing a law or obligation.

evasive Elusive, shifty, vague, nebulous.

event Occurrence, activity, case.

every Each one of all, without exception.

evict (1) To recover possession of real property by operation of law; (2) to expel, eject, oust.

eviction Legal process by which one in possession of real property is removed therefrom in favor of the owner.

evidence Any form of proof used to induce belief or establish a fact.

evidence of debt Written instrument importing obligation to repay a loan.

evidence of title Deed or other documentary indicia of ownership.

evident Clear, plain, manifest, obvious, apparent.

evidentiary [ev i DEN shuh ree] Having the quality of evidence.

evil -adj. (1) Bad, immoral, wicked, sinful; (2) foul, offensive, painful; -n. (3) wickedness, sin; (4) misfortune, calamity, disaster.

evolution Expectable development from precedents, organic development, process of change.

evolve To develop by experience, derive, unfold.

ex [eks] From, out of, on account of, according to, by, without.

ex aequo et bono [eks EK woh et BOH noh] According to what is equitable and good.

ex cathedra [eks kuh THEE druh] (from the chair) With authority, by virtue of one's office.

ex contractu [eks kuhn TRAK too] Upon, from a contract.

ex delicto [eks duh LIK toh] By reason of a wrong, arising from a wrongful act.

ex gratia [eks GRO tee uh] As a matter of grace, favor or indulgence, gratuitous, not compelled by law.

ex mero motu [eks ME roh MOH too] Of his own accord, voluntarily, by his own mere motion.

ex officio [eks uh FISH ee oh] By reason of office, without appointment other than by holding a particular office.

ex parte [eks PAHR tay] On one side, done in behalf of or on application of only one party.

ex post facto [eks pohst FAK toh] (after the fact) Having retroactive effect.

ex post facto law [eks pohst FAK toh law] Law passed after occurrence of an event which retrospectively changes legal consequences of such event.

ex rel. [eks rel] (ex relatione) On the relation of.

ex relatione [eks ruh lo tee OH nay] (upon relation or information) Term used in caption of a legal proceeding instituted in name of the state but on information of an individual who has a private interest in the matter, as in a writ of habeas corpus (People ex rel Jones v. The Warden).

ex tempore [eks TEM puh ray] By lapse of time.

exact -adj. Strict, particular, in complete accord; -v. to demand, force, compel, extort.

exaction (1) Wrongful act of one compelling payment of a fee or reward for services rendered under color of official authority, where no payment is due; (2) levying of tribute, extortion; (3) something exacted; a payment secured by severity or injustice.

exalt To raise in rank, dignity, wealth, power or character.

examination (1) Preliminary investigation of an accusation made against one for a crime; (2) interrogation on oath before a court or by an examiner; (3) search, scrutiny, investigation, interrogation.

examination before trial Pre-trial interrogation under oath of a party to an action or a witness.

examination in chief Direct examination by the party calling the witness.

examine To investigate, search, interrogate, test, seek to ascertain, scrutinize.

examiner (1) One charged with conduct of examinations; (2) person who inspects a given thing or situation, as, an examiner for an administrative board.

except (1) To protest against, object; (2) but, not including, other than, unless.

exception (1) Act of excepting, excluding, omitting; (2) objection; (3) formal objection to action of a court in overruling an objection or denying a request to charge the jury upon some point.

excess (1) Amount by which one quantity is greater than another; (2) state of going beyond limits, surplus.

excess insurance (1) Insurance coverage of a risk arising only after loss exceeds a stated amount; (2) insurance in amount greater than required by a co-insurance clause; (3) insurance coverage on a second policy insuring the same risk.

excessive (1) Greater than what is usual or proper, exceeding normal and reasonable limit or measure; (2) intemperate, immoderate, extreme, exorbitant.

exchange -n. (1) Transfer of goods, trade, barter; (2) place where securities and commodities are sold; (3) substitution of one thing for another; -v. to barter, swap, trade.

excise -n. Duty or tax on articles produced or consumed within the country; -v. to cut out, delete, expunge.

exclude To keep out, prevent entry, rule out.

exclusion Denial of entry, rejection, act of excluding.

exclusionary Tending to exclude. Exclusionary rule in law of evidence is the principle, now applicable in state as well as Federal courts, that evidence illegally obtained may not properly be received at the trial.

exclusive Vested in one alone.

excommunication Ecclesiastical censure in nature of exclusion from fellowship and communion of a church.

exculpate [eks KUL payt] To acquit, prove innocence, absolve, exonerate, vindicate.

exculpation [eks kul PAY shuhn] Clearing of alleged fault or guilt.

exculpatory [eks KUL puh taw ree] Tending to acquit or absolve.

excusable Capable of being excused, forgiven, justified, acquitted of blame.

excusable homicide [eks KYOO zuh buhl HOM i sahyd] Killing of a human in self defense or by misadventure without criminal intent.

☆ **excusable homicide** [eks KYOO zuh buhl HOM i sahyd] The intentional but justifiable causing of the death of another, or the unintentional causing of the death of another by accident or misadventure, without gross negligence.

excusable neglect Failure to take proper action at proper time by reason of some unexpected or unavoidable hindrance or accident, or reliance on promises made by one's adversary.

excuse -n. Reason given in justification of fault or defect, absolution, justification, release; -v. to forgive, pardon, condone, overlook, grant exemption for, condone.

execute (1) To accomplish, put into effect, complete, obey, do; (2) to put to death a criminal in pursuance of a death sentence.

executed (1) Completed, performed; (2) put to death.

executed contract One that has been carried out according to its terms.

execution (1) Process of performance or accomplishment; (2) act of signing, sealing and delivering a legal instrument, or otherwise putting it into valid legal form; (3) judicial writ by which the order of a court is directed to be carried out; (4) imposition of death penalty on a person pursuant to court order.

executioner One who puts criminals to death pursuant to court order.

execution of judgment Process by which order of court is put into effect.

executive Head of executive department, one holding chief position of administrative or managerial responsibility.

executive agency One of government agencies under jurisdiction of the President, as, a cabinet department is an executive agency.

executive officer Military officer who is second in command of an organization.

executive pardon Act of grace which exempts an individual from punishment judicially ordered, as, an executive pardon granted by a governor of a state.

executive warrant Order for arrest issued by a governor.

executor [eg ZEK yoo tawr] Person appointed by a testator to carry out provisions of his will.

executor de son tort [eg ZEK yoo tawr duh sohn tawrt] (see **de son tort**) Person who acts as an executor although not having legal authority.

executory [eg ZEK yoo taw ree] That which remains to be carried out, future, incomplete.

executory contract [eg ZEK yoo taw ree KON trakt] One wherein something remains to be done by one or more parties.

executory interest [eg ZEK yoo taw ree IN trest] Future estate or interest, not presently in effect.

executrix [eg ZEK yoo triks] Female executor.

exemplary [eg ZEMP luh ree] (1) Serving as a pattern or form, deserving imitation; (2) commendable.

exemplary damages [eg ZEMP luh ree DAM uh jiz] Punitive damages by way of punishment for injury caused by aggravated circumstances or malice, in addition to compensation for the injury.

exempli gratia [eg ZEM plee GRO tee uh] For instance, for example; usually appears as e.g.

exemplification (1) Authentication of an official record for use in evidence, by additional proof as to capacity of person attesting it to be an official record; (2) act of showing or illustrating by example.

exemplify (1) To authenticate an official record for use in evidence, by use of additional proof as to the capacity of the person attesting it to be an official record; (2) to show or illustrate by example.

exempt To release or deliver from a liability or obligation.

exemption Immunity, freedom from a duty, burden, tax or charge.

exercise -n. Exertion, use, practice; -v. to make use of, to execute, bring into play.

exhaust To use up, consume, evacuate, tire.

exhaustion Process of exhausting, state of over-exertion.

exhibit -n. (1) Physical evidence produced for examination; (2) collection of articles displayed in a public showing; -v. (3) to show, display, present for inspection, produce in public, explain.

exhibition (1) Public showing; (2) display of athletic or other skill.

exhumation Disinterment, removal of that which has been buried.

exhume To disinter, remove from the earth.

exigency Imperativeness, urgency, pressure.

exigent Demanding, pressing, critical, exacting.

exile -n. (1) Banishment, expulsion from home; (2) person banished; -v. (3) to banish, expel, drive away.

exist To live, be in effect, come into being.

existence (1) Actual or present occurrence; (2) state of being.

existing (1) Having actual or real being; (2) presently effective.

exit -n. Departure, means of egress; -v. to go out, depart.

exonerate To relieve, exculpate, clear from accusation or blame.

exoneration (1) Discharge; (2) removal of a burden, charge or duty.

exorbitant Excessive, going beyond appropriate limits.

expatriate -n. One who abandons or renounces allegiance to his country and becomes a subject of another; -v. to quit allegiance to one country in favor of another; to drive into exile.

expatriation Act of abandoning and renouncing allegiance to one country in favor of another.

expect (1) To await, look forward to an event; (2) to suppose, think, believe, hope for.

expectancy (1) That which is expected or hoped for; (2) condition of being deferred to a future time; (3) act of waiting.

expectancy of life Number of years which a person of a given age may expect to live, based upon actuarial computation.

expectant Waiting in anticipation; pregnant.

expediency (1) Utility, convenience, fitness, suitability; (2) haste, dispatch.

expedient Apt, suitable, appropriate, advisable.

expedite To hasten, speed, facilitate.

expedition (1) Journey or excursion for a specific purpose; (2) speed, haste.

expeditious Quick, speedy.

expel To eject, dislodge or put out with force.

expend To pay out, consume.

expenditure Disbursement, laying out of money.

expense Outlay, charge, cost.

experience (1) Skill, facility, practical wisdom gained by personal knowledge; (2) repeated performance of process through which one attains knowledge or wisdom; (3) something personally encountered or lived through.

experiment -n. Test, observation, trial; -v. to try, test, experience.

expert -adj. Having special skill or knowledge derived from training or experience; -n. one specially qualified in a field by reason of training, skill, or familiarity with the subject matter.

expert evidence Testimony offered by person qualified by training, skill or familiarity with subject matter to give an opinion based upon a particular state of facts presented or assumed.

expert witness One possessing special or peculiarly unique knowledge, skill or familiarity acquired from experience or training.

☆ **expert witness** A person who, on the basis of his training, work or experience as an expert in the field, is qualified to testify on the standard and scientific facts in a particular science, trade or art.

expiration (1) Termination, cessation, death; (2) exhalation.

☆ **expiration of sentence** *recommended statistical terminology* In correctional usage, the termination of the period of time during which an offender has been required to be under the jurisdiction of a state prison or parole agency as the penalty for an offense.

expire (1) To end, cease, terminate; (2) to die.

explicate To give a detailed account of, interpret, clarify, extricate.

explicit Clear, precise, without ambiguity or reservation, definite, unequivocal.

explode (1) To burst suddenly, detonate, usually with a loud noise; (2) to release pressure suddenly; (3) to shatter.

exploit -n. Deed, act, feat; -v. to use for advantage of another, utilize.

exploitation Process of using for one's benefit or turning to one's account.

exploration Examination, investigation, search.

explore To search, look for, investigate, examine.

explosion Sudden and violent expansion accompanied by bursting of container and loud noise.

explosive -adj. Tending to burst suddenly; -n. substance used to generate sudden and violent expansion.

export -n. Commodity sent from one country to another for purpose of trade; -v. to carry or send to another country.

expose To show publicly, display, exhibit, make accessible, reveal.

exposition (1) Explanation, interpretation; (2) public display.

exposure Act of placing on display, exhibiting, disclosure.

express -adj. (1) Clear, definite, explicit, unmistakable; -n. (2) common carrier for speedy transport of persons or goods; -v. (3) to force out, press, squeeze, empty by pressure; (4) to utter, voice, broach.

express authority Permission given in direct terms, exactly and plainly stated.

expression Manifestation, utterance, sign.

express warranty Definite statement guaranteeing a material fact.

expropriate To take property of another for one's own use.

expropriation (1) Act of appropriation to one's own use; (2) taking of property for government purpose under right of eminent domain.

expulsion Ejectment, banishment, act of driving out.

expunge To destroy, obliterate, strike out, omit.

expurgate To purge, cleanse, remove objectionable portions.

extend To lengthen, proffer, prolong, protract, advance.

extended Lengthy, prolonged, protracted, widespread.

extended insurance Status of life insurance policy which is continued in **force** in its original face amount without further payment of premium for the period allowed by its cash value.

extension Addition, enlargement, lengthening.

extensive (1) Widely dispersed; (2) thorough, far-reaching.

extent Amount, scope, dimension, magnitude.

extenuate To palliate, mitigate, excuse.

extenuating circumstances Those which render an act less aggravated.

extenuation Excuse, pardon, mitigation.

exterior Outside, external.

external Apparent, outward, exterior.

extinct Extinguished, defunct, deceased.

extinguish To put an end to, quench, bring to an end, crush, nullify.

extinguishment Destruction, cancellation, act of putting out, extinction.

extort To compel, coerce, gain by unlawful means.

extortion Act of unlawfully obtaining money from another by enforcing oppressive conditions or circumstances.

☆ **extortion** Unlawfully obtaining or attempting to obtain something of value from another by compelling the other person to deliver it by the threat of eventual physical injury or other harm to that person or his property, or a third person.

extra (1) Beyond, additional; (2) unusually, uncommonly, extremely.

extract -n. (1) Portion, fragment, summary, outline; (2) certified copy of a record or document; (3) essence, concentrate; -v. (4) to draw out, pull from a fixed position; (5) obtain by effort, separate.

extradite To secure physical presence of an alleged fugitive in the demanding state, from the jurisdiction where he may presently be.

extradition Process by which one state (asylum state) surrenders an alleged fugitive found within its territory to the jurisdiction wherein the crime was allegedly committed (demanding state) for purposes of criminal prosecution.

☆ **extradition** The surrender by one state to another of an individual accused or convicted of an offense in the second state.

extrajudicial (1) Effected outside the scope of regular judicial proceedings; (2) not founded upon or connected with a court of law.

extraneous Not relevant, derived from outside sources not pertinent to the issue under consideration.

extraordinary Unusual, irregular, rare, uncommon, beyond average or normal.

extrapolate To arrive at conjectured knowledge of the unknown by inference from known or observed data.

extraterritoriality Operation of law of a jurisdiction beyond its geographical boundaries.

extravagant (1) Lavish, prodigal; (2) excessive, intemperate; (3) strange, curious.

extreme -adj. (1) Existing in highest or greatest possible degree; (2) going to exaggerated lengths; (3) immoderate, excessive; (4) most remote, utmost; -n. (5) critical circumstance, strait, hardship, maximum.

extremis [eks TREE mis] Near death. Person is in extremis when he is sick, death is imminent and he is beyond hope of recovery.

extremity (1) Furthest point or projection; (2) an arm, leg, hand or foot; (3) severe, violent, desperate act or measure.

extrinsic Foreign to the subject matter, from an outside source, extraneous.

extrinsic evidence That not contained in the body of an agreement or instrument.

extrovert Person whose interests are external and outside of self.

eyewitness One who has seen the events he is called upon to describe.

☆ **eyewitness** A person who directly perceives an event or thing related to a criminal case, via sight, hearing, touch, or smell, usually a person other than the victim.

F

fabricate (1) To falsify or create with intent to deceive; to tell a lie; (2) to manufacture, form, build.

fabricated evidence Falsehood deceitfully contrived so as to furnish needed proof.

fabrication (1) Creation or statement calculated to deceive; (2) process of assembling materials to form a product.

face value (1) Amount shown on face of instrument; (2) par value of corporate stock; (3) apparent value, as, to accept something at face value.

facias [FO kee uhs] That you do, or cause.

facile [FAS uhl] (1) Easily accomplished, easy, superficial; (2) lacking in sincerity or depth.

facilitate To make easier, remove difficulty or impediment.

☆ **facilitation** Unlawful conduct on the part of a person by which he or she knowingly aids another person to commit a crime.

facility (1) Ease, readiness; (2) institution or object designed for a particular purpose.

☆ **facility** Generally, a structure or location built or established to serve a particular purpose.

facsimile [fak SIM i lee] Exact copy.

fact Thing having reality, actual occurrence, event, circumstance.

factor (1) One acting as agent for a principal in sale of principal's goods and having authority to receive payment; (2) one of matters to be considered in production of a result; (3) organization or person providing funds to a business in exchange for assignment of its accounts receivable.

factoring Purchase of accounts receivable from a business to provide operating funds for the business and give to the purchaser of the accounts (factor) the burden and right of collection.

factory Business establishment for manufacture of goods.

faculty (1) Skill, ability, aptitude; (2) teaching body of an educational institution.

fail (1) To neglect, omit, refuse, lack; (2) to lose vigor, decline in health.

failure Want, neglect, defeat, omission, default.

failure of consideration Neglect, refusal, or omission of a party to a contract to perform or furnish the consideration agreed upon.

failure of issue Death without surviving descendants to receive one's estate.

failure of proof Lack of evidence to support allegations of a pleading, complaint or charge.

failure of title Inability to establish good and marketable title.

failure to bargain collectively Refusal by employer or union to negotiate in good faith on terms and conditions of employment.

fair Equitable, reasonable, justifiable, valid.

fair and reasonable value Largest amount obtainable at voluntary and public sale.

fair cash value Largest cash amount obtainable at voluntary and public sale.

fair comment Honest expression of reasonable criticism or opinion concerning established facts on matters of public interest, as a defense to charge of libel or in summation by counsel to a jury.

fair consideration Valid, reasonable payment, given in good faith, by one party to a contract to the other.

fair equivalent Equivalent, reasonable amount or quantity in exchange for another.

fair hearing One conducted in accordance with due process and fundamental principles of law.

fair market price Price currently obtainable for goods at voluntary and public sale.

fair market value Price obtainable as result of negotiation between a willing buyer and a willing seller, where both parties have reasonable knowledge to relevant facts, and neither is under any compulsion to buy or sell.

fair on its face In proper form, so that extraneous evidence would be required to establish unfairness or illegality.

fair preponderance Quantity greater or weightier, more convincing on one side than on another.

fair return Reasonable income secured from an investment of capital.

fair trial One conducted in accordance with due process and fundamental rules of law by an impartial court.

fair value Market value reasonably obtainable in public sale by willing seller from a willing buyer.

fait accompli [fet uh kom PLEE] Accomplished act.

faith Belief, trust, reliance, credence, confidence.

faithful Trustworthy, reliable, loyal, conscientious.

fake adj. False, counterfeit; -n. imitation intended to deceive; -v. to falsify.

faker Swindler, one who deceives.

false Not true, artificial, contrary to fact, counterfeit, erroneous, sham, dishonest.

false and misleading Intentionally untrue and intended to deceive.

false arrest Unlawful or unauthorized taking into custody.

falsehood Untruth wilfully made and intended to deceive.

false imprisonment Arrest and detention of a person unlawfully, illegal deprivation of liberty.

false pretenses Untrue representations of fact made to obtain money or deceive.

false representation Untrue statement of an existing fact or circumstance, knowingly and wilfully made to deceive.

false statement Untrue and deceitful oral or written expression, made with intent to deceive.

false swearing Knowingly and wilfully giving false statement or testimony under oath.

false witness Giving of untrue testimony, knowing it to be untrue.

falsus in uno, falsus in omnibus [FAWL suhs in OO noh, FAWL suhs in OM nuh buhs] (false in one thing, false in everything) Doctrine or maxim by which a jury may, if they find a witness has testified falsely in one material respect, disregard all the other testimony of that witness.

family (1) Household; (2) persons living in one house under one head or management; (3) group descending from a common ancestor.

fanatic -adj. (1) Extravagant, mad, unreasonable; -n. (2) lunatic; (3) enthusiast.

faro [FAY roh] Illegal card game, in which all other players play against the banker or dealer.

f.a.s. (free alongside ship) Delivery without charge at a dock, from which goods are loaded on a ship by others.

fascism Political system based upon centralized totalitarian authority, abolition of democratic practices and civil liberties, and fostering of strong nationalist sentiment.

fascist One espousing fascism, member of fascist political party.

fatuous Silly, absurd, stupid, simple.

fault -n. Neglect, error, failing, vice, defect, impairment of excellence, want of care, improper act or omission, imperfection, blemish; -v. to blunder, fail, blame.

favor -n. (1) Act of kindness or generosity; (2) partiality, interest, behalf; -v. (3) to aid, show partiality for, encourage.

fealty [FEEL tee] Fidelity, allegiance, loyalty.

fear -n. Apprehension of distress, harm or punishment; -v. to stand in awe of, be afraid of, be apprehensive.

feasance [FEE zuhns] Doing of an act, performance.

feasible [FEE zuh buhl] Capable of being done or accomplished, suitable, reasonable.

feasor [FEE zawr] Doer, maker.

federal Belonging to a union of states which have surrendered their sovereignty to the central government, retaining limited and residuary power in themselves.

federation (1) Organization of states; (2) organization or association for some purpose.

fee (1) Payment for official or professional services; (2) estate in land; (3) fixed charge for admission or privileges, as, an entrance fee.

fee simple Estate in land without limitation or condition.

fee tail Estate in land in which there is a fixed line of inheritable succession so that general succession of heirs, as well as power of alienation, is cut off, and possibility of reversion exists if there is no issue that can inherit.

feign To pretend, simulate.

fellatio [fuh LAY shee oh] Sexual contact involving male sex organ of one party and mouth of another.

fellow servant One of several engaged in a common activity for same master.

fellow servant rule Doctrine that where several employees of the same employer are engaged in a common endeavor under such circumstances that their employer, having observed due care, cannot reasonably guard against their negligence, the employer will not be held liable for an injury to one caused by negligence of another.

felo de se [FEL oh de say] (a felon as to himself) A suicide.

felon [FEL uhn] One who has committed felony, one convicted of felony.

felonious [fuh LOH nee uhs] (1) Criminal, malicious, wicked, unlawful; (2) of the grade or quality of a felony.

felony [FEL uh nee] (1) Serious crime as defined by statute, usually punishable by death or imprisonment in a state prison, or other severe penalty; (2) criminal offense greater than a misdemeanor.

☆ **felony** A criminal offense punishable by death, or by incarceration in a prison facility.

feme covert [fom koh VAYR] Married woman.

feme sole [fom sohl] Single woman, including one widowed, divorced, or in some cases, separated.

fence (1) One who receives stolen property; (2) dealer in stolen property.

feoffee [fef EE] One to whom an estate in land (fee) is conveyed.

feoffment [FEF muhnt] Granting of an estate in land by actual delivery of possession.

feoffor [FEF awr] One who conveys an estate in land.

ferae naturae [FE rahy NA chuh rahy] Wild animals in their native state.

fetishism (fetichism) (1) Abnormal sexual desire aroused by an object; (2) extravagant and irrational devotion to an object, idea or practice.

fetus (foetus) Unborn child.

feud (1) Inheritable right to use and occupation of land, held on condition of rendering services to the lord or proprietor who retained title to the property; (2) form of private war, enmity, quarrel.

feudal (1) Growing out of the feudal system as it existed in Europe during the 11th, 12th and 13th centuries; (2) characterized by impressive, imperious style and manner of citizenry; (3) relating to control by a ruling class.

fiat [FEE ot] (let it be done) Order, warrant, command or decree by constituted authority.

fiction (1) Assumption in law that something is true when it is or may be false; (2) fabrication of the mind; (3) literary work based on its author's imagination.

fictitious Arbitrarily invented, pretended, counterfeit, false, imaginary.

fidelity Loyalty, reliability, devotion.

fidelity bond Form of insurance on personal honesty of an employee.

fides [FEE des] Faith, honesty, confidence, trust, as, bona fides (good faith).

fiduciary [fi DOO shee e ree] -adj. (1) Founded upon trust or confidence; -n. (2) trustee of property having duty to act faithfully for another's benefit; (3) legal status accorded to person acting in particular relationship to others, based upon good faith, loyalty and confidence, including executors, administrators, trustees, partners, corporate directors, brokers, attorneys, receivers and others.

fiduciary capacity [fi DOO shee e ree kuh PAS uh tee] Status of person acting for the benefit of another in a relation of confidence, trust and good faith.

fiduciary relation [fi DOO shee e ree ruh LAY shuhn] Mutual relationship of trust, confidence, reliance and good faith.

fieri [FEE uh ree] To be made, to be done.

fieri facias [FEE uh ree FO kee uhs] (that you cause to be made) Common law writ of execution commanding sheriff to levy an execution on goods of a judgment debtor to satisfy the judgment.

filch To steal, pilfer.

file -n. (1) Court record of a case; (2) collection of papers and records of a legal matter; (3) place where records are kept; -v. (4) to place papers in custody, as, to file a legal instrument in a court or with a recording officer, for its permanent preservation as a public record.

filiate [FIL ee ayt] To determine male parentage of an illegitimate child.

filiation [fil ee AY shuhn] (1) Relationship of parent and child; (2) adjudication of paternity.

filiation, order of [fil ee AY shuhn, AWR duhr uv] Written finding by a court declaring one to be the father of an illegitimate child.

☆ **filing** I. *recommended general court caseload statistical terminology* The initiation of a case in court by formal submission to the court of a document alleging the facts of a matter and requesting relief.
II. *recommended criminal justice statistical terminology* The initiation of a criminal case in a court by formal submission to the court of a charging document, alleging that one or more named persons have committed one or more specified criminal offenses.

filius [FIL ee uhs] Son, child.

fill To make full, occupy whole extent of, complete, satisfy.

final Last, conclusive, completed, decisive.

final determination Ultimate settling of rights of parties to an action.

final order Judgment of a court which determines a fact and prevents further litigation upon the matter.

final settlement Ultimate determination of monies paid and payable.

find -n. (1) Discovery; -v. (2) to discover, come upon, detect; (3) to ascertain, declare, determine a controversy in favor of one of the parties.

finder (1) One who discovers lost property of another; (2) one who originates a financial transaction for a fee.

finder's fee Payment given by one who receives a profit as result of a business deal brought to him.

finding (1) Conclusion reached upon some matter by a judge, jury, examiner, coroner or referee; (2) result of an inquiry or investigation.

☆ **finding** Commonly, a decision by a judicial officer or a jury as to a matter of fact; occasionally used to mean a decision by a judicial officer as to a matter of law, that is, a "judgment."

finding of fact Specific determination or conclusion made as to facts established by evidence.

fine -n. Sum paid as a punishment; -v. to impose pecuniary punishment.

☆ **fine** The penalty imposed upon a convicted person by a court, requiring that he or she pay a specified sum of money to the court.

firearm Weapon that propels shot, shells or bullets by explosion of gunpowder.

firebug Incendiary, pyromaniac, arsonist.

fire wall Noncombustible partition, as defined in a building code.

fireworks Flammable and explosive contrivances used for display and exhibition.

firm -adj. Unyielding, immovable; definite; -n. business organization.

firmly Fixedly, steadfastly, solidly.

first Preceding all others, foremost.

first blush Initial reaction, original impression.

first class Of superior grade or kind.

first class mail Sealed matter containing writing, as defined by postal regulations.

first impression New or novel point of law, question on which precedent is not available.

first in, first out rule In accounting, assumption that merchandise first sold is that which was first bought, as a procedural device for valuation of inventory.

fiscal Pertaining to finances.

fiscal year Any twelve month period used for budgeting, computation of income and expenditures, and preparation of financial reports.

fit Suitable, appropriate, qualified.

fix -v. (1) To determine, to make permanent or certain as to value;
(2) to arrange, prepare; (3) to repair, adjust, regulate; -n. (4) corrupt arrangement to obtain a desired result; (5) predicament, dilemma.

fixed (1) Determined, agreed on, settled; (2) permanent, stationary;
(3) corruptly arranged to obtain a desired result.

fixed asset One used in conduct of a business, such as land, buildings and
equipment.

fixed capital Investment in plant and equipment.

fixed charges Expenses such as rent, insurance and depreciation, which continue regardless of income.

fixed opinion Prejudgment, determination made before hearing evidence in a
case.

fixed price (1) Price agreed on; (2) established and unchanging price;
(3) uniform price for all customers.

fixing bail Setting amount of security required by a court to insure
appearance of a defendant when necessary.

fixture (1) Personal property so attached to realty that it may, under
particular circumstances, be legally regarded as part of the realty;
(2) chattel attached to realty for purpose of trade, such as store fixtures.

flagellate To whip, drive, punish.

flagellation Act of whipping, beating.

flagrant Notorious, glaring, gross, as, a flagrant neglect of duty.

flagrante delicto [fluh GRAN tay duh LIK toh] In the act of committing a crime or
misdeed.

flattery False or excessive praise, insincere compliments.

flee To leave in haste with purpose of avoiding or evading.

flight Voluntary and hasty departure to avoid arrest, detention or danger.

flim-flam Confidence game, trick, swindle.

float -n. Total amount of checks outstanding and in process of collection at any
given time; -v. to raise capital by issue of securities for sale to investors.

floater Policy insuring specific articles wherever they may be found, as, furs,
jewelry, money, securities or similar items.

floating debt Loans for which no permanent provision has been made as to
repayment.

floating policy Insurance to provide coverage on property frequently changing in
location and quantity.

flog To thrash, beat with a whip.

floor plan (1) Drawing showing arrangement of walls, doors, windows, partitions
and passages of a horizontal level of a building; (2) financing of merchandise
for dealers, whereby finance company advances funds to dealer secured by
inventory of merchandise on dealer's floor.

flotsam Wreckage of a ship or its cargo found floating on the water, as
distinguished from jetsam, which is that part of a ship, its equipment or cargo
that has been cast overboard in time of distress to lighten the load.

flourish (1) To brandish or wave, as, to flourish a gun; (2) to prosper, thrive,
blossom.

f.o.b. (free on board) Delivery of merchandise to a carrier without charge, for
further delivery by the carrier at the expense of the consignee.

focal Main, having a focus.

focus Central point, center of attention.

foetus (fetus) Unborn child.

folio (1) Prescribed number of words in a writing, generally one hundred; (2) number of a page; (3) largest size of a book; (4) leaf of a manuscript or book.

follow (1) To conform to, comply with, be determined by; (2) to pursue a trade or profession; (3) to occur later in time or sequence; (4) to trail, pursue.

for (1) In behalf of, in place of, equivalent to; (2) during, throughout, during the period of; (3) belonging to, by reason of, concerning; (4) as preparation toward, to bring about.

for collection Form of conditional indorsement on a note or check, by which transferee is authorized only to collect the face amount, and cannot transfer title to another.

for value received Term used in a bill of exchange or promissory note as prima facie evidence that a consideration has been given for it.

forbearance Restraint, delay, leniency, restraining from action.

force -n. Power or strength directed to a purpose, vigor, violence, compulsion; -v. to compel, do violence, exert maximum effort, coerce.

forced sale Sale made at time and place prescribed by law in furtherance of execution of a judgment.

force majeure [fawrs muh ZHOOR] (1) Superior or irresistible force; (2) event that cannot be anticipated or controlled.

☆ **forcible rape** Unlawful vaginal penetration of a female of any age against the will of the victim with use or threatened use of force, or attempting such an act.

☆ **forcible rape** *Uniform Crime Reports usage* Sexual intercourse or attempted sexual intercourse with a female against her will, by force or threat of force.

foreclose To shut out, bar, prevent, hinder, terminate rights of mortgagor.

foreclosure Equity proceeding by which the right of a mortgagor to redeem the mortgaged premises upon payment of the debt with interest is barred or foreclosed.

foreclosure decree Order of court to foreclose a mortgage or sell the mortgaged premises in order to satisfy the mortgage.

foreclosure sale Sale held to obtain satisfaction of a mortgage out of its proceeds.

foreign (1) Belonging to another nation, country or jurisdiction; (2) situated outside one's own country; (3) alien, strange, inappropriate.

foreign exchange (1) Credit instruments payable in the currency of another country; (2) process of settling accounts between residents of different countries.

foreign jurisdiction Jurisdiction other than the one having the matter under consideration.

foreign trade Export and import transactions.

foreman (1) Presiding member of a jury; (2) one who directs employees for a master, an overseer.

forensic [fuh REN zik] (1) Belonging to or applied in courts of justice and legal proceedings; (2) argumentative, rhetorical.

foresaid (aforesaid) Previously referred to.

foresee To anticipate, expect, consider beforehand.

foreseeability Concept in tort law for determining liability for accident or injury based on the predictability of its occurrence.

foresight (1) Prudence; (2) action directed to the future.

forfeit -n. (1) Misdeed, fine, penalty; -v. (2) to lose due to error, fault, offense or crime; (3) to subject to confiscation.

☆ **forfeit** Something to which the right is lost by failure to perform an obligation or by commission of a crime.

forfeiture Loss of some right or property as a penalty for illegal act, negligence, breach of contract or breach of obligation.

forge (1) To counterfeit or make falsely; (2) to sign name of another with fraudulent intent; (3) to fashion, make, produce.

☆ **forgery** The creation or alteration of a written or printed document, which if validly executed would constitute a record of a legally binding transaction, with the intent to defraud by affirming it to be the act of an unknowing second person; also the creation of an art object with intent to misrepresent the identity of the creator.

☆ **forgery and counterfeiting** In Uniform Crime Reports terminology, the name of the UCR offense category used to record and report arrests for offenses of making, manufacturing, altering, possessing, selling, or distributing, or attempting to make, manufacture, alter, sell, distribute, or receive "anything false in the semblance of that which is true."

form -n. (1) Manner, as of a pleading; (2) model to guide preparation of a legal document; (3) formality, ceremony, ritual; (4) figure, shape, conformation; -v. (5) to fashion, make, construct.

formality Requirement as to method, order, arrangement, technical expression, execution or performance.

former jeopardy [FAWR muhr JEP uhr dee] Plea offered as a defense to criminal prosecution that one has previously been subject to prosecution or punishment for the same offense.

formula (1) Recipe, schedule of ingredients; (2) prescribed or fixed form or method.

fornication (1) Sexual intercourse between two unmarried persons; (2) sexual intercourse between two persons, one of whom is unmarried.

forswear (1) To reject, deny or renounce, upon oath; (2) to swear falsely.

forthwith Immediately, without delay, promptly.

fortuitous Accidental, unexpected, happening by chance.

forum (1) Judicial tribunal; (2) place of jurisdiction; (3) meeting for discussion.

forum contractus [FAW ruhm kuhn TRAK tuhs] Jurisdiction of the place where a contract is made.

forum non conveniens [FAW ruhm nohn kuhn VEEN yens] Doctrine whereby one of two courts having jurisdiction declines to exercise it on the ground that interests of justice would be better served if the case were tried in the other jurisdiction.

forward (1) To advance, promote, hasten; (2) to transmit.

forwarder One who receives, assembles, transships, forwards and delivers goods as an agent.

foster parent One who rears a child as his own, without other legal relationship between them.

foundation (1) Basis upon which something is built; (2) incorporated or endowed institution or fund for philanthropic purposes.

founded Based upon, arising from, growing out of.

foundling Deserted infant.

four corners Entire area comprising something, as, that which is apparent on the face of a legal instrument is said to be within its four corners.

fraction Portion of a thing, less than the whole.

fragment Piece, part broken off.

frame-up Conspiracy to incriminate a person on false evidence.

franchise (1) Special privilege conferred by government, as, a franchise to a private person or corporation to operate a bus route; (2) privilege, jurisdiction or immunity accorded to an individual or class; (3) right given a person or group of persons to sell another's goods or services or use another's trade name or trademark for retail purposes in a particular area.

franchise tax Business tax on privilege given by a franchise.

frank -adj. Without concealment, marked by honesty and candor; -n. privilege of sending material through the mail without payment of postage, as, the franking privilege accorded to members of Congress.

fraternal (1) Brotherly; (2) relating to a fraternity or similar association.

fraternal benefit association Society for mutual aid and benefit of its members, usually including a prescribed form of customs and observances and deriving its income from dues and assessments.

fraternal insurance Life or accident insurance furnished by a fraternal benefit association to its members.

fraternity (1) Body of persons associated for their common interest, purpose or pleasure; (2) organization of male college students for scholastic or extracurricular activities.

fratricide Killing of one's brother or sister.

fraud (1) Deceitful practice or device used with intent to deprive or injure; (2) any artifice or misrepresentation by one to deceive another.

☆ **fraud** In Uniform Crime Reports terminology, the name of the UCR offense category used to record and report arrests for offenses of conversion or obtaining of money or other thing of value by false pretenses, except forgery, counterfeiting and embezzlement.

☆ **fraud offenses** *tentatively recommended national category for prosecution, courts and corrections statistics* The crime type comprising offenses sharing the elements of practice of deceit or intentional misrepresentation of fact, with the intent of unlawfully depriving a person of his property or legal rights.

fraudulent Deceitful, false, done with intent to carry out a fraud.

free (1) Having civil and political liberty limited only by laws which reasonably protect against infringement upon another's rights or liberties; (2) having no cost, charging nothing, supplied without payment, cost or obligation.

free on board Delivery of merchandise to a carrier, without charge, for further delivery by the carrier at the expense of the consignee (usually abbreviated f.o.b.).

freight (1) Compensation paid for transportation of goods; (2) goods being transported.

frenetic Frenzied, hectic, frantic.

frequent -adj. Common, habitual, familiar; -v. to visit often, to practice or partake of often.

fresh (1) Immediate, recent; (2) pure, brisk.

fresh pursuit Pursuit instituted immediately with intent to capture a wrongdoer, following his escape or commission of wrong.

friend of the court One not a party to a legal action who is permitted by a court to introduce argument, authority or evidence by reason of some interest in the subject matter.

friendly suit (1) One brought by an executor or administrator in the name of a creditor, against himself, in order to secure judicial approval for distribution of assets; (2) action brought by agreement of parties to obtain judicial decision on a doubtful matter.

frisk To run hands over another's person in search for weapons or contraband.

frivolous Insufficient in law, untenable, insufficient in substance, so bad as to indicate lack of good faith, superficial, irrelevant.

frolic and detour Act of a servant outside of and departing from the scope of his employment.

frontage Portion of land abutting upon a road or body of water.

frontier Portion of territory of a country which lies along the border line of another country.

fructus [FROOK tuhs] Fruit, increase, that which results or springs from a thing.

fructus industriales [FROOK tuhs in dus tree OL uhs] Fruits of industry such as crops of grain produced by one's labor and industry.

fructus naturales [FROOK tuhs na chuh ROL uhs] Products from the yield of nature, as, wool,milk, fruit.

fruit (1) Product of a tree or plant; (2) product, proceeds, result, as, the fruits of crime.

frustrate To hinder, delay, impede, hamper, circumvent.

frustration Defeat, disappointment.

fugitive One who flees.

☆ **fugitive** In FBI usage, includes both escapees and persons avoiding prosecution or custody: "fugitives from justice."

fugitive from justice One who commits a crime in one jurisdiction and goes to another to evade prosecution.

full Sufficient in quantity or degree, complete, entire, unabbreviated.

full age Age of legal majority as defined by statute.

full blood Descent from parents both of one pure breed, as, to be a full-blooded Indian is to be descended from parents both of whom in turn were descended from full-blooded Indians.

full court Court duly organized with all its judges sitting.

full faith and credit Requirement in the United States Constitution (Article IV) that the public acts, records and judicial proceedings of one state shall be given the same effect by the courts of other states that they have in the state wherein they were created.

☆ **full opinion** An opinion in writing, usually lengthy, presenting in detail the reasons and reasoning leading to the decision.

☆ **full pardon** An executive act completely and unconditionally absolving a person from all consequences of a crime and conviction.

full settlement Complete adjustment of differences, mutual release of obligation between parties.

☆ **full-time temporary release** *recommended statistical terminology* The authorized temporary absence of a prisoner from a confinement facility, for a period of 24 hours or more, for purposes relating to such matters as the prisoner's employment or education, or personal or family welfare.

function -n. Office, duty, appropriate activity, occupation; -v. to perform, serve, work.

functional Utilitarian, practical, connected with a function.

functionary Public officer or employee.

fund -n. (1) Sum of money set apart for a specific purpose; -v. (2) to provide an account to pay interest or other special purpose; (3) to make provision for payment of interest and reduction of principal and to convert a number of different debts into one.

fundamental law Constitution, organic law.

fungible goods [FUN juh buhl guhdz] Things that can be replaced by equal quantities and qualities of the same kind, as for example, wheat, sugar, rice.

furious Fierce, violent, turbulent.

furnish To supply, provide, equip.

further Additional, farther, moreover.

furtherance Advancement, promotion.

futures Contracts for the purchase or sale of given units of a commodity for future delivery at a specified price and date.

G

gage Pawn, pledge, security.

gain -n. (1) Profit, increase of advantage, value, benefit; (2) increase in amount, magnitude or degree; -v. (3) to obtain, secure, acquire, increase.

gainful Profitable, advantageous, remunerative.

gainful employment Ordinary employment such as an insured may fairly be expected to follow.

gambit (1) Remark designed to launch a conversation or make a point; (2) topic; (3) device, maneuver.

gamble -n. (1) Act of playing a game of chance for money; (2) chance, risk; -v. (3) to bet money on an event whose outcome is uncertain; (4) to expose to risk or hazard in the hope of gain.

gambler (1) One who habitually engages in games of chance to win money; (2) one who takes risks, speculator.

☆ **gambling** I. Staking or wagering of money or other thing of value on a game of chance, or on an uncertain event. II. *tentatively recommended national category for prosecution, courts and corrections statistics* Offenses relating to unlawful games of chance or wagering systems.

☆ **gambling** In Uniform Crime Reports terminology, the name of the UCR category used to record and report arrests for offenses relating to promoting, permitting, or engaging in gambling.

gambling device Apparatus or device designed and intended for playing games of chance for money.

game (1) Wild birds and animals; (2) athletic contest of skill; (3) amusement, pastime, diversion; (4) racket, trick.

game laws Statutes enacted to preserve wild birds and animals and prevent their unreasonable destruction.

game of chance One in which success depends on accidental or fortuitous circumstances rather than on skill.

gaming Gambling, playing games of chance for money.

gaming house Place maintained for gambling.

gang (1) Group jointly engaged in same work or under same direction; (2) group of persons joined in antisocial activity.

gangster (1) Member of gang of criminals; (2) one associated with others in violence, coercion or intimidation; (3) thug, gunman.

gaol [jayl] Jail.

garnish To attach the wages or other property of a debtor to secure repayment of the debt.

garnishee Person having money or property of a debtor which has been attached to secure repayment of the debt.

garnishment Attachment of money or property of a debtor in the hands of a third party, in order to obtain payment of the debt.

garnishor (1) One who obtains a garnishment; (2) creditor of the person whose property is garnished.

gauge -n. (1) Measurement according to a standard or system; (2) instrument used for testing, measuring; -v. (3) to measure exactly; (4) to estimate, appraise, judge.

general (1) Common to many, universal, not restricted; (2) a person or rank of highest military significance.

general appearance Appearance in a competent court, by a party for all purposes, giving a court complete jurisdiction as to that party.

general assignment Transfer of all property of a debtor for the benefit of creditors, with authority to liquidate debtor's property and distribute proceeds to creditors.

general verdict Jury verdict of guilty or not guilty on the entire case, both on the law and the facts.

genocide Crime of exterminating whole races, nationalities or religious groups.

genuine (1) True, authentic; (2) natural, sincere.

genus [JEE nuhs] General class or division marked by common characteristics.

germane [juhr MAYN] Appropriate, pertinent, relevant.

gerrymander [JE ree man duhr] -n. Pattern of election districts varying greatly in size, population or electorate as a result of change of district boundaries; -v. to divide an area into election districts in an unnatural and unfair way in order to favor one party by concentrating its strength while dispersing strength of the opposition.

gestation Period from conception to birth during which a fetus is carried in the womb.

gift (1) Voluntary transfer of property for which no consideration is given; (2) faculty, aptitude, talent, knack.

gift causa mortis [gift KOU zuh MAWR tis] Gift made in fear or anticipation of death but revocable until death.

gift inter vivos [gift IN tuhr VEE vohs] Gift between living persons, effective when made.

gist Main point in question, ground or foundation of a legal argument.

give To transfer, yield, bestow, confer ownership, allot, bequeath, present, award, permit, contribute, donate.

give bail To furnish security for one's required appearance in a legal proceeding.

give judgment To render or pronounce judgment in court.

give notice To communicate in proper or permissible manner information or warning of an existing or intended matter or course of conduct.

give way To deviate from a course so that another may pass without alteration of direction.

going concern Existing and solvent business.

going price Prevailing, current market price.

good (1) Valid, legally sufficient, responsible, appropriate; (2) useful, wholesome, sound.

good behavior (1) Conduct in conformity with law; (2) proper or correct conduct.

good cause (1) Legally sufficient reason, justification; (2) provocation that would motivate a reasonable man in the same circumstances.

good consideration (1) Valuable inducement or influence; (2) inducement or influence deemed legally sufficient to sustain a contract; (3) consideration of blood relationship or natural love and affection; (4) moral obligation founded on a previous legal obligation presently unenforceable.

good faith (1) Honesty of intention; belief in lawfulness of purpose; belief that known circumstances do not warrant further investigation; absence of fraud or collusion; (2) as defined in the Uniform Commercial Code, honesty in fact in the conduct or transaction concerned.

☆ **good time** In correctional usage, the amount of time deducted from time to be served in prison on a given sentence(s) and/ or under correctional agency jurisdiction, at some point after a prisoner's admission to prison, contingent upon good behavior and/or awarded automatically by application of a statute or regulation.

good title Property ownership that is marketable and free from doubt as to its validity.

good will (1) Favor which business management wins from the public, with probability that customers will continue their patronage; (2) capitalized value of excess earning power over normal rate; (3) benevolence, cheerful consent, zeal.

goods (1) Personal property of every description; (2) personal property not including animals or chattels real.

goods and chattels [guhdz and CHA tuhlz] (1) General and inclusive denomination of personal property to include living animals, right to crops, leaseholds and choses in action; (2) animate or inanimate personal property that is visible, tangible and movable, and has intrinsic value, as distinguished from choses in action or freehold property.

govern To direct, control, regulate, guide, administer, restrain.

government (1) Supreme political power in a nation, state or other political entity; (2) act or process of governing; (3) body of persons comprising governing authority of a political unit.

grace (1) License, dispensation, special favor from a person in power; (2) mercy exercised by an executive such as a governor in granting a pardon; (3) favor shown by postponing an action or granting a reprieve or temporary exemption from a penalty; (4) equitable relief.

grace, days of Extension of time allowed for payment.

grace period Time allowed after due date for payment of insurance premium, during which time policy continues in force and, thereafter, upon timely premium payment, coverage is extended.

grade -n. (1) Quality, value, rank, relative position, standard of quality; (2) elevation line of street in relation to a reference point; (3) to bring street surface to established level.

graft (1) Payment paid to or received by public employee as compensation for dishonest and corrupt act(s) or the omission of legal and obligatory act(s); (2) illegal practice for profit or personal gain.

grand jury Body of citizens of a county, who are legally drawn, empanelled and sworn, as defined by statute, to inquire into crimes allegedly committed or triable in the county.

☆ **grand jury** *recommended statistical terminology* A body of persons who have been selected according to law and sworn to hear the evidence against accused persons and determine whether there is sufficient evidence to bring those persons to trial, to investigate criminal activity generally, and to investigate the conduct of public agencies and officials.

grand larceny [grand LAHR suh nee] (1) Stealing of property above a specified value; (2) aggravated larceny of any amount, as defined by statute.

grandfather clause Provision in a statute exempting from its operation a class of persons who have, prior to its effective date, been engaged in activities now prohibited by the statute.

grant -n. (1) Transfer of real property from a grantor to a grantee; (2) consent, permission, acknowledgment; (3) allotment of monies for a particular purpose usually associated with educational or societal benefit objectives; -v. (4) to bestow, confer, convey, transfer; (4) to allow, accord, award.

grant, bargain and sell Operative words in a conveyance of real property.

☆ **grant of parole** *recommended statistical terminology* A release from prison by discretionary action of a paroling authority, conditional upon the parolee's fulfillment of specified conditions of behavior.

grantee (1) One to whom a conveyance of real property is made; (2) one to whom a grant is made.

grantor (1) One who makes a conveyance of real property; (2) one who grants.

gratification Pleasure, reward, something that pleases.

gratis [GRA tis] Free, without consideration.

gratuitous Without consideration, voluntary, free.

gratuity (1) Something freely given in return for a favor or service; (2) tip, bounty, benefit.

gravamen [GRAV uh men] (1) Substantial cause of a grievance or charge; (2) grievance complained of.

grave -adj. Serious, weighty, important; -n. place of burial.

great (1) Extraordinary; (2) of considerable magnitude, power or degree; (3) extreme, marked.

great writ [grayt rit] Habeas corpus to inquire into an alleged illegal deprivation of liberty.

grievance Injury, injustice, wrong, annoyance, displeasure, distress.

grievous Harmful, painful, offensive, oppressive, onerous, intense, severe.

gross -adj. (1) Great, excessive,entire, whole; (2) common, cheap, inferior; -n. (3) quantity of 144.

gross income Total receipts before deduction of any expenses.

gross negligence Failure of care, marked by total or nearly total disregard for the rights of others as well as total or nearly total indifference to consequences.

gross profit Excess of receipts over cost of goods sold, before deducting expenses.

gross weight Total weight including containers.

ground (1) Surface of earth; (2) foundation, basis, point relied on.

ground of action Fundamental theory and facts on which a legal proceeding is based.

ground rent Annual sum paid by a tenant or grantee for occupied land and the right to erect improvements thereon.

group insurance Master policy between insurer and an organization, by which insurer assumes liability for insurance of participating members of the organization, each of whom receives a certificate of coverage under the group policy.

guarantee (1) One to whom a guaranty is given; (2) agreement to answer as a guarantor for payment of debt or performance of duty.

guarantor [GA ruhn tawr] One who promises and is secondarily liable to pay a debt or perform a duty where person obligated in first instance fails to pay or perform.

guaranty [GA ruhn tee] (1) Promise by one to be responsible (secondarily liable) for payment of debt or performance of duty if person obligated in first instance fails to pay or perform; (2) assurance of responsibility for something.

guardian One who has control or management of the person or property, or both, of another who is incapable of acting for himself, as, a guardian for an infant or insane person.

guardian ad litem [GAHR dee uhn ad LAHY tuhm] Person appointed by a court to represent a minor or incompetent for purpose of some litigation.

guerilla [guh RIL uh] Member of independent body of armed men carrying on irregular warfare.

guest (1) One who lodges at an inn; (2) one who rides in automobile or occupies premises of another, without payment or compensation.

guild (1) Voluntary association of persons engaged in some trade, art, profession or business; (2) fellowship, society, association.

guilt (1) Delinquency, failure, fault; (2) state of being liable to penalty for an offense against law.

guilt by association Assumption of wrongdoing or unfitness by reason of one's companions, without other proof.

guilty (1) Responsible for delinquency, crime or evil; (2) blameworthy, culpable.

☆ **guilty plea** *recommended statistical terminology* A defendant's formal answer in court to the charge(s) contained in a complaint, information, or indictment, admitting that he or she did in fact commit the offense(s) listed.

☆ **guilty verdict** *recommended statistical terminology* In criminal proceedings, the decision by jury or judicial officer on the basis of the evidence presented at trial, that the defendant is guilty of the offense(s) for which he or she has been tried.

gun Weapon capable of discharging projectiles by use of gunpowder; portable firearm.

H

☆ **habeas corpus** [HAY bee uhs KAWR puhs] In criminal proceedings, the writ which directs the person detaining a prisoner to bring him or her before a judicial officer to determine the lawfulness of the imprisonment.

habeas corpus ad prosequendum [HAY bee uhs KAWR puhs ad pro suh KWEN duhm] Form of habeas corpus writ to produce a person held in custody before a court having jurisdiction of a charge against him, so that he may be prosecuted therein.

habeas corpus ad subjiciendum [HAY bee uhs KAWR puhs ad sub ji see EN duhm] The Great Writ, the usual remedy for a person unlawfully deprived of his liberty, addressed to him who detains a person in custody, and commanding that the person detained be produced before the court at the date and time specified, together with the authority by which detained, so that the court may inquire into the cause of detention and do that which is proper in the premises.

habeas corpus ad testificandum [HAY bee uhs KAWR puhs ad tes ti fi KON duhm] Form of habeas corpus writ used to bring a witness into court to testify, when the witness is in custody at the time.

habendum [ho BEN duhm] Clause of a real property deed, containing the words "to have and to hold," which defines the extent of the conveyance.

habit (1) Customary conduct, usual practice, behavior pattern; (2) an acquired mode of behavior that has become nearly or completely involuntary.

habitation Residence, dwelling.

habitual Customary, usual.

habitual criminal (1) One subject to increased surveillance, suspicion, or penalty, by reason of previous criminal conviction, as defined by statute; (2) one so adjudged by a court in accordance with statute.

☆ **habitual offender** A person sentenced under the provisions of a statute declaring that persons convicted of a given offense, and shown to have previously been convicted of another specified offense(s), shall receive a more severe penalty than that for the current offense alone.

habitually Customarily, frequently.

half-blood Person born of the same mother or father as another, but not having both parents in common.

half-brother Brother by one parent only.

half-sister Sister by one parent only.

hallmark Stamp or impression affixed by the maker of an object, as evidence of its genuineness or origin.

hallucination Sensing of an object or idea which does not exist, delusion.

hallucinogen [ha loo SIN uh jen] Substance, usually taken orally, that induces hallucinations.

hamlet Small village.

hand down (1) To announce or file a decision in a legal proceeding; (2) to transmit in succession, as, to hand down an object from father to son.

handle -n. (1) Part of an object designed for grasping it; (2) total amount wagered on a race or other event; -v. (3) to control, deal with, act on, manage.

handwriting Anything written by hand, including a mark made by one unable to write.

harbor -n. (1) Safe anchorage, port for ships; (2) place of security and shelter; -v. (3) to provide a refuge, to furnish shelter, lodging and food, as, to harbor a criminal; (4) to entertain or cherish, as, to harbor an idea.

hard cases make bad law Legal maxim which indicates that matters difficult to decide may not always be decided in accordance with optimum or minimal standards of equity and justice.

hard labor Compulsory work which may be required of imprisoned criminals.

hardship Suffering, onerous burden, privation, difficulty.

harmful Damaging, injurious.

harmless Inoffensive, free from guilt or loss, unhurt.

harmonize To reconcile, bring into accord.

harmony Agreement, accord, tranquility.

haul -n. (1) Result of an effort to collect; (2) (slang) proceeds of a crime; -v. (3) to pull, drag, transport.

have To keep, own, retain, include.

have and hold Phrase used in real property conveyances ("to have and to hold") as the operative words of the conveyance.

haven Place of safety, refuge.

hawk -v. To sell by calling out in the street; -n. sometimes used to denote a person favoring aggressive national policy in foreign relations.

hawker Peddler, one who sells his wares by calling in the street.

hazard Risk, peril, exposure to loss or injury, danger.

hazardous Perilous, risky, involving danger or loss.

headnote Summary of a legal principle or decision placed before its text in reported cases.

healthy Free from disease or bodily ailment; salutary, flourishing.

hearing (1) Trial of an action; (2) preliminary examination in case of a person charged with crime; (3) consideration of a matter by an executive, legislative or administrative body, including taking of testimony from witnesses; (4) court proceeding in which arguments and testimony are received on preliminary or interlocutory matters, as, the hearing of argument on a motion.

☆ **hearing** A proceeding in which arguments, witnesses, or evidence are heard by a judicial officer or administrative body.

hearsay Generally, information heard from someone else, as opposed to information based on personal observation or knowledge.

hearsay evidence Legal testimony of a witness (usually oral) based on something heard from another.

hedge -n. (1) Purchase or sale of commodity futures to offset risk of loss from variations in market price; (2) any purchase or sale made primarily for protection against a known risk; (3) ambiguous or equivocal statement or position; -v. (4) to eliminate or reduce risk of loss in a wager by placing offsetting wager on the opposing position; (5) to buy or sell as protection against loss due to price fluctuations; (6) to avoid decision or commitment.

heedless Unmindful, unobservant.

hegemony [he JEM uh nee] Dominance, leadership.

heir [ayr] One who inherits, or is entitled to receive under laws of intestacy, an estate upon the death of its owner.

heir apparent [ayr u PAR uhnt] One who is next in line of succession to an ancestor.

heir at law [ayr at law] Person who would receive a decedent's property if decedent dies without a will.

heir by devise [ayr bayh duh VAHYZ] One to whom real property is given (devised) by will.

heirloom [AYR loom] Personal chattel received by an heir.

heirs [ayrz] Persons who inherit, or are entitled to receive under laws of intestacy, an estate upon the death of its owner.

heirs and assigns [ayrz and u SAHYNZ] Term formerly required at common law to convey an estate in fee simple.

held (1) Decided (in reference to a court's decision); (2) kept or retained in custody.

henceforth From the present time forward.

hereditaments [he ruh DIT uh muhnts] Every kind of property that can be inherited.

hereditary Acquired from an ancestor.

heredity Transmission of qualities from ancestor to descendant.

hereinafter Following this.

heresy (1) Offense against religion, in the public denial of established dogma of a church; (2) dissent from prevailing view, in any field.

heretofore Previously, before this.

heritage Legacy, inheritance, something acquired from a predecessor.

hermaphrodite [huhr MAF ruh dahyt] Individual having both male and female reproductive organs.

heterosexual Relating to sexual preference directed towards members of the opposite gender.

he who seeks equity must come with clean hands Legal maxim applicable to equity jurisdiction by which one seeking equitable relief must himself be fair and just, and not seek judicial sanction of his own misconduct or oppression.

hierarchy [HAHY rahr kee] A graduating series of ranks or degrees of power and authority.

high water mark That part of the seashore to which the water ordinarily reaches when the tide is highest.

highway (1) Any public road; (2) roadway having specific limitations defined by statutes.

hijack (highjack) To steal or kidnap, as, to hijack a truck and make off with its load or driver.

☆ **hijacking** Taking control of a vehicle by the use or threatened use of force or by intimidation; or, taking a vehicle by stealth, without the use or threatened use of force, in order to steal its cargo.

hinder To delay, impede, obstruct, retard.

hire -n. (1) Payment for temporary use of something; (2) payment for services: -v. (3) to engage a person's services for wages or to secure temporary use of something for compensation, as, to hire a horse for some period of time.

☆ **hit and run** *tentatively recommended national category for prosecution, courts and corrections statistics* Unlawful departure by the vehicle operator from the scene of a motor vehicle accident which resulted in injury to a person or damage to property of another.

hitherto In past time, previously, before the present.

hold (1) To possess, occupy, as a tenant, grantee or owner; (2) to bind under a contract; (3) to decide, as, a judge holds in deciding a case; (4) to conduct or preside, as, to hold a public meeting; (5) to keep or retain in custody.

holder Payee or endorsee in possession of a negotiable instrument.

holder in due course Payee or endorsee in possession of a negotiable instrument, good on its face, received for value and without knowledge of any defect in the title of the person from whom it is received.

holding (1) Possession, ownership, as, a holding of common stock; (2) actual decision or ruling of a court.

holding company Corporation organized to hold the stock of other corporations.

holdover (1) Possession of premises by a lessee after expiration of his term (2) possession of an office or position after expiration of earlier term.

holograph [HOL uh graf] Instrument entirely written in the handwriting of its maker.

holographic will [hol uh GRAF ik wil] One written wholly in handwriting of the testator.

home rule Practice or right of local self-government.

homestead (1) Home and land of a family; (2) tract of land formerly held by United States Government, given to an individual to live on and farm.

homicidal [hom i SAHY duhl] Relating to homicide, murderous.

homicide [HOM i sahyd] Killing of one human being by another.

☆ **homicide** *recommended statistical terminology* The causing of the death of another person without legal justification or excuse.

☆ **homicide** In Uniform Crime Reports terminology, the name of the UCR category which includes and is limited to all offenses of causing the death of another person without justification or excuse.

homosexual (1) Referring to a sexual preference directed to one's own gender; (2) one having a sexual preference directed to one's own gender.

honi soit qui mal y pense [OH nee swo kee MOL y pahns] Evil to him who thinks evil.

honor -n. (1) Reputation, glory, outward respect or admiration, deference, privilege, chastity, purity, integrity; -v. (2) to live up to, fulfill, as, to honor a check or conform to an obligation; (3) to exalt, praise, respect.

honorable (1) Title of courtesy accorded to public officials of rank or distinction; (2) worthy of honor.

honorarium [on uh RAY ree uhm] Voluntary reward in consideration of services, where custom or propriety forbids any fixed amount, or where payment cannot legally be enforced.

honorary (1) Arising out of an honor or dignity; (2) with honor but without compensation, as, an honorary appointment to an office.

hope Desire, expectation, reliance, promise.

hornbook Book containing elementary principles of law.

hornswoggle To overcome by trickery.

hostage Person held as security for performance of an act by another.

hostile Unfriendly, adverse.

hostile possession Continuous, adverse, open, actual, notorious and exclusive possession and enjoyment of real property under claim or color of title continuing for period required by statute so as to ripen into legal ownership.

hostile witness Person called to testify who manifests so much hostility or prejudice under examination in chief that the court allows the party calling him to subject him to cross-examination.

hostility Enmity, opposition, animosity.

house (1) Dwelling; (2) institution, firm.

House of Commons Lower body of British Parliament.

house of ill fame Brothel.

House of Lords Upper body of British Parliament.

House of Representatives Lower body of United States Congress.

house of worship Building used for religious services.

housebreaking Breaking into and entering a dwelling with intent to commit a crime therein.

household Domestic establishment, social unit of persons living together in one dwelling.

household goods Articles of permanent nature used in a home.

householder One who keeps house with his family, head of a household.

huckster Peddler, hawker.

hue and cry (1) Outcry made on pursuit of a felon by which, formerly, all persons hearing it were required to join in pursuit until the felon was captured; (2) hubbub.

humane Kind, considerate, marked by compassion and sympathy.

humanitarian Philanthropic, humane, concerned for human welfare and social reform.

hung jury One whose members are unable to agree upon a verdict.

☆ **hung jury** A jury which after long deliberation is so irreconcilably divided in opinion that it is unable to reach any verdict.

hurt -n. Injury, wound, mental distress or anguish, harm, detriment; -v. to damage, impair, weaken, cause pain.

husbandman Farmer.

husbandry (1) Farming; (2) conservation, thrift.

hush money Payment as a bribe given to secure silence.

husting (1) Election platform; (2) name of a local court in some jurisdictions.

hybrid Animal or plant formed of union of different species.

hypnosis Mental state in which subject involuntarily acts in obedience to will of the hypnotizer.

hypochondria [hahy poh KON dree uh] (1) Morbid anxiety about one's health by exaggeration of symptoms; (2) extreme mental depression centered on imaginary physical ailments.

hypothecate [hahy POTH uh kayt] To pledge something without delivery of title or possession.

hypothecation [hahy poth uh KAY shuhn] (1) Act by which property is pledged as security for a loan without delivery of title or possession; (2) right of a creditor or claimant to cause pledged property to be sold to satisfy his claim, if payment of debt is not made.

hypothetical question Question put to an expert witness containing an assumed state of facts and requiring the witness to state his opinion thereon.

I

ibid. [IB id] (ibidem) In the same place.

id. [id] **(idem)** [ID em] The same, something previously mentioned.

idem sonans [ID em SOH nans] Having the same sound, sounding alike.

identical (1) Exactly the same; (2) essentially the same.

identification (1) Proof of identity; (2) recognition of a person or thing as having been seen before.

identity Fact that a person or thing is same as represented, claimed or charged.

id est [id est] (abbreviated i.e.) That is.

idiocy Extreme mental deficiency due to incomplete or abnormal brain development, usually congenital.

idiot (1) Feeble-minded person having a mental age not exceeding two years and requiring complete custodial care; (2) ignorant person; (3) person who fails to use normal discrimination and judgment, as, he acted like an idiot in driving his car.

i.e. (id est) That is.

ignorance Absence of knowledge, unawareness, lack of information.

ignore To disregard wilfully, decline to take notice of, reject as false or ungrounded.

illegal Forbidden by law, unlawful, illicit.

☆ **illegal search and seizure** An act in violation of the Fourth Amendment of the U.S. Constitution: "The right of people to be secure in their persons, houses, papers and effects, against unreasonable searches and seizures, shall not be violated, and no warrants shall issue but upon probable cause, supported by oath or affirmation, and particularly describing the place to be searched and the persons or things to be seized."

illegitimacy Condition of one whose parents were not married to each other at time of his birth.

illegitimate (1) Born of parents not married to each other at time of birth; (2) contrary to law; (3) not recognized as legal.

ill fame Having a reputation for vice, as, a house of ill fame.

illicit Unlawful, not permitted.

illiteracy Condition of one who is unable to read or write.

illiterate -adj. (1) Unable to read or write; (2) marked by lack of knowledge and education generally, or in a particular field, as, one who is musically illiterate; - n. (3) person unable to read or write.

illness Disease or ailment

illusion (1) Something that deceives the mind so as to produce a false or misleading impression; (2) misapprehension, fancy.

illusory Deceptive, unreal.

illustrious Famous, distinguished, eminent.

imagine (1) To create a mental image; (2) to think, suppose, guess.

imbecile (1) Feeble-minded person with mental age between three and seven years and requiring special care; (2) in general usage: fool, idiot.

imbecility (1) State of being mentally weak; (2) futility, complete nonsense.

imitation Object made in likeness of another, copy.

immaterial Unimportant, without weight or significance, not necessary.

immediate (1) Without delay, at once; (2) next in line, directly connected, proximate.

immediate cause Last of a series of events tending to bring about a given result and by its action directly producing the result.

immediate issue Children of a parent, as distinguished from grandchildren or other descendants.

immediately (1) Without delay; (2) closely, in direct connection or relation.

immemorial Beyond memory, ancient.

immigration Act by which persons enter a country for permanent residence therein.

imminent (1) Near at hand, impending; (2) threatening, menacing.

immobile Incapable of movement, stationary, fixed.

immoderate Not within suitable limits, extravagant, unreasonable.

immoral Unprincipled, wicked, contrary to morality.

immunity Freedom from conviction for any offense or imposition of any penalty or forfeiture concerning evidence given by a witness. Immunity does not protect an individual from conviction for perjury if the evidence given is false.

    transactional immunity the form of freedom from conviction or imposition of any penalty or forfeiture applying to an entire transaction, matter or thing about which evidence is given.

    use immunity the form of freedom from conviction or imposition of any penalty or forfeiture applying only to evidence given by a witness, but not barring conviction, penalty or forfeiture for the transaction, if that can be obtained without the evidence for which use immunity has been given.

impair To damage, lessen in power, diminish in value or condition.

impanel To enter on a panel, as, to impanel a jury and enroll names of those serving.

impartial Equitable, treating all alike, not favoring one above another.

impeach (1) To challenge, accuse, charge, inform against; (2) to charge one before a competent tribunal with impropriety or misconduct in office, as, to impeach a public official; (3) to challenge as biased, not credible or invalid, as, to impeach the testimony of a witness.

impeachment (1) Proceeding against a public officer before a competent tribunal pursuant to articles of impeachment charging misconduct, corruption or other offense in office; (2) calling into question one's honesty and integrity.

impeachment of waste Restraint of a tenant from committing injury or destruction upon lands, or demand for compensation for injury or destruction done by a tenant.

impeachment of witness Discrediting testimony of a witness by showing that the witness is dishonest or acting from impure motives.

impede To obstruct, hinder, block.

impediment Hindrance, bar, disability, as, being a minor is an impediment to exercising voting rights.

imperative -adj. Mandatory, binding, compulsory; -n. obligatory duty or act.

imperfect Defective, incomplete, lacking some legal or formal requisite, inadequate.

impertinent (1) Not pertinent, irrelevant, inappropriate, frivolous; (2) insolent, uncivil, presumptuous.

impleaded Included in an action between other persons.

implicate (1) To involve in incriminating connection; (2) to connect intimately.

implication (1) Inference, connotation, suggestion; (2) incriminating involvement.

implied Indicated by deduction, inference or necessary consequence.

implied authority Authority reasonably appropriate and necessary to the exercise of actual and express authority.

implied contract Binding agreement inferred from particular circumstances, general language or conduct of the parties.

implied easement Such use of the grantor's land as is reasonably necessary for beneficial enjoyment of the land conveyed.

implied power Such power as may be reasonably necessary to make effective an express power.

implied warranty Guaranty arising by operation of law but not expressly stated, as, an implied warranty that an article is fit for its intended use, such as food being fit for human consumption.

imply To indicate by logical inference, association or necessary consequence, to communicate by allusion.

import -n. (1) Article of foreign manufacture; (2) meaning, consequence, significance; -v. (3) to cause articles made in foreign countries to be brought to one's own country, usually for sale; (4) to mean, signify, imply.

importation Act of bringing in articles from a foreign source.

Importunity Unreasonable request, repeated solicitation.

impose (1) To levy or exact by authority, as a burden, tax, duty or charge; (2) to inflict, establish forcibly.

imposition (1) Levy, tax, burden; (2) act of imposing upon another or being imposed upon.

impossibility (1) Impracticability, inability to achieve by reasonable means; (2) something unable to be attained.

impost Tax, duty, tribute.

Impotence (1) Physical inability of a male to consummate sexual intercourse; (2) weakness, feebleness, helplessness.

impound To take into legal custody for safekeeping or other disposition.

impress -n. (1) Mark made by pressure; (2) impression, effect; -v. (3) to apply with pressure, imprint; (4) to affect forcibly or deeply, arouse interest or admiration of another.

impression (1) Identification of form resulting from physical contact under pressure; (2) subjective perception of quality or nature.

imprimatur [im pri MO toor] (1) (let it be printed) License to print or publish; (2) sanction, approval.

imprison To confine, restrain.

imprisonment Confinement in a prison, restraint of a person against his will.

improbable Unlikely, not readily believable.

improper (1) Unfit, unsuitable, indecorous, indecent; (2) incorrect, inaccurate.

improve To make more desirable, enhance in value.

improvement (1) Building or other betterment of real property; (2) desirable modification or useful addition to an existing machine, object or process.

improvidence Lack of care and foresight, failure to foresee or provide for the future.

improvident Not providing for the future.

impugn [im PYOON] To call into question, make insinuations against.

impulse Sudden urge.

impunity Exemption from punishment, harm or loss.

imputation Insinuation, accusation, attribution.

impute To ascribe, attribute, lay responsibility or blame for.

in absentia [in ab SEN shee uh] In absence.

in action Not in possession but obtainable by legal suit.

inadequate Insufficient, deficient.

inadmissible That which cannot be received or allowed in evidence.

inadvertence Carelessness, inattention oversight, mistake.

inalienable Incapable of being transferred or surrendered, as, human rights are said to be inalienable.

inapposite [in AP uh zit] Not pertinent, irrelevant.

inaugurate (1) To begin; (2) to install, induct into office.

in being Presently in existence.

inboard (1) In maritime law, applying to a cargo so placed that it does not project over the side of a vessel; (2) inside the line of a ship's hull.

in bulk Not packaged for ultimate distribution, as, sugar is shipped in bulk from a refinery.

inc. Incorporated.

in camera [in KAM ruh] In chambers, in private.

incapacity Lack of power, ability or qualification.

incarceration Imprisonment.

incendiary [in SEN dee e ree] One who deliberately sets a building on fire.

inception Beginning, commencement, initiation.

incest Sexual intercourse of persons related to each other within the prohibited degree of consanguinity, as, incest between father and daughter, or mother and son.

☆ **incest** Unlawful sexual intercourse between closely related persons.

incestuous Partaking of or relating to incest.

in chief Principal, primary, as, testimony in chief is that adduced by the party calling the witness (direct testimony).

inchoate [in KOH ayt] Imperfect, partial, unfinished, potential, as, an inchoate contract is one not executed by all parties.

inchoate dower [in KOH ayt DOU uhr] Wife's interest in husband's real property during his lifetime, which upon his death may become a right of dower.

☆ **inchoate offense** [in KOH ayt uh FENS] An offense which consists of an action or conduct which is a step to the intended commission of another offense.

incident (1) Event, happening; (2) something relating to, dependent upon or inherent in another matter of principal importance, as, homework is an incident of school.

incidental (1) Subordinate, non-essential, secondary to the main purpose; (2) occurring by chance, as, an incidental meeting with a friend;
(3) occasional, casual, accidental.

incinerate To consume by fire.

incise To cut into, carve, engrave.

incite To arouse, urge, instigate, provoke.

inclose (enclose) To surround, bound, confine.

inclosure (enclosure) Confined area.

include To contain, inclose, involve, confine.

☆ **included offense** An offense which is made up of elements which are a subset of the elements of another offense having a greater statutory penalty, and the occurrence of which is established by the same evidence or by some portion of the evidence which has been offered to establish the occurrence of the greater offense.

inclusio unius est exclusio alterius [in KLOO zee oh OO nee uhs est eks KLOO zee oh ol TEE ree uhs] The inclusion of one is the exclusion of another.

inclusive Embracing, encompassing, broad in orientation or scope.

income Gain from business, labor or capital.

in common Held by several for their equal use, advantage and enjoyment.

incommunicado [in kuh myoo ni KOD oh] Without means of communication, as, to hold a prisoner incommunicado is to deny him the right to communicate with friends or relatives.

incompatible Not capable of association with something else, mutually repellent, unable to exist in harmony.

incompetence Lack of ability, fitness or legal qualification.

incompetency State of being unqualified or unable to perform given tasks.

incompetent -adj. (1) Unable, unqualified, unfit, inadmissible; -n. (2) one who is unable to manage his own affairs by reason of insanity, imbecility or other mental condition as defined by statute; (3) one incapable of doing what is required.

☆ **incompetent to stand trial** *recommended statistical terminology* In criminal proceedings, the finding by a court that a defendant is mentally incapable of understanding the nature of the charges and proceedings against him or her, of consulting with an attorney, and of aiding in his or her own defense.

inconclusive Not leading to a definite result or decision, open to further proof or consideration.

incontestability clause Provision in a life insurance policy that payment by the insurer shall not be avoided by insurer's claim that the policy was invalid at inception or thereafter became invalid by reason of action by the insured.

incontestable (incontestible) Not subject to any challenge as to its validity.

incontinence (1) Inability to retain a bodily discharge; (2) inability to resist desire or impulse, as, to live in sexual incontinence.

incontinent (1) Lacking control, unrestrained; (2) sexually dissolute; (3) unable to retain a bodily discharge.

inconvenience Disadvantage, handicap, misfortune, trouble.

inconvenient Not suitable, unfit, inopportune.

incorporate (1) To create a corporation; (2) to include the terms of one document as though made within the confines of another; (3) to combine into one.

incorporation (1) Process of creating a corporation; (2) act by which one document is considered as part of another (incorporation by reference) or is physically included in the other (actual incorporation); (3) combination of matters into a whole.

incorporeal [in kawr PAW ree uhl] Without body, not tangible.

incorporeal hereditaments [in kawr PAW ree uhl he ruh DIT uh muhnts] That which may be inherited, but is not tangible or visible.

incorrigible [in KO ri juh buhl] Not capable of being corrected, disciplined or improved in conduct.

incorruptible Not subject to bribery or other corrupt acts.

increase -n. Enlargement, increment, addition, growth; -v. to increase, grow, enlarge.

increment That which is gained or added.

incriminate To charge with crime, to involve in criminal prosecution.

incriminatory Tending to establish guilt.

incroachment (encroachment) Unlawful or improper intrusion upon right or property of another.

inculcate To indoctrinate, teach by frequent repetition, instill.

inculpate [in KUL payt] To impute blame or guilt, involve in guilt.

inculpatory [in KUL puh taw ree] Tending to establish guilt.

incumbent One presently in possession of an office or status.

incumber (encumber) To subject to charge, liability or obligation.

incumbrance (encumbrance) Claim, lien, charge, liability on real property, but sometimes used loosely in relation to personal property, in the same context.

incur To receive or have placed upon one, as, to incur an obligation.

in custodia legis [in kuh STOH dee uh LEG is] In legal custody.

indebtedness State of being in debt, extent to which one is in debt.

indecent Offensive to propriety, unfit to be seen or heard, tending to be obscene.

☆ **indecent exposure** Unlawful intentional, knowing, or reckless exposing to view of the genitals or anus, in a place where another person may be present who is likely to be offended or alarmed by such an act.

indefeasible That which cannot be defeated or revoked.

indefinite Without fixed boundaries or precise limits, vague, uncertain, unlimited.

indemnification Act of making good for loss or damage caused by another.

indemnify To secure against loss or damage, to compensate one who has sustained loss or damage.

indemnitor One who is under an obligation to compensate another who has incurred loss or damage.

indemnity (1) Security against loss or damage; (2) exemption from penalty or liability; (3) amount paid as compensation under an indemnity agreement.

indemnity bond Surety agreement providing for payment of a sum in event of hurt, loss or damage.

indemnity policy Insurance policy to indemnify one for loss of money actually paid pursuant to an indemnity agreement.

indenture (1) Deed by which two or more persons enter into reciprocal grants or obligations towards each other; (2) formal document under seal, such as a deed; (3) apprenticeship agreement binding apprentice to work for master for a given period.

independent Not subject to control, modification or restriction; self-governing.

independent contractor One who contracts to do some work or accomplish a desired result, free of any authority or control as to how the work shall be done, and having the right to hire and direct other workers.

indeterminate [in duh TUHR min uht] Uncertain, not precisely fixed.

indeterminate sentence [in duh TUHR min uht SEN tens] Period of punitive imprisonment within certain limits allowed by law as to minimum and maximum term, subject to action of a parole board or similar administrative authority.

☆ **indeterminate sentence** [in duh TUHR min uht SEN tens] A type of sentence to imprisonment where the commitment, instead of being for a specified single time quantity, such as three years, is for a range of time, such as two to five years, or five years maximum and zero minimum.

index (1) Alphabetically arranged table of reference to contents of a book or other material; (2) relative standard for purpose of comparison, as, a cost-of-living index; (3) sign, token, indication.

☆ **Index Crimes** In Uniform Crime Reports terminology, the Index Crimes are: murder and nonnegligent manslaughter, forcible rape, robbery, aggravated assault, burglary, larceny-theft, motor vehicle theft, and arson.

indication Sign, token, signal.

indicia [in DISH ee uh] Signs, indications, circumstances showing the existence or nature of a given situation.

indict [in DAHYT] To charge with a crime by formal written accusation presented by a grand jury.

☆ **indictment** [in DAHYT muhnt] A formal, written accusation submitted to the court by a grand jury, alleging that a specified person(s) has committed a specified offense(s), usually a felony.

indifferent (1) Impartial, disinterested; (2) passable, mediocre.

indigent [IN duh juhnt] Needy, poor, incapable of self-support.

indignity Insult, outrage, humiliating or injurious treatment to one's self-respect.

indirect Not having immediate bearing or application, roundabout.

indirect evidence Collateral facts from which the main fact may be inferred.

indispensable That which cannot be spared or omitted; necessary, requisite, essential.

indispensable party In an equitable action, one having such an interest in the subject matter that a final decree cannot be made without affecting his interests or rendering a decree inconsistent with equity and good conscience.

individual Pertaining to a single being; not divisible.

individually Separately, personally.

indivisible Inseparable, entire, incapable of division or separation.

indorse (endorse) (1) To place one's signature on the back of a check, bill, note or similar instrument in order to obtain the proceeds or to transfer its possession to another; (2) to show approval or acceptance, as, to indorse a country's foreign policy.

indorsee (endorsee) One to whom an instrument such as a check or note is assigned by act of indorsement.

indorsement (endorsement) (1) Act of one assigning or transferring his property right in a negotiable instrument by signing his name upon the back of the instrument; (2) signature on back of a negotiable instrument as evidence of transfer of ownership; (3) support, approval.

indorser (endorser) One who signs his name on the back of an instrument in order to transfer ownership from himself.

indubitable Beyond doubt or question.

induce To bring about, persuade, influence, motivate, prevail on.

inducement (1) Cause or reason why a thing is done; (2) that which incites a person to do an act.

induct (1) To put into possession or enjoyment, as, to induct one into an office with appropriate ceremony; (2) to enroll one into military service by conscription.

induction (1) Formal and ceremonial introduction of one into an office or organization; (2) acceptance by government of a person for military service, including completion of all steps prescribed by statute and regulations.

indulgence Forbearance, special leniency, self-gratification.

industry (1) Group of businesses in fields of activity related to each other, conducted for profit and employing labor and capital; (2) diligence, steady attention to business.

inebriated Tipsy, intoxicated.

ineligible Lacking legal qualification or capacity.

in esse [in ES uh] In being, actually existing.

in evidence Actually received and accepted for consideration as an exhibit in the course of a legal proceeding.

inevitable Unavoidable, beyond human care and foresight to avoid or prevent.

in extenso [in ek STEN soh] In its full extent, at full length, from beginning to end.

in extremis [in ek STREE mis] In one's last moments, at point of death, in the last illness.

infamous Detestable, abhorrent, vicious, criminal, contemptible.

infamous crime Treason, felony or other crime involving moral turpitude of such nature as to create a presumption that accused person is unworthy of belief.

infamy (1) Loss of honor and reputation; (2) shocking, brutal act.

infancy Minority, state of one below age of legal majority.

infant Person under age of majority, as defined by statute.

infanticide Killing of a newly or recently born child.

infection Abnormal state of an organism caused by invasion of a harmful foreign organism.

inference Deduction or conclusion whose logical validity is drawn from one or more facts.

inference on inference Deduction or conclusion whose validity in logic is based upon another deduction or conclusion.

inferior (1) Lower; (2) mediocre; (3) of less quality than another.

infirm Weak, feeble.

infirmity (1) Unsound or debilitated state; (2) defect, omission, failing.

in flagrante delicto [in fluh GRAN tay duh LIK toh] In the very act of committing a crime.

influence -n. (1) Production of an effect without apparent exertion of tangible force; (2) corrupt manipulation of authority; -v. (3) to have effect on condition or development of some matter or object.

informal (1) Carried out without prescribed or ceremonious procedure; (2) appropriate to casual and familiar use.

in forma pauperis [in FAWR muh PAWpuh ris] In the manner of a poor person.

☆ **information** In criminal justice usage, a formal, written accusation submitted to the court by a prosecutor, alleging that a specified person(s) has committed a specified offense(s).

informer One who gives information about another, usually concerning criminal activities.

infra [IN fruh] Below, under, with in, after.

infraction Breach, violation, or infringement; as, infraction of a law, right or duty.

☆ **infraction** A violation of state statute or local ordinance punishable by a fine or other penalty, but not by incarceration, or by a specified, unusually limited term of incarceration.

☆ **infraction (corrections)** A statutory offense or a violation of prison or jail administrative regulations committed by an offender while incarcerated or in a temporary release program such as work release.

infringe To trespass or encroach upon right or property of another.

infringement (1) Encroachment or trespass on a right or privilege; (2) unlawful use of a patent, copyright, trademark or trade name.

in futuro [in fyoo CHOO roh] In the future, from present time forward.

ingenuity Inventiveness; cleverness in design, contrivance or mental process.

ingress [IN gres] (1) Entrance; (2) right of entrance or access.

in gross In total, in a large amount, without division.

ingross (engross) [in GROHS] To write a fair copy of an instrument.

inhabit To dwell, live, occupy.

inhabitant One who resides permanently in a given place, one who is domiciled there.

in haec verba [in hahyk VUHR buh] In these words.

inhere To exist in and be inseparable.

inherent Within itself, intrinsic, essential.

inherit (1) To take by inheritance; (2) to receive by descent on the death of an ancestor.

inheritance (1) Estate or property which is or may be transmitted to another as an heir; (2) act of inheriting; (3) something derived from the past.

inheritance tax Excise tax payable by an heir or next of kin on privilege of succession to property.

inhibit (1) To hinder, restrain, discourage; (2) to prohibit, forbid.

inhibition Prohibition, prevention, impediment.

iniquity Wickedness, sin, injustice.

initial -adj. Beginning, first; -n. first letter of a name; -v. to indicate approval by affixing one's initials, as, to initial changes on a document.

☆ **initial appearance** *recommended statistical terminology* In criminal proceedings, the first appearance of an accused person in the first court having jurisdiction over his or her case.

initiate To begin, originate.

initiative (1) Self-reliant action; (2) power of electorate to propose new laws.

injunction Legal process issued by a court requiring a person to refrain from doing or to continue doing a certain act.

injure To hurt, offend, do harm to, violate another's legal right.

injuria [in JOO ree uh] Injury, wrong.

injuria absque damno [in JOO ree uh AB skway DAM noh] (injury without damage) A wrong from which no loss or damage results, hence, not actionable.

injury Damage, harm, hurt.

injustice (1) Act, fault or omission of a court; (2) violation of the rights of another.

in kind (1) Of the same kind, class or genus; (2) non-monetary.

inland bill of exchange One where both the drawer and drawee reside within the same state or country.

in limine [in LIM i nay] Preliminarily.

in loco parentis [in LOH koh puh REN tis] In place of a parent.

inmate Person confined in an institution.

innocence Absence of guilt, blamelessness, simplicity.

innocent (1) Free from guilt; (2) acting in good faith and without knowledge of any defects or objections.

innocent purchaser One who acquires an interest in property without knowledge or reasonable means of knowledge of any defect or infirmity in the seller's title.

innovation (1) Change, novelty; (2) exchange of one obligation for another.

Inns of Court Private unincorporated associations of the legal profession, located in London, and having the exclusive privilege of admitting persons to the practice of law.

innuendo [in yoo EN doh] (1) Oblique allusion to something not directly set forth; (2) hint, insinuation.

in pais [in PAY is] Without legal proceedings (in the country, as distinguished from in court).

in pari delicto [in PO ree duh LIK toh] Equally at fault.

in pari materia [in PO ree muh TEE ree uh] Upon the same subject, in a similar case.

in particeps criminis [in PAHR ti seps KR IM uh nis] In criminal association.

in perpetuity [in puhr puh TOO i tee] Forever.

in personam [in puhr SOH nuhm] Directed to a specific person to impose a personal liability on him.

in propria persona [in PROH pree uh puhr SOH nuh] In his own person, not by attorney.

inquest (1) Trial of an issue of fact where plaintiff alone gives testimony; (2) examination before a coroner and jury as to cause of violent or suspicious death; (3) inquiry, investigation.

inquire (enquire) (1) To ask about; (2) to search, investigate, examine.

inquisition (1) Inquiry, examination; (2) judicial or official inquiry; (3) severe questioning.

in re [in ray] In the matter of, concerning.

in rem [in rem] (1) Against a right, status or property; (2) action not directed to a specific person, but rather to right, status or title to property.

insane (1) Mad, disordered, unsound; (2) foolish, ridiculous.

insanity (1) Such lack of reason, memory and intelligence as to disable one from mental capacity required by law for entering into a particular relationship or status; (2) in some jurisdictions, a defense provided by statute which may serve to mitigate responsibility in criminal actions; (3) extreme foolishness or unreasonableness.

inscription (1) Writing or engraving upon a metallic or other solid substance, for durability; (2) entry in a public record.

insecure (1) Unsafe, dangerous; (2) not confident, uncertain.

insensible (1) Without consciousness; (2) meaningless, not intelligible.

insidious Cunning, deceitful, subtle.

insignia Distinctive marks, badges, characteristics.

insolvency Condition of being unable to pay one's debts as they become due.

insolvent -adj. Condition of one who is unable to pay his debts as they become due; -n. person unable to pay his debts.

in specie [in SPEE shee] In the same or like form.

inspect (1) To examine with care; (2) to ascertain quality and condition by examination.

inspection Physical examination, as, inspection of an injury for which one seeks damages.

install (1) To give a place to, put in possession of an office; (2) to set up or fix in position for use.

installation (1) Act or ceremony by which one is put in possession of an office; (2) process by which objects such as machines are placed in position for use; (3) something placed in position for use.

installment Portion of a debt payable at successive periods as agreed.

instant case The matter presently under consideration.

instanter [in STAN tuhr] Immediately, instantly.

instantly Directly, without delay, at once.

in status quo [in STAT uhs kwoh] In the existing state of affairs.

instigate To incite, urge, provoke, solicit another to commit an act.

instigation Urging, solicitation, incentive.

institute -n. (1) Organization for promoting a worthy cause; (2) association of persons or organizations having authority and competence in a study or profession; (3) brief course of instruction; -v. (4) to commence, set up, establish.

institution (1) An establishment, as, a charitable institution; (2) firmly established and, accepted custom or relationship; (3) act of commencing.

☆ **institutional capacity** An officially stated number of inmates which a confinement or residential facility is or was intended to house.

instruct (1) To teach a particular subject or area of knowledge; (2) to convey commands or directions.

instruction (1) Order, direction; (2) direction by judge to jury on law of a case.

instrument (1) Written legal document such as a deed or contract; (2) in law of evidence, anything tangible that may be presented for consideration; (3) means whereby something is achieved or furthered.

instrumentality Means, intermediary, agent.

insubordination Disobedience to authority.

insufficiency Inadequacy, inability, lack of value.

insufficient Inadequate, unfit.

☆ **insufficient evidence** In criminal proceedings, evidence that is not enough to constitute proof at the level required at a given point in the proceedings.

insurable Affording a sufficient ground for insurance.

insurable interest Such relationship to the subject matter of the policy as will make the happening of the damage or risk insured against a matter of right, benefit, advantage or liability.

insurance (1) Contract whereby for a specified consideration one party (insurer) agrees to pay the other (insured) for losses due to specified damage or perils; (2) plan whereby risks or perils are predicted or estimated and an agreed sum is paid to those incurring the risk or peril, by persons joining in the plan for their mutual protection.

insure To make sure; underwrite.

insured (1) Person who obtains insurance; (2) person whose life is insured.

insurgent One who or that which rises in revolt against constituted authorities.

insurrection Combined resistance to lawful authority of the state, manifested by acts of violence.

☆ **intake** The process by which a juvenile referral is received by personnel of a probation agency, juvenile court or special intake unit, and a decision made to close the case at intake, or refer the juvenile to another agency, or place him or her under some kind of care or supervision, or file a petition in a juvenile court.

intangible Incapable of being touched or perceived, not in physical existence, as, an idea is intangible.

intangible property Property having no intrinsic or marketable value, but which may be evidence of value, such as stocks, bonds and judgments.

integrate To bring several things together into one so as to form a harmonious entity.

integrated bar Status in which every attorney is required to be a member of an association of attorneys as a condition precedent to his practice of law.

integration (1) Act or process of making whole or entire; (2) process of unifying divergent groups.

integrity (1) Uncompromising adherence to a code of values; (2) honesty, uprightness, candor; (3) completeness.

intelligible Understandable.

intemperance (1) Excessive use of intoxicants; (2) excess or lack of moderation in some action.

intend To design, resolve, plan, signify, mean.

intendment Intention, true meaning, design.

intent (1) State of mind to do or omit an act; (2) aim, meaning, purpose.

☆ **intent** The state of mind or attitude with which an act is carried out; the design, resolve or determination with which a person acts to achieve a certain result.

intention (1) Determination to act in a particular way; (2) resolve, objective.

intentional Willful, designed, voluntary.

intentionally Having a conscious objective to cause a particular result or engage in specific conduct.

inter [IN tuhr] Among, between.

inter alia [IN tuhr OL ee uh] Among other things.

inter alios [IN tuhr OL ee ohs] Among other persons, between strangers to the matter.

intercede (1) To intervene, mediate; (2) to act between parties for reconciliation of differences

interception Act of taking or seizing before arrival at destination.

interchange (1) Junction of highways providing passage of traffic from one to another, at different levels for free movement; (2) act of giving one article for its duplicate or substantial equivalent.

interchangeable Capable of exchanging one for another.

intercourse (1) Communication, dealings; (2) sexual connection.

interdict [in tuhr DIKT] To prohibit, forbid.

interdiction [in tuhr DIK shuhn] Prohibition, restraint.

interest -n. (1) Any property right in realty or personalty; (2) claim, concern or share in something; (3) compensation payable for use of money; -v. (4) to involve the concern of.

interfere To hamper, hinder, intervene, take part in affairs of others.

interference (1) In patent law, situation where a claimed patent conflicts with one already issued or pending; (2) act of hampering an activity or process.

interim Meanwhile, in the meantime, temporary.

interline To insert written matter between lines of a legal instrument.

interlocutory [in tuhr LOK yoo taw ree] Provisional, temporary, something done between the beginning and end of an act that decides a point but is not a final decision of the whole matter, as, an interlocutory divorce decree.

☆ **interlocutory appeal** A request, made at some point before judgment in trial court proceedings, that a court having appellate jurisdiction review a prejudgment decision of the trial court before judgment is reached.

interloper Person who interferes or intrudes without authority or invitation.

intermarriage Marriage between two persons considered as members of different nations, tribes, ethnic or religious groups.

intermediary One who acts as a negotiator between two parties.

intermediate Between limits, between the beginning and end.

☆ **Intermediate appellate court** *recommended statistical terminology* An appellate court of which the primary function is to review the judgments of trial courts and the decisions of administrative agencies, and whose decisions are in turn usually reviewable by a higher appellate court in the same state.

intermediate order Incidental order made during the pendency of an action, which does not finally determine the cause, and is usually not appealable.

☆ **intermittent sentence** *recommended statistical terminology* A sentence to periods of confinement interrupted by periods of freedom.

intern (interne) One acquiring practical experience in a profession, such as a medical intern.

internal waters Those lying wholly within territorial boundaries.

International Court of Justice United Nations agency having jurisdiction of international legal disputes voluntarily presented to it.

interpellate [in tuhr PEL ayt] To address with a question, as for the court to interpellate a question to counsel during course of an argument.

interpleader Action by which one having possession of an article or fund claimed by two parties may compel them to litigate the title between themselves, instead of with him.

interpolate To insert words in a written or oral statement.

interpolation (1) Act of inserting words in a document or statement; (2) process of determining unknown values by their position between values already known.

interpose To place between, intrude, intervene.

interpret (1) To explain meaning; (2) to translate from one language to another.

interpretation (1) Process of discovering and expounding meaning, explanation of what is not plain or explicit; (2) act of translating from one language to another.

interregnum [in tuhr REG nuhm] (1) Interval or vacancy between death of one sovereign and accession of another; (2) vacancy when there is no government or authority.

interrogate To question.

interrogation Act of questioning.

interrogatories Series of formal written questions used in judicial pre-trial examination of a party or a witness.

interruption Act of stopping normal sequence, temporary cessation, suspension.

intersect To meet and cross.

intersection Space where two roadways cross each other.

interstate Between two or more states.

interstate commerce Traffic, trade and transportation of persons and property between different states.

☆ **interstate compact** An agreement between two or more states to transfer prisoners, parolees, or probationers from the physical or supervisory custody of one state to the physical or supervisory custody of another, where the correctional agency that first acquired jurisdiction over the person usually retains the legal authority to confine or release the prisoner.

interstate rendition Extradition, process by which an alleged fugitive is delivered from state where he is found to state requiring his presence therein for criminal prosecution.

intervene To come between, interfere.

intervening agency Independent means which interrupts a natural sequence of events so as to produce a different or unexpected result.

intervening cause One which turns aside a natural sequence of events, destroys causal connection, and produces an unexpected result.

intervening force One which operates to produce harm after another's negligent act or omission.

intervenor One who voluntarily and with leave of a court interposes himself in an action.

intervention (1) Interference; (2) act by which a third party becomes joined in an action pending between others in order to protect his own interests.

inter vivos [in tuhr VEE vohs] Between living persons, as, an inter vivos trust is one created during life of donor.

intestacy [in TES tuh see] Status of one dying without a will.

intestate [in TES tayt] Person dying without leaving a will; condition of one dying without leaving a will.

intimacy (1) Close friendly relationship between persons; (2) sexual liberty, sexual intercourse; (3) relationship marked by depth of knowledge.

intimate -adj. (1) Close, confidential, familiar, personal; -v. (2) to hint, give notice of, suggest.

intimation Hint, notification, announcement.

intimidate To put in fear, to coerce, to secure compliance by threat.

intimidation Coercion, duress, putting in fear.

intolerable Extreme, unbearable, excessive, irresistible.

in toto [in TOH toh] Wholly, completely, altogether.

intoxicate (1) To excite or stupefy by alcohol or narcotics; (2) to elate excessively.

intoxicated (1) Under marked influence of an intoxicant; (2) emotionally exhilarated or excited.

intoxicating liquor Beverage, usually containing alcohol, which when consumed in sufficient quantity will produce partial or complete state of drunkenness.

intoxication (1) State of being poisoned; (2) drunkenness produced by consumption of alcohol; (3) strong excitement of mind, as, intoxication from joy or pleasure.

☆ **intoxication** *tentatively recommended national category for prosecution, courts and corrections statistics* The offense of being in a public place while intoxicated through consumption of alcohol, or intake of a controlled substance or drug.

intra [IN truh] In, near, within, underneath.

intramural Within the walls, as, intramural powers of a municipality are those exercised within the corporate limits.

in transitu [in TRAN zi too] In transit.

intrastate Within the state.

intra vires [IN truh VEE res] Within the power (as distinguished from ultra vires, beyond the power).

intrinsic Belonging to, essential to or inherent in nature of something.

intrinsic evidence That derived from a document or article without further explanation.

introduce (1) To present, lead or bring in for the first time; (2) to bring into play or consideration, as, to introduce a document in evidence.

intrude To enter without right, consent or welcome.

intruder One who enters without authority.

intrusion Unauthorized entry, trespassing, encroachment; (2) wrongful possession of property of another.

intuition (1) Act of coming to direct knowledge without reasoning; (2) revelation by insight.

inundation Overflow of waters from their bed.

inure [in YOOR] To accustom, accrue, take effect, be available.

invade (1) To enter in a hostile manner; (2) to encroach, intrude or trespass upon; (3) to penetrate, engulf.

Invalid -adj. Not legally effective, indefensible, unjustified, without foundation; -n. one who is sickly or disabled.

invalidate To negate legal effect of, discredit, weaken, make valueless.

invasion (1) Intrusion, encroachment upon rights of another; (2) hostile entrance on property of another.

invective Vehement verbal attack, critical language, violent abuse.

inveigle To delude, mislead, hoodwink.

invent To originate, fabricate, develop something new.

invention Original and useful device or process reflecting creative imagination and contributing to advancement of its area of application.

inventory Itemized list of articles of property with their value.

in ventre sa mere [in VAHN truh so mayr] In his mother's womb, referring to a child conceived but not yet born.

inverse Reverse, contrary, opposite.

invest (1) To advance money for purpose of securing revenue or income; (2) to install in an office or honor; (3) to infuse, enrich, clothe, adorn.

investigation Examination, study, survey, research.

investiture Ceremony or formality by which one is placed in possession of property or an office.

investment Expenditure of money to secure income or profit from its use.

Inviolate Pure, unbroken, intact, free from charge or blemish.

Invite (1) To provide opportunity or occasion for; (2) to request one's presence or participation.

invitee One who is upon another's premises by express or implied invitation of the owner or person having control of the premises, under such circumstances as to impose an obligation to use reasonable care for protecting the safety of the invitee.

invoice Written itemized account showing prices of merchandise and terms of sale, given to a purchaser by a seller.

involuntary (1) Without will or power of choice, spontaneous, unintentional; (2) compulsory, dictated by circumstance.

involuntary manslaughter Unlawful killing of a human being by one acting in a negligent or improper manner while performing a lawful act or by reason of failure to perform a legal duty expressly required for protection of human life.

☆ **involuntary manslaughter** Causing the death of another person without intent to cause death with recklessness or gross negligence, including by reckless or grossly negligent operation of a motor vehicle.

involuntary servitude (1) Slavery; (2) condition of one compelled by force, fear or threat to labor for another, with or without payment.

iota [ahy OH tuh] Infinitesimal amount.

ipse dixit [IP say DIK sit] (he himself said it) A bare assertion unsupported by other authority.

ipso facto [IP soh FAK toh] By the fact itself.

ire Anger.

irrational Lacking power of reasoning or understanding, lacking normal menta clarity or coherence.

irrebuttable Conclusive, incapable of being rebutted or refuted.

irregular Improper, departing in some way from prescribed course.

irregularity Lack of. adherence to prescribed rule or manner of proceeding in doing or not doing an act, or in untimely or improper performance thereof.

irrelevant Not relative or pertinent to the matter in issue, not tending to prove or disprove the issue.

irreparable (1) That for which reparation cannot be given; (2) that which is impossible to make good, repair or remedy.

irresistible (irresistable) Superior to opposition, uncontrollable.

irresistible impulse In criminal law, an impulse to commit a criminal act which cannot be resisted or overcome because mental disease has destroyed freedom of will, choice of action and power of self-control.

irrevocable Unable to be revoked, recalled or altered.

irrevocable letter Letter of credit which requires no formal acknowledgment or acceptance, and constitutes an agreement to pay on compliance with its terms.

irritant Agent producing irritation or inflammation.

irritation Annoyance, anger, impatience.

isolate To place by itself, separate from others, single out.

isolated transaction Single and unusual transaction of such transitory character that it does not constitute evidence of continuing conduct.

issuable (1) Tending to produce or producing an issue; (2) authorized for issuing.

issue -n. (1) In a legal action, what is advanced by one party and denied by the other; (2) offspring, progeny; (3) final outcome, result, consequence; (4) act of putting forth, as, publication of a book, release of a new postage stamp, offering of securities for sale to investors; (5) in a controversy, the point of disagreement; (6) proceeds from a source of revenue; -v. (7) to come out, go forth, emerge, result, eventuate; (8) to discharge, emit; (9) to publish, distribute.

item (1) Separate or distinct particular of an account or bill; (2) portion into which anything is divided, piece, fragment, part, article, single detail of any kind.

itemize To specify each particular or article separately.

itinerant Wandering, travelling, journeying from one place to another.

J

J. Judge or justice.

jail Prison, place of confinement for persons held in lawful custody.

☆ **jail** *recommended statistical terminology* A confinement facility administered by an agency of local government, typically a law enforcement agency, intended for adults but sometimes also containing juveniles, which holds persons detained pending adjudication and/or persons committed after adjudication, usually those committed on sentences of a year or less.

☆ **jail commitment** *recommended statistical terminology* A sentence of commitment to the jurisdiction of a confinement facility system for adults which is administered by an agency of local government and of which the custodial authority is usually limited to persons sentenced to a year or less of confinement.

jaywalking Crossing of a street by a pedestrian illegally, dangerously or at an inappropriate place.

J.D. Juris Doctor, Doctor of Law.

jeopardy [JEP uhr dee] (1) Hazard, peril, danger; (2) risk incurred by one tried for a criminal offense.

jetsam Part of a ship, its equipment or cargo which sinks or is grounded after being thrown overboard to lighten the ship's load in an emergency.

jettison (1) Voluntary sacrifice of cargo of a vessel, in time of danger, to lighten its load; (2) abandonment, as, the jettison of an idea or course of action.

jewel Ornament of precious metal or precious stone.

JJ. Judges.

jobber (1) One who buys and sells articles in bulk and resells to dealers; (2) middleman; (3) merchant trading in job lots.

John Doe Fictitious name used in legal proceedings in place of or to conceal a true name. Mary Doe is used to indicate a fictitious female person; Richard Roe is used to indicate a second male fictitious person.

join To combine, unite, associate, connect.

joinder [JOYN duhr] (1) Union, conjunction, putting together; (2) joining of causes of action or defense or of parties in an action.

☆ **joinder** [JOYN duhr] I. In the broadest usage, the combining of multiple defendants and/or charges for purposes of any legal step or proceeding. II. In criminal proceedings, the naming of two or more defendants and/or the listing of two or more charges in a single charging document.

joinder of issue [JOYN duhr uv ISH yoo] Act by which one party in a suit joins in or accepts an issue raised by the other party as being the basis of controversy, usually when answer is made by defendant to complaint of plaintiff.

joint United, combined, coupled in interest or liability, shared between two or more.

joint account Account held by two or more persons either of whom can effect transactions independently of the other.

joint and several Relating to duties and liabilities of two or more persons for which they may be held liable either together or separately.

joint debtor One of two or more persons having common responsibility for the same debt.

joint enterprise Undertaking by several persons of a common object under such circumstances as to give each party express or implied authority to act for all parties in the execution of their common purpose, and to subject each party to liability to others for the negligence of the other parties to the joint enterprise.

joint estate Common ownership of property by several persons as joint tenants, each having unity of interest, title, time and possession, accruing under the same conveyance.

joint executors [joynt eg ZEK yoo tawrz] Two or more persons designated to act together as executors.

joint liability Pecuniary obligation of several who must be sued together to enforce the liability.

joint lives Life of two or more persons considered together as one limiting event, so that on the death of any one, the interest is determined.

jointly Held or shared in common by two or more.

jointly acquired property Property acquired by joint industry of husband and wife during their marital relationship.

jointly and severally Relating to duties and liabilities of two or more persons for which they may be held liable either together or separately.

joint offense One offense committed by two or more persons jointly.

joint resolution Proposition winning affirmative vote of both houses of a legislative body.

joint stock company Association or company consisting of a number of persons organized in the conduct of a profit-making business with joint stock, each member being able to transfer his shares without consent of the others.

joint tenancy [joynt TEN uhn see] Ownership of real or personal property by two or more persons concurrently, whereby upon death of any joint tenant the title remains in the surviving joint tenants and ultimately in the last survivor.

joint tort-feasor [joynt tawrt FEE zuhr] One who, in conjunction with another, commits a wrongful act or breach of a legal duty not founded on contract, resulting in damage.

joint venture Enterprise for profit of two or more persons, for which purpose they combine their property, money, skill and knowledge.

joker Ambiguous, misleading or misunderstood clause in a legal instrument or legislative bill to make it inoperative or uncertain or to alter its apparent terms.

jostling Pushing, shoving, elbowing others (sometimes used in referring to opportunity for pickpocketing).

journal (1) Permanent record book for keeping daily entries of transactions or events; (2) record of proceedings of a legislative body; (3) book of original entry in double-entry bookkeeping for recording transactions.

journey Travel from one place to another.

journeyman (1) Worker who has acquired proficiency in a skill or trade and is qualified to work for others on a daily wage; (2) experienced, reliable workman.

☆ **joyriding** Unlawful taking of a motor vehicle with intent to temporarily deprive the owner of possession.

J.S.D. Doctor of Juristic Science.

judge Public officer appointed or elected to preside and administer law in a court of justice.

☆ **judge** An official having broad authority granted by statute or constitution to preside over sessions of courts of general jurisdiction or to conduct appellate court business.

judge advocate Legal officer of a military court who acts as prosecutor, swears in other members of the court and performs other specified functions as a legal adviser.

☆ **judge pro tem.** [juj proh tem] (**pro tempore**) [proh TEM puh ray] A judge who sits in lieu of a regularly appointed or elected judge, and who is appointed with full authority to hear all of the cases scheduled for, and to exercise all functions of, the regular judge.

judge's order Order made by a judge in chambers or out of court.

☆ **judgment** I. In the broadest usage, any decision or determination of a court. II. *recommended criminal justice statistical terminology* The statement of the decision of a court, that the defendant is acquitted or convicted of the offense(s) charged.

judgment creditor One having a legal right to enforce execution of judgment for a sum of money due him.

judgment debtor Person obligated to pay money pursuant to a judgment.

judgment docket List of judgments entered in a given court, kept by clerk or other proper officer, so as to give official notice to interested parties of the existence of judgments.

judgment in personam [JUJ muhnt in puhr SOH nuhm] Judgment against a particular person, binding only upon the parties and their privies.

judgment in rem [JUJ muhnt in rem] Adjudication of a particular subject matter, operating directly on the property and binding upon all persons.

judgment of conviction Sentence in criminal case duly entered on court's minutes.

judgment of his peers Trial by jury.

judgment proof Status of person who has no property or who has fraudulently concealed or removed his property.

judgment record Entire proceedings in a case, signed, filed and docketed by the clerk of the court.

judgment roll Inclusive proceedings in a case to entry of judgment, duly prepared and certified by clerk of the court as record for purpose of appeal.

judicature [JOO dik uh choor] (1) The judiciary; (2) scope or extent of jurisdiction; (3) administration of justice.

judicial Relating to or connected with the administration of justice.

judicial administration Management of business affairs of court system.

judicial authority Official power of a judge to hear and determine matters in controversy.

judicial circuit Geographical subdivision of the United States, or other governmental unit, for administration of justice.

judicial decision Opinion or determination by a court on a matter before it.

judicial department One of three coordinate branches of government, having power to interpret and apply the law in determination of legal actions and proceedings.

judicial dictum [joo DISH uhl DIK tuhm] Expression of personal opinion by a judge in his decision, not decisive of any question before him and not controlling upon parties.

judicial discretion Latitude in exercise of judgment accorded to a judge in deciding a case on principles of equity and justice.

judicial district Geographical subdivision of a state or political entity for purposes of judicial administration.

judicial notice Acceptance by a court of the existence and truth of matters of common knowledge without necessity for production of evidence, such as court taking judicial notice that a day has 24 hours.

☆ **judicial officer** *recommended statistical terminology* Any person authorized by statute, constitutional provision, or court rule to exercise those powers reserved to the judicial branch of government.

judicial power Authority vested in courts and judges as distinguished from executive and legislative power.

judicial proceeding Any proceeding where judicial action is requested and taken.

judicial separation Separation of husband and wife pursuant to court decree.

judiciary [joo DISH ee e ree] Branch of government having judicial power.

judiciously Directed by sound judgment, wisely.

jump bail To abscond, withdraw, or secrete one's self as principal in violation of the obligation of a bail bond.

junior (1) Younger; (2) inferior.

junk shop Place buying and selling worn-out and discarded material of any kind.

junta [HUHN tuh] (1) Select council for taking cognizance of political or governmental affairs of great consequence; (2) closely knit group of persons dominating new government after a revolution.

jural [JOO ruhl] Relating to law, legal rights or obligations.

jurat [JOO rot] That part of an affidavit showing before whom it was made.

juridical [juh RID i kuhl] Relating to administration of justice.

jurisdiction (1) Legal power, right and authority to hear and decide cases; (2) geographical area within which authority may be exercised.

☆ **jurisdiction** The territory, subject matter, or persons over which lawful authority may be exercised by a court or other justice agency, as determined by statute or constitution.

☆ **jurisdiction (corrections)** The authority to confine or release a person, to remove a person from or return a person to a correctional caseload, or to otherwise direct or set conditions for behavior.

jurisdictional facts Actual matters which must exist before the court can properly take jurisdiction of a particular case, such as proper service of process on defendant or amount in controversy being within the court's jurisdiction.

jurisprudence [joo ris PROO duhns] Philosophy of law, science of positive law and legal relations.

jurist (1) One skilled in law, lawyer, judge; (2) one distinguished as a writer on legal subjects.

juror (1) Member of a jury sworn to deliberate on matters charged by the court; (2) person selected for jury service.

jury Body of persons selected according to law and sworn to deliberate on matters charged by the court.

jury box Enclosed place in a court where jury sits during trial.

jury commissioner Officer charged with selection of names for jury wheel and drawing panel of jurors therefrom for a particular term of court.

☆ **jury panel** The group of persons summoned to appear in court as potential jurors for a particular trial, or the persons selected from the group of potential jurors to sit in the jury box, from which second group those acceptable to the prosecution and the defense are finally chosen as the jury.

☆ **jury poll** A poll conducted by a judicial officer or by the clerk of the court after a jury has stated its verdict but before that verdict has been entered in the record of the court, asking each juror individually whether the stated verdict is his own verdict.

☆ **jury sentencing** In criminal proceedings, upon a jury verdict of guilty, the recommendation or determination of a sentence by the jury.

☆ **jury trial** *recommended statistical terminology* In criminal proceedings, a trial in which a jury is empaneled to determine the issues of fact in a case and to render a verdict of guilty or not guilty.

jury wheel Drum containing names of persons qualified for jury service, which is revolved in order to draw names therefrom by chance.

jus [yoos] Right, justice.

just (1) Conforming to what is morally right; (2) correct, true, accurate; (3) reasonable, well-founded, equitable.

just compensation (in reference to property taken for public use) (1) Fair market value; (2) settlement leaving one no poorer or richer than before the property was taken.

just debts Legal, valid and incontestable obligations.

justice (1) Title of certain judicial officers; (2) constant and perpetual disposition to render every man his due; (3) impartial adjustment of conflicting claims; (4) fairness, integrity, honesty, righteousness.

justice of the peace Judicial officer having limited civil jurisdiction, and criminal jurisdiction with respect to minor offenses or to hold persons for trial by a higher court.

justiciable [jus TISH uh buhl] Proper to be examined in courts of justice or decided by legal principles.

justifiable Excusable, defensible, warranted or sanctioned by law.

justifiable homicide [JUS ti fahy uh buhl HOM i sahyd] Killing of one human being by another when done in self-defense, or in defense of one's home or family, or in performing a legal duty.

☆ **justifiable homicide** The intentional causing of the death of another in the legal performance of an official duty or in circumstances defined by law as constituting legal justification.

justification (1) Showing of sufficient reason; (2) lawful excuse, vindication; (3) act of qualifying as bail or surety by taking oath as to the ownership of sufficient property.

justified (1) Done on adequate reasons sufficiently supported by credible evidence; (2) guided by common sense and correct rules of law.

justifying bail Proving the sufficiency of one's property to qualify as bail or surety for person being released on a bail bond.

just value (1) Fair, honest and reasonable value; (2) actual market value.

juvenile Young person; youth as defined by statute.

☆ **juvenile** In the context of the administration of justice, a person subject to juvenile court proceedings because a statutorily defined event or condition caused by or affecting that person was alleged to have occurred while his or her age was below the statutorily specified age limit of original jurisdiction of a juvenile court.

☆ **juvenile adjudication** *recommended statistical terminology* The juvenile court decision terminating an adjudicatory hearing, that the juvenile is a delinquent, status offender, or dependent, or that the allegations in the petition are not sustained.

☆ **juvenile complaint** Petition alleging that a juvenile is a delinquent or status offender.

☆ **juvenile court** *recommended statistical terminology* The name for the class of courts which have, as all or part of their authority, original jurisdiction over matters concerning persons statutorily defined as juveniles.

☆ **juvenile court judgment** *recommended statistical terminology* The juvenile court decision terminating an adjudicatory hearing, that the juvenile is a delinquent, status offender, or dependent, or that the allegations in the petition are not sustained.

☆ **juvenile disposition** *recommended statistical terminology* The decision of a juvenile court, concluding a disposition hearing, that an adjudicated juvenile be committed to a juvenile correctional facility, or placed in a juvenile residence, shelter, or care or treatment program, or required to meet certain standards of conduct, or released.

☆ **juvenile facility** A building or part thereof, set of buildings or area enclosing a set of buildings or structures, which is used for the custody and/or care and treatment of juveniles who have been administratively determined to be in need of care or who have been formally alleged or adjudged to be delinquents, status offenders or dependents.

☆ **juvenile justice agency** A government agency, or subunit thereof, of which the functions are the investigation, supervision, adjudication, care or confinement of juvenile offenders and non-offenders subject to the jurisdiction of a juvenile court; also, in some usages, a private agency providing care and treatment.

☆ **juvenile petition** *recommended statistical terminology* A document filed in juvenile court alleging that a juvenile is a delinquent, a status offender, or a dependent, and asking that the court assume jurisdiction over the juvenile, or asking that an alleged delinquent be transferred to a criminal court for prosecution as an adult.

juxtaposition (1) Placing of two or more objects in nearness or contiguity; (2) condition of being placed in comparative relationship.

K

K. B. King's Bench (English court).

kangaroo court (1) Mock court, acting in disregard of basic principles of justice; (2) court or similar body whose procedures are irregular and irresponsible.

keep (1) To continue, maintain continuously, observe, fulfill; (2) to preserve, tend, harbor, shelter, take care of; (3) to have, retain.

keeper One who has possession, care, custody or management.

key (1) Implement for opening and closing a lock; (2) reference or guide to explain or solve something.

key number Permanent number assigned by West Publishing Company to a specific legal topic, so that a researcher may find that topic so identified in all West publications.

kickback Payment made, usually secretly, for using influence or giving assistance which benefits person making the payment.

kidnapping Unlawful seizing or carrying away of a person with intent to detain or imprison him against his will.

☆ **kidnapping** *tentatively recommended national category for prosecution, courts and corrections statistics* Transportation or confinement of a person without authority of law and without his or her consent, or without the consent of his or her guardian, if a minor.

kill -v. To deprive of life; to put an end to; -n. river, stream, channel.

kin Relation by blood or consanguinity.

kind -adj. Gentle, lenient, obliging; -n. generic class, grade, species, type.

kindred -adj. Related, similar, congenial; -n. group of related individuals.

kleptomania [klep toh MAY nee uh] A mental condition consisting of an irresistible compulsion to steal.

knock down (1) To complete a transaction at auction by the knock of the auctioneer's hammer, which signifies the closing of bids and acceptance of last offer; (2) to take apart or disassemble something; (3) to reduce price of an object.

know (1) To have knowledge, cognizance, awareness; (2) to perceive, apprehend, understand.

know all men Phrase of long usage in commencing formal written instruments, intended as a form of public address.

knowingly With awareness of the particular nature of one's conduct, or of particular circumstances.

knowingly and willfully Consciously and intentionally.

knowledge Range of person's information, comprehension, learning, information.

known Familiar, recognized, understood.

L

labor -n. Service rendered, physical exertion, toil; -v. to work, strive, exert physical effort.

laborer One who performs physical work (usually unskilled) for another for wages.

labor organization Association of workers to secure for themselves improved conditions and terms of employment by collective bargaining with employers.

labor union Worker's organization to advance interests of its members in their employment, by collective bargaining with employers and by other means.

laches [LACH uhz] Neglect or delay in asserting a right or claiming a privilege.

laches, estoppel by [LACH uhz, e STOP uhl bahy] Failure or undue delay by one party in performing a duty or enforcing a right, induced by conduct, misrepresentation or silence of the other party.

lack of jurisdiction (1) Complete failure of authority to act in a matter; (2) failure of authority to act in a case because of non-compliance with some essential condition.

lacuna [luh KOO nuh] (pl. **lacunae**) [luh KOO nahy] (1) Missing part, gap or blank space in a written instrument; (2) defect, flaw.

lading, bill of [LAY deeng, bil uv] Written instrument, signed by a carrier, acknowledging receipt of described goods for delivery to a specified person and place.

lame duck (1) Office holder who has been defeated for re-election but continues in office for remainder of his term or until inauguration of his successor; (2) person on stock exchange unable to pay his business debts.

land Real property, soil and similar matter on or below its surface.

landed (1) Having an estate in land, derived from land; (2) delivered, as, the merchandise was landed.

land grant Donation of public land for a particular purpose such as a railroad or a college.

landlocked Entirely surrounded by land of others, so that access can be had only by travelling over their land.

landlord Owner of real property, who rents or leases to another.

landlord and tenant Contractual relationship by parties whereby the landlord, as owner of real property, gives to the tenant the right to use and occupy landlord's premises on agreed terms.

landmark (1) Monument marking a boundary line between adjoining estates; (2) fixed object serving as a reference point to a geographical area; (3) established guiding principle, such as a landmark decision on a legal question.

lands, tenements and hereditaments [lanz, TEN e muhnts and he ruh DIT uh muhnts] Comprehensive description of real property.

lapse -n. (1) Failure or curtailment of a privilege or right by reason of neglect or failure to exercise it within prescribed time; (2) interruption, as, lapse of time; -v. (3) to terminate, fall, fail.

lapsed legacy Bequest which cannot be made because the legatee has died before the legacy is payable, and the proceeds therefore go into the residuary estate.

lapsed policy Insurance contract on which payment of premiums is in default.

larcenous [LAHR suh nuhs] Having character of stealing.

larcenous intent [LAHR suh nuhs in TENT] Intent to deprive the owner of personal property which has been taken from him without his consent.

larceny [LAHR suh nee] Unlawful taking, obtaining, or withholding of another's property, with intent to deprive him of the property or to appropriate it to the wrongdoer's use or to the use of a third person.

☆ **larceny** [LAHR suh nee] *recommended statistical terminology* Unlawful taking or attempted taking of property other than a motor vehicle from the possession of another, by stealth, without force and without deceit, with intent to permanently deprive the owner of the property.

larceny by trick [LAHR suh nee bahy trik] Obtaining property of another by means of fraud, trick or device, with intent to convert it to the wrongdoer's use or to the use of a third person.

☆ **larceny-theft** *Uniform Crime Reports usage* Unlawful taking, carrying, leading, or riding away by stealth of property, other than a motor vehicle, from the possession or constructive possession of another, including attempts.

lascivious [luh SIV ee uhs] Lewd, lustful, tending to cause sexual desire.

last Final, latest, at the end of a series, terminal.

last clear chance Doctrine that plaintiff's contributory negligence will not bar his action where defendant had an evident final opportunity to avoid damage or injury but failed to do so.

last illness Illness terminating in death.

last in, first out Method for determining value of inventory, in accounting practice, by using price last paid for an article as basis for unit cost of all such articles in inventory on assumption that last article purchased will be the first article sold.

last resort Court of last resort is one from which no appeal can be taken.

last will Written and formal direction of a person for the disposition of his estate after death.

late -adv. Formerly, recently; -adj. recent, tardy.

latent Hidden, potential, dormant.

latent defect Hidden flaw, flaw not discoverable by reasonable inspection.

lateral support Right to have land supported by adjoining land or soil beneath

law (1) Body of principles, standards and rules prescribed and enforced by government for its own regulation and the conduct of its inhabitants; (2) rules of behavior made mandatory by society.

☆ **law enforcement agency** *recommended statistical terminology* A federal, state, or local criminal justice agency or identifiable subunit of which the principal functions are the prevention, detection, and investigation of crime, and the apprehension of alleged offenders.

☆ **law enforcement officer** I. In some usages, any government employee who is an officer sworn to carry out law enforcement duties, whether or not employed by an agency or identifiable subunit which primarily performs law enforcement functions. II. *recommended statistical terminology* An employee of a law enforcement agency who is an officer sworn to carry out law enforcement duties.

lawful Rightful, legal, authorized by law, legitimate.

lawful age Age at which one attains full legal status in regard to legal rights and duties.

lawless (1) Not observing legal forms and rules; (2) without control of law.

law of the land Body of substantive and procedural law, binding upon all persons and derived from a Constitution.

laws Statutes enacted by legislatures.

lawsuit Legal action before a court.

lawyer Person whose profession is to represent an interest of a party in a judicial proceeding and give advice and assistance on legal matters.

☆ **lawyer** A person trained in the law, admitted to practice before the bar of a given jurisdiction, and authorized to advise, represent, and act for other persons in legal proceedings.

lay -adj. (1) Non-professional, not of the clergy; -v. (2) to state or allege in pleading; (3) to deposit, as a bet.

laying the venue [LAY eeng *th*uh VEN yoo] Determination and designation by plaintiff in his pleadings of the jurisdiction he proposes for further proceedings in an action.

layman (1) One not belonging to a particular profession; (2) one of laity as distinguished from one of clergy.

layoff Termination of employment by act of employer.

leading case One so well reasoned and of such importance that it has commanded attention and support as a precedent for subsequent decisions on the same point or related points.

leading question One which by its wording suggests or implies the answer to be given.

league Agreement, treaty or alliance between states or parties.

learn To gain knowledge or comprehension.

lease Formal contract between lessor and lessee for lessee's possession and use of lessor's property for a specified term and consideration (usually used in relation to real property between landlord and tenant).

leaseback Transaction by which real property is sold and immediately leased to the vendor.

leasehold Interest in property by reason of a lease.

leasing Act of giving to another temporary possession, custody and use of one's property, by formal instrument setting forth agreed terms.

leave -n. (1) Departure, absence, vacation; (2) permission to do something; liberty; -v. (3) to abandon, depart; to allow, permit without interference; (4) to devise bequeath.

leave of court Permission from a court to take some action not otherwise allowable.

ledger Account book containing debits and credits.

legacy [LEG uh see] Personal property given by will.

legal Conforming to law, created by law, pertaining to law, permitted by law.

legal cap Writing paper for legal use, usually 8½ inches wide ´ 13 inches long, and sometimes ruled.

legal representative One who represents or succeeds another in legal status, such as an executor, guardian, receiver or trustee.

legal tender Currency which the law authorizes a debtor to offer to a creditor in satisfaction of a money obligation.

legality Lawfulness, conformity to law.

legalization Act of making legal or lawful.

legalize To provide legal authority or sanction.

legally in accordance with law.

legatee [leg uh TEE] One to whom property is given by will.

legation (1) Diplomatic mission in a foreign country; (2) official residence of a diplomatic minister in a foreign country.

legislate To enact laws.

legislation (1) Bills passed by a legislature; (2) process of enacting new laws.

legislative Pertaining to law-making power and function.

legislative history Legislative documents which may be consulted to provide meanings and interpretations of a particular statute.

legislator One who makes laws as a member of a legislative body.

legislature Organized law-making body of a government.

legitimacy (1) Status of being legal; (2) status of one born of a legal marriage.

legitimate -adj. (1) Genuine, law-abiding, valid; (2) born in wedlock; -v. (3) to make lawful.

legitimation Act of making lawful.

lend To give to another the temporary possession, custody and use of some article.

lender One who gives temporary possession, custody or use of his property to another.

lesbian Female homosexual.

lese majesty [lez MA jes tee] (1) High treason against a sovereign; (2) detraction from dignity or importance of duly constituted authority.

lesion Abnormal structural change of a bodily organ due to injury or disease.

lessee [les EE] One having possession of property in accordance with a lease.

lesser Inferior, smaller.

lesser included offense An offense of lesser grade or degree necessarily committed by the same conduct of one who commits an offense of greater grade or degree; as, for example, one who steals property in a grand larceny has by the same conduct necessarily committed the lesser included offense of petit larceny. When it is legally possible to attempt to commit a particular crime, such attempt constitutes a lesser included offense as to the object crime.

☆ **lesser included offense** An offense which is made up of elements which are a subset of the elements of another offense having a greater statutory penalty, and the occurrence of which is established by the same evidence or by some portion of the evidence which has been offered to establish the occurrence of the greater offense.

lessor [LES awr] Owner of property who grants a lease to a tenant or lessee.

let -n. (1) Obstruction; -v. (2) to award a contract by competitive bidding; (3) to permit, admit, release, as, to let to bail.

lethal Deadly, fatal.

letter of credit Written instrument by which its maker authorizes a correspondent to advance credit to bearer or person named, for which the maker guarantees payment.

letters of administration Written authority issued by a competent court showing designation and power of one as administrator in administering the estate of a deceased person.

letters of guardianship Written authority issued by a competent court empowering and designating one to act as guardian.

letters patent Formal instrument from a government acknowledging grant and recording of a patent in favor of designated individual and setting forth its details.

letters rogatory [LET uhrs ROG uh taw ree] Written request issued by a court to a foreign court, requesting that testimony of a witness therein resident be taken in accordance with request and forwarded to the requesting court for its use in a pending proceeding.

letters testamentary [LET uhrs tes tuh MEN tuh ree] Court certification granting authority and appointment to an executor to carry out a will.

letting (1) Awarding of a contract by competitive bidding; (2) leasing.

☆ **levels of proof** The degrees of certainty required at different stages in the criminal justice process.

levy -n. (1) Imposition or collection of an assessment, fine or tax; (2) act of taking goods of a judgment debtor for their sale to satisfy the debt;
-v. (3) to impose, collect, seize, as, to levy a tax or execution.

lewd Obscene, lascivious, vulgar.

lex [leks] Law.

lex contractus [leks kuhn TRAK tuhs] Law of the place where a contract was entered into.

lex delictus [leks duh LIK tuhs] Law of the place where a wrong was committed.

lex fori [leks FAW ree] Law of the forum, Law of the jurisdiction wherein an action is pending.

Lexis [LEK sis] The name given to a major computerized legal research system developed by Mead Data Central.

lex loci [leks LOH kee] Law of the place where the rights or liabilities were created.

lex loci contractus [leks LOH kee kuhn TRAK tuhs] Law of the place where a contract was made or to be performed.

lex loci delicti [leks LOH kee duh LIK tahy] Law of the place where a wrong occurred.

lex talionis [leks ta lee OH nis] Law of retaliation, by which formerly a wrongful act was punished by similar infliction upon the wrongdoer, as, an eye for an eye.

liability Obligation, debt, burden, drawback.

liable Bound, responsible, chargeable, answerable.

libel [LAHY buhl] -n. (1) Statement which ridicules, shames, disgraces or injures one's reputation unjustly (N.B. although libel is usually by publication and slander is oral, libel is frequently used to include either written or oral defamation); (2) first pleading in an admiralty action; -v. (3) to injure one's reputation unjustly and maliciously;
(4) to proceed in an admiralty action by filing a libel against a ship or goods.

☆ **libel** Defamation by any non-spoken communication, most commonly by some written or printed matter.

libellant (libelant) [LAHY buhl uhnt] (1) One who publishes a libel;
(2) plaintiff in an admiralty action.

libellee (libelee) [lahy buhl EE] (1) Person libelled; (2) defendant in an admiralty action.

libelous (libellous) [LAHY buhl uhs] Having the quality of libel, defamatory.

libelous per se [LAHY buh luhs puhr say] (1) Of such intrinsic character as to constitute libel without proof of special damage; (2) that which is presumed, due to its derogatory nature, to have injured the reputation and standing of the person libelled, so that proof of damage will not be required but only proof of publication.

liber [LAHY buhr] Record book for preservation of legal or official records, as, a liber of deeds or wills.

liberal (1) Generous, abundant, bountiful; (2) broadminded, not conforming to traditional or established views.

liberal interpretation Concept that ideas or words should receive broad interpretation in respect to the matter under consideration, so that a particular issue may be considered to be within the spirit of a law although no precise authority for it can be found.

liberate To set free.

liberation Act of setting free or removing from domination.

liberty Freedom, exemption from control.

license -n. (1) Permission to act; (2) formal instrument showing authority for some act or status; -v. (3) to permit, authorize, allow.

licensee (1) One to whom some particular authority or permission has been given by license; (2) person on the premises of another by permission or invitation, or under legal authority.

licensor One who grants or issues a license.

licentiate [lahy SEN shee uht] (1) One holding a license to practice a profession, such as medicine or law; (2) European academic degree, ranking below Doctor of Philosophy.

licentious [lahy SEN shuhs] (1) Marked by freedom of individual will without restraint; (2) lascivious, unchaste.

lie -n. (1) Falsehood; (2) position, as, the lie of a golf ball; -v. (3) to utter falsehood; (4) to rest, sojourn, exist.

lie detector Polygraph machine which records fluctuations in blood pressure, pulse, respiration and perspiration of a subject while he is being questioned and which uses data so obtained in determination of truth or falsity of answers given. Use of lie-detector tests for admissibility of evidence has not been established.

lien [leen] Encumbrance on property, used to secure payment of a debt.

lienee [leen EE] One whose property has incurred a lien.

lienor [LEEN uhr] One placing a lien on property to secure payment of a debt.

life State of being, existence, period of activity ending with permanent stoppage of organic functions.

life annuity Contract providing for payments during life of an annuitant.

life estate Estate in property limited by life of a given person, and its reversion thereafter as provided or prescribed by law.

life in being Span of time measured by continued life of a person actually alive when the measuring period commences.

life insurance Plan, usually administered by a life insurance company, whereby number of anticipated deaths in a group of persons of a given age is actuarially calculated, and premiums paid by members of the group are used to pay insurance to beneficiaries of those who die.

life interest Estate in property, given for the life of a person, and its reversion thereafter as provided or prescribed by law.

life table Statistical table showing mathematical life expectancy of persons by age group.

lift -n. (1) Mechanical device for raising or lowering; (2) rise in position or condition; -v. (3) to raise, elevate; (4) to plagiarize.

ligan [LAHY guhn] Goods tied to a buoy and thrown into the sea in time of danger, so that they may later be recovered.

light -adj. (1) Bright; (2) trivial; (3) inconsiderable; -n. (4) physical illumination; (5) intellectual illumination.

lighterage [LAHY tuh ruhj] (1) Movement of goods between vessels; (2) price paid for movement of goods between vessels.

like -adj. Equal, corresponding, same, similar; -v. to enjoy, approve.

likelihood Probability.

likely Probable, credible, qualified.

likewise In like manner, similarly, moreover.

limit -n. Boundary, border, limitation; -v. to bound, restrain, confine.

limitation (1) Restriction, restraint; (2) establishment of a lesser estate by deed or will, out of a fee.

limited Restricted, bounded, confined.

limited jurisdiction Authority effective within a prescribed area or amount, as, a court has limited jurisdiction to try cases in which recovery claimed does not exceed a prescribed amount.

limited liability Restriction of obligation that may be incurred, as, shareholders of a corporation possess limited liability as to corporate obligations.

limited partnership Partnership having one or more partners whose liability is expressly limited to extent of their capital contribution, unlike that of the general partners.

limited payment plan Form of life insurance wherein premiums needed to provide coverage for life span of a person according to his attained age are paid during a given term, such as 20 or 30 years.

limited power of appointment Authority given, as in a will, to name another to act in some capacity, where the choice must by the grant of authority be made from a specific group.

line (1) Boundary between parcels of real property; (2) order of one's descent or ancestry; (3) amount of credit available to a borrower.

lineage [LIN ee uhj] Family line of descent from ancestors.

lineal [LIN ee uhl] Relating to a line, hereditary, in a direct line of descent.

lineal consanguinity [LIN ee uhl kon sang GWIN i tee] Family relationship in a direct line as, for example, son and father, grandfather or great-grandfather.

lineal descent [LIN ee uhl duh SENT] Family succession in direct line, as, a father to son or grandfather to grandson.

link Connection, bond, tie, unifying element.

liquid -adj. (1) Undisputed, as a debt; (2) in cash or readily converted into cash; -n. (3) free-flowing fluid having volume without definite shape except as given by its container.

liquidate (1) To adjust, settle, determine an amount, such as a debt, damages or an account; (2) to terminate affairs of a business, convert its assets into cash, and make appropriate legal disposition of the proceeds.

liquidated claim Claim whose amount has been agreed upon or provided for by law.

liquidated damages (1) Amount stipulated and agreed to by parties to a contract as proper payment by either to the other for breach of contract; (2) amount of damages fixed by judgment.

liquidated debt One whose amount and date of payment has been made certain.

liquidation (1) Process of settling or making definite an amount claimed as debt, damages or account due; (2) termination of a business, sale of its assets, and distribution thereof appropriately to creditors and others.

liquidator One designated to convert assets of a business into cash.

liquor Strong, distilled alcoholic beverage, as defined by statutes.

☆ **liquor laws** In Uniform Crime Reports terminology, the name of the UCR category used to record and report arrests for offenses relating to regulation of the manufacture, sale, distribution, transportation, possession, or use of intoxicating liquor, except public drunkenness and driving under the influence of alcohol.

lis mota [lis MOH tuh] Legal action begun.

lis pendens [lis PEN duhns] (1) Pending legal action; (2) recorded notice of pending legal action.

list -n. (1) Docket, schedule, registry, roll, roster; -v. (2) to lean to one side, as, the ship listed to port; (3) to enroll on a schedule, registry or similar compilation; (4) to enter securities for sale on a stock exchange; (5) to offer real property for sale through a broker.

listed (1) Included in a list; (2) traded on a stock exchange.

listing (1) Offering of real estate for sale or rental through a broker to sell or rent; (2) admission of securities for trading on a stock exchange.

liter (litre) [LEE tuhr] Metric system measure of volume, equal to 61.022 cubic inches or 2.113 American pints.

literal In accord with primary meaning, exact, unadorned.

literary Relating to study or use of books and writing.

literary composition Original written work and its preparation.

literary property Author's right of ownership in his original written work, as a common-law right or by statutory copyright.

literate (1) Able to read and write; (2) educated, lucid.

litigant [LIT uh guhnt] Party to a legal action.

litigate [LIT uh gayt] To contest an issue by its submission to a court or quasi-judicial body.

litigation [lit uh GAY shuhn] Legal contest between adverse parties before a court or quasi-judicial agency.

litigious [li TIJ uhs] Inclined to engage in lawsuits, fond of litigation.

littoral [LIT uh ruhl] -adj. (1) Belonging to shore of sea or lake; -n. (2) coastal region including land along coast and water nearby; (3) area of shore between high and low water marks.

livery (1) Delivery of possession of lands; (2) servant's uniform; (3) care of horses for compensation; (4) business of renting vehicles, such as boats and autos.

livery of seisin [LIV uh ree uv SEE zin] Common law ceremonial transfer of possession of land.

lives in being Measurement of time, based on lives of persons presently alive as the limiting period, in creating a future interest.

livestock Domestic animals kept for use or pleasure, such as dairy cattle and horses.

live storage Safekeeping of property subject to active use, as, the live storage of an automobile.

L. J. Law Journal.

LL. B. Bachelor of Laws.

LL. D. Doctor of Laws.

loading (1) Act of placing a load or burden on a carrier, as in the loading of a truck or vessel; (2) in insurance premiums, that portion of the premium in excess of anticipated liability to policyholder.

loan Act of giving property for temporary use, upon promise of its repayment or return.

loan shark Person who lends money at exorbitant rate of interest.

lobby -n. (1) Anteroom, foyer, entrance of a building; (2) group seeking to influence legislators in behalf of their particular interest; -v. (3) to promote passage of particular bills pending before a legislature by seeking to influence its members.

lobbying Act of urging, persuading or inducing favorable consideration of pending legislation.

lobbyist One engaged for compensation in urging and working for legislative enactment of pending bills.

local Confined to a particular place.

☆ **local law enforcement agency** *recommended statistical terminology* A law enforcement agency which is an organizational unit, or subunit, of local government.

☆ **local law enforcement officer** *recommended statistical terminology* An employee of a local law enforcement agency who is an officer sworn to carry out law enforcement duties.

local option Privilege given by a state legislature to a city or other subdivision to determine by vote of its own citizens whether a particular state law shall apply in such subdivision.

location Site, particular land area, land having some distinguishing feature.

loc. cit. [lohk sit] (loco citato) In the place cited.

lockout Refusal of an employer to permit his employees to enter his premises and work.

lockup -n. Local jail; -v. to arrest, take into official custody.

loco parentis [LOH koh puh REN tis] (**in loco parentis**) [in LOH koh puh REN tis] In place of a parent.

locus [LOH kuhs] Locality, place.

locus delicti [LOH kuhs duh LIK tahy] Place of the offense.

locus in quo [LOH kuhs in kwoh] Place in which, place under consideration.

locus poenitentiae [LOH kuhs pen i TEN shee ahy] (1) Area for repentance (referring to mental rather than physical area); (2) opportunity to change one's mind, relinquish a criminal intent before acting, withdraw from a bargain before it results in definite contract.

locus sigilli [LOH kuhs suh GIL ee] (abbreviated L.S.) Place of the seal, place for the seal.

lodging house Premises offering sleeping accommodations for rent, as further defined by statute.

logic Science of reasoning, intellectual process of proceeding from the known to the unknown.

logical In accordance with reasonable inferences and accepted principles of logic.

log rolling Trading of votes between legislators to secure approval of pending bills on a reciprocal basis.

loiter To stand around idly, linger, lag behind, delay.

long In security exchange parlance, one is long on stock when he has presently a quantity for future sale in anticipation of price increase.

longevity Long life-span.

long ton 2,240 pounds.

lookout (1) Person on a vessel charged with duty of detecting obstructions to navigation; (2) participant in a crime whose function is to give warning to his fellow-criminals in event of danger; (3) one engaged in keeping watch; (4) elevated place used for keeping watch.

lose To be deprived of, part with, ruin, destroy.

loss (1) Decrease in amount; (2) deprivation, damage, detriment.

lost property One or more articles which an owner has casually and involuntarily parted from, without knowing where or how to recover them.

lot (1) Division of land; (2) determination by chance; (3) considerable quantity or number.

lottery Plan for distribution of prizes by chance among persons who have paid to participate.

☆ **lottery** An unlawful game of chance in which a set amount of money is wagered for a chance to win a set prize.

low water Furthest receding point of a tide.

loyal Faithful, devoted, unswerving in allegiance.

loyalty Fidelity to a government, person or principle.

L. S. (locus sigilli) Place of the seal, place for the seal.

lucid interval Temporary period during which an insane or delirious person is restored to use of his reason and mental capacity.

lucrative Profitable, money-making.

lucre [LOO kuhr] Profit, reward, money.

lucri causa [LOO kree KOU zuh] For the sake of gain.

lump sum payment Payment in one installment of a sum due, as, for example, lump sum payment of proceeds of a life insurance policy in event of insured's death.

lump sum settlement In workmen's compensation, matrimonial and other matters, agreement to pay a sum certain at one time in satisfaction of an obligation, rather than in periodic payments during continuation of status.

lunacy State of one having a deranged or unsound mind so as to lack legal capacity or responsibility.

lunar Measured by revolutions of the moon.

lunatic Person legally incapable or irresponsible by reason of abnormal mental condition.

lying in wait Remaining concealed in ambush for the purpose of making sudden and violent attack upon one arriving.

lynch To seize out of legal custody persons charged with crime and inflict violence or death upon them without trial or process of law.

lynch law A contradiction in terms, but as so used denoting rule and force exerted by a mob unlawfully and in defiance of legal standards and institutions, whereby persons charged with crime are taken from legal custody and assaulted or killed.

M

mace (1) Chemical used as a weapon by spraying into the eyes:
(2) ornamented staff used as a ceremonial symbol of authority by
certain public bodies.

machine Useful mechanical device.

magisterial [maj is TEE ree uhl] (1) Relating to office of a magistrate;
(2) authoritative, dignified, sedate.

magistrate Local judicial officer having limited original criminal jurisdiction.

☆ **magistrate** The judicial officer of a court of limited jurisdiction who sets bail and
may conduct misdemeanor trials and felony preliminary (probable cause)
hearings.

Magna Charta [MAG nuh KAHR tuh] Charter of rights granted by King John of
England at Runnymede, June 15, 1215 to the barons. By its provisions for
regulating the administration of justice, securing the liberty and property of
individuals, and defining temporal and ecclesiastical jurisdiction, it is
considered as the cornerstone of English constitutional liberty and the
forerunner of American constitutional government.

maim To inflict injury which deprives one of use of a limb or body member, or is
disfiguring.

maiming Act of inflicting injury which has permanent effect, such as loss of or
loss of use of a limb or body member, or disfigurement.

main -adj. Principal, leading, chief; -n. principal utility conductor, as, a gas, water
or electric main.

maintain (1) To keep in repair, as, to maintain a building; (2) to sustain, as, to
maintain a legal action; (3) to support, as, to maintain a family; (4) to uphold in
argument, as, to maintain one's views.

maintenance (1) Act of supporting, providing sustenance; (2) unlawful
interference in a legal action between others by providing funds or means to
carry it on; (3) act of preserving, keeping in repair.

majority (1) Status of full age; (2) more than half of a total number;
(3) preponderant quantity.

majority of stockholders Number representing more than half of the interest in
stock held by stockholders, when each share is entitled to one vote.

☆ **majority opinion** An opinion of the majority of the judges hearing a case.

majority rule Decision determined by agreement of more than half of those who
vote.

make over (1) To transfer title of property; (2) to alter, renovate.

maker Person signing a negotiable instrument, such as a promissory note.

mala fide [MOL uh FEE day] In bad faith, falsely maliciously.

mala in se [MOL uh in say] (singular: **malum in se**) Wrongs in themselves, acts
morally wrong irrespective of statute.

mala prohibita [MOL uh proh HIB i tuh] (singular: **malum prohibitum**) Wrongs
prohibited by statute and not inherently evil.

malconduct Dishonest conduct of public affairs.

malefactor [MAL uh fak tuhr] One guilty of an offense, evildoer.

malfeasance [mal FEE zuhns] (1) Doing of an act which one has no right to do;
(2) act of wrongdoing by a public officer under color of authority of his office.

malice Intention or desire to do harm to another, willful wrongdoing.

malice aforethought Predetermination to commit an unlawful act.

malicious (1) Done with intent to harm another; (2) done wrongfully and intentionally.

malicious injury Wrongful and intentional act which damages, harms or hurts.

malicious mischief Willful or wanton damage of another's property.

☆ **malicious mischief** Intentionally destroying or damaging, or attempting to destroy or damage, the property of another without his consent, usually by a means other than burning.

malicious prosecution Commencement of a legal action without probable cause and with intent to harm the defendant.

malign [muh LAHYN] To slander, libel, vilify, utter injuriously false reports.

malingerer One who feigns an ailment in order to escape performance of work or duty.

malo animo [MOL oh AN uh moh] With wrongful intent.

malpractice (1) Unreasonable lack of professional skill; (2) illegal or improper professional conduct.

maltreatment Rough or improper treatment.

malum in se [MOL uhm in say] Wrong in itself, morally evil in its own nature irrespective of statute.

malum prohibitum [MOL uhm proh HIB i tuhm] Wrong prohibited by statute but not inherently evil.

manage To control, take charge of, administer, conduct.

management Direction, regulation, control, supervision.

manager One having charge of an activity and vested with discretion and authority to conduct and supervise it.

mandamus [man DAY muhs] Judicial order commanding performance by a public officer of a specified act or duty.

mandate Command, order, direction.

mandatory Essential, required, obligatory.

☆ **mandatory sentence** A statutory requirement that a certain penalty shall be set and carried out in all cases upon conviction for a specified offense or series of offenses.

mania [MAY nee uh] (1) Mental condition accompanied by a high degree of excitement, hallucinations and illusions; (2) excessive, unreasonable enthusiasm.

manifest -adj. (1) Clearly visible, evident, obvious; -n. (2) list of cargo or passengers for transportation, such as on a ship, plane or train.

manifesto Public statement of opinion or policy.

manner Mode, method, kind, character.

manslaughter Unlawful killing of a human being without deliberate or willful intent.

manual adj. (1) Performed by hand, requiring physical skill and effort; -n. (2) book used by insurance underwriters for rate and classification data; (3) concise treatise on some subject.

manual delivery Actual physical delivery.

manual rates Uniform insurance premium rates determined by a rating bureau composed of participating companies and published as a prescribed schedule.

manufacture Production of goods by labor and machinery.

manufacturing establishment Place where machinery and labor are used in production of goods.

manumission [man yoo MISH uhn] (1) Delivery of a person from another's control; (2) act of liberation.

manuscript Handwritten or typewritten composition.

marauder One who roams about and attacks or enters premises with criminal intent.

mare clausum [MO ray KLOU zuhm] Navigable body of water controlled by one nation and closed to others.

mare liberum [MO ray LI buh ruhm] Navigable body of water open to all nations.

margin (1) Border; (2) security transaction by which customer makes partial payment for his purchase to a stockbroker, who advances the balance required and holds the securities for his customer's account.

marijuana (marihuana) [ma ri WO nuh] Plant source of a drug producing psychic disturbances, properly called cannabis sativa.

marine carrier Freight-carrying vessel.

marine insurance Branch of casualty insurance business concerned with loss or damage in transport on land, sea or air, further divided into inland marine and ocean marine categories.

marital Relating to marriage.

marital portion Amount of a deceased husband's estate to which his widow is entitled.

mark (1) Substitute for a signature; (2) token, indication, visible sign of identification.

market Any place for commercial transactions between buyers and sellers.

marketable Salable.

marketable title Condition of property ownership in which title is free from material defects and reasonable possibility of litigation.

market order Direction given to a broker to buy or sell for customer's account at market price when order is executed.

market price Amount actually paid in current market dealings.

market value Amount which can be obtained by mutual agreement between buyer and seller in regular course of business.

marque and reprisal, letters of [mahrk and ruh PRAHY zuhl, LET uhrs uv] Letters issued by a government to one of its subjects, purporting to authorize the seizure of commercial goods of subjects of another state, when found on the high seas, in alleged reprisal for similar acts.

marriage Social and legal status of man and woman united in mutual relationship as husband and wife.

marriage articles Agreement as to financial matters made between prospective parties to a marriage.

marriage portion Property given by husband to wife on marriage, dowry.

marriage settlement Financial agreement fixing rights of the parties to a marriage in each other's property, and made in consideration of marriage or in connection with divorce or separation.

marshal -n. (1) Ministerial officer for United States judicial districts to execute orders and processes of the court; (2) local law enforcement officer; (3) local officer having authority to seize assets of a judgment debtor in aid of execution of judgment; -v. (4) to assemble, arrange in order, as, to marshal assets or marshal the evidence in a case;

(5) to determine order of priority with respect to payment of claims from assets of a debtor.

marshaling assets (also spelled **marshalling**) Arrangement of assets in order of priority for payment to creditors.

marshaling evidence Review of evidence in a case by a court as part of its instructions to a jury.

martial law Military government imposed and executed by military authority over civilian population.

masher Man who makes sexual advances to a woman he does not know.

masochism [MAS uh kiz uhm] (1) Pleasure derived from physical or mental suffering inflicted on oneself; (2) sexual or other gratification obtained by acceptance of beating, mistreatment and humiliation.

Massachusetts rule In banking, rule that each bank handling a check for collection acts in turn as agent for the depositor.

Massachusetts trust Form of unincorporated business organization by which trustees hold title to corporate assets which they administer for benefit of holders of transferable certificates similar to corporate stock.

mass picketing Use of large number of pickets in a labor dispute so as to discourage persons from passing picket line.

master -n. (1) One who controls services and performance of another as an employer; (2) one having some particular authority, as, a master in chancery appointed by a court, master of a ship, master of a school;
(3) one possessing great skill or proficiency in an art or technique;
-v. (4) to overcome, bring under control.

master and servant Employer and employee.

master in chancery [MAS tuhr in CHAN suh ree] One appointed by a court of equity to conduct designated proceedings, such as conduct of a hearing, taking of testimony, examination of accounts, submission of a report and recommendation to the court, or executing a conveyance of property owned by a person who has refused to convey property pursuant to order of the court.

Master of the Rolls Title of English equity judge, who serves usually as presiding judge of the Court of Appeal and ranking next below the Lord Chancellor.

material -adj. Important, relevant, substantial; -n. goods such as building material or textiles, from which finished articles are made.

material allegation One having such relevance to a pleading as to be an essential part.

material fact Something having existence, and essential to or having serious bearing on an issue.

materiality (1) Quality of relevance; (2) state of being vital or requiring serious consideration.

materialman Person supplying building materials for use in construction.

material misrepresentation Untrue oral or written statement which is substantial and relevant, presented as true.

material witness Person whose testimony on some issue has been judicially determined as relevant and substantial, so that bail may be required of the witness to insure his testimony when required.

materials Articles from which finished products are made.

materiel [muh tee ree EL] Supplies and equipment of an organization.

maternal line Line of descent traced through a mother.

matricide Murder of a mother by her son or daughter.

matrimonial Pertaining to marriage.

matrimonial action Legal proceeding relating to marital status, such as separation, divorce or annulment.

matrimonial domicile [mat ruh MOH nee uhl DOM uh sahyl] Place where husband and wife live together.

matrimonial res [mat ruh MOH nee uhl rayz] Legal status of marriage, usually in relation to determination of jurisdiction in a matrimonial action.

matrimony Union of man and woman as husband and wife.

matron (1) Married woman; (2) female official or attendant of an asylum, jail or similar institution.

matter Subject of consideration, topic of discussion or contention, substance.

matter in issue Factual or legal question to be determined in a proceeding by evidence and proof.

matter of course (1) Done in regular order of procedure; (2) natural and logical result.

matter of fact That which exists and is perceivable by the senses, actual occurrence.

matter of form That which does not go to the merits of an issue but is required by proper procedure.

matter of law That which is determined and ascertained by rules of law.

matter of record That which may be established by official record of a court or other record required to be kept.

matter of right That to which one is legally entitled.

mature -adj. (1) Based on careful consideration; (2) fully grown and developed, due; (3) having normal adult qualities; -v. (4) to bring to full development, ripen, age.

maturity (1) Time when a debt or other obligation becomes due; (2) state of full development.

maxim (1) Established and widely accepted principle; (2) general truth; (3) saying of proverbial nature.

maximum -adj. Highest, greatest; -n. greatest quantity, upper limit allowed.

☆ **maximum sentence** I. In legal usage, the maximum penalty provided by law for a given criminal offense, usually stated as a maximum term of imprisonment or a maximum fine. II. In correctional usage in relation to a given offender, any of several quantities (expressed in days, months or years) which vary according to whether calculated at the point of sentencing or at a later point in the correctional process, and according to whether the time period referred to is the term of confinement or the total period under correctional jurisdiction.

mayhem Malicious, permanent and unlawful deprivation of a person's body member or of its use.

☆ **mayhem** Intentional inflicting of injury on another which causes the removal of, or seriously disfigures, or renders useless or seriously impairs the function of, any member or organ of the body.

mayor Chief executive of a city.

mean -adj. (1) Common, low, humble, inferior, shabby, stingy, low-minded; -n. (2) middle point of something; (3) instrument, agent or plan for accomplishing a purpose (**means**); -v. (4) to signify, express, intend.

meaning Intent, aim, purpose, sense.

means Instrument, intermediate agency, resources.

means test Examination of a person's assets in order to determine his eligibility for a specified payment of public funds.

measure of damages Applicable rule governing computation of money damages in a legal action.

mechanic's lien [muh KAN iks leen] Claim on real property pursuant to law for amount of labor or material used in constructing, altering or repairing the property.

mediation Intervention by a third person to settle or reconcile a controversy between conflicting parties.

mediator One not a party to a controversy who seeks to reconcile the parties.

medical examiner Public medical officer having duty to make post-mortem examination in case of violent or suspicious death.

medical jurisprudence [MED i kuhl joo ris PROO duhns] (also called forensic medicine) Formal application of medical science to resolution of legal questions in courts.

medicine (1) Scientific discipline concerned with health and the prevention, treatment and cure of disease; (2) substance possessing curative properties used in treatment of disease.

meeting of minds Essential requirement in formation of a contract, in that the mental faculties of both parties have met on the same subject matter and been in agreement as to terms, conditions and subject matter.

membership corporation Non-profit corporate association.

memorandum Informal written record or inter-office communication.

memorandum decision Brief opinion or decision of a court on a litigated question, giving the court's conclusion on factual and legal issues.

☆ **memorandum opinion** An opinion in writing, which is a very brief statement of the reasons for a decision, without detailed explanation.

memorandum sale Transaction by which vendee is given possession of the subject matter by signing a receipt for it, with title remaining in vendor until merchandise is paid for or returned by the vendee (frequently used in jewelry trade).

memorial Document in nature of a petition, presented to a legislative body or an executive of government.

memory Process of reproducing or recalling something previously learned.

menace Threat, danger.

menial Humble, lowly, not requiring special skill or intellect.

mensa et thoro [MEN suh et THAW roh] Bed and board.

mens rea [mens RAY uh] Criminal intent.

mental anguish Emotional suffering, such as grief or humiliation.

mental capacity (1) Degree of understanding and memory legally required to make one responsible for his acts; (2) such conscious understanding, memory and judgment as will enable a person to transact some particular act.

mental cruelty Course of conduct by one spouse, without physical cruelty, which endangers the other's mental health and physical efficiency to the extent of rendering the marital relationship intolerable.

mental deficiency Such failure of mental development as to result in social incompetence.

mental incapacity Lack of intellectual ability to understand and act with discretion in the usual affairs of life.

mental reservation Exception existing in the mind of a party to a promise or agreement.

mercantile [MUHR kuhn tahyl] Relating to trade, commerce and merchants.

mercantile agency [MUHR kuhn tahyl AY juhn see] (1) Credit investigating firm; (2) business of a factor who customarily has authority to buy, sell, pledge or consign goods of his principal.

mercantile paper [MUHR kuhn tahyl PAY puhr] Notes, bills of exchange and acceptances used in trade and commerce.

merchandise All commodities bought and sold.

merchant One engaged in business of buying and selling goods.

merchantable Salable, acceptable to buyers.

merchantman Privately owned ship for transport of passengers or freight.

merchant seaman Sailor on privately owned vessel.

mercy (1) Judicial discretion to mitigate or remit punishment in a criminal case; (2) leniency, compassion, forbearance, clemency.

meretricious [me ruh TRISH uhs] (1) Relating to a prostitute; (2) false, insincere.

merger Absorption of two entities into one, as, a merger of two business concerns.

meritorious Worthy, deserving.

merits -n. Points of legal substance and right, as distinguished from matters of form or practice; -v. earns, deserves.

merit system Competitive civil service, based on competence.

mero motu [ME roh MOH too] Mere motion.

message Any form of transmitted communication.

metes and bounds [meets and bounz] Boundaries and dimensions to describe areas of land.

method Process employed in attaining an objective.

metric system Decimal system of standards for weights and measures, generally used in Europe.

middleman (1) Broker, agent between two parties; (2) dealer in goods, between manufacturer and retailer or consumer.

might Power, capacity or resources of an individual or group.

mileage Allowance or charge for traveling expenses based upon distance traveled.

mileage tax License tax on business operating on public roads, determined by number of miles travelled.

milestone (1) Mark of achievement; (2) monument formerly erected on a road to mark distance from a point of reference.

military government Exercise by military commander of authority over civil administration of an occupied area, superseding local law.

military law Legal system applicable to military establishment and its personnel.

military offense Violation of military regulations, such as desertion, insubordination or absence without leave.

militia Body of citizens enrolled by a state as a military force available for service in emergencies.

mill run Ordinary course of production, without special preparation or finish.

mineral Usually, a natural solid element or compound extracted from the ground.

mineral deed Real estate conveyance of title to minerals, as distinguished from title to fee.

mineral lease Contract permitting exploration for and removal of minerals from land.

☆ **minimum eligible parole date** In data systems, the date on which the offender is or was first eligible for parole, as determined at the time of admission to prison or as first set by paroling authority action, depending on the statutes and other rules of the jurisdiction.

☆ **minimum sentence** The minimum penalty provided by law for a given offense, meaning in most statistical contexts, the minimum term of confinement to be served.

mining Process of withdrawing desired valuable minerals from the earth.

ministerial (1) Relating to an official act or duty prescribed by law as belonging to exercise of executive function of government; (2) relating to an act done in obedience to legal mandate, without exercise of judgment or discretion.

ministerial act Duty performed in response to legal mandate, without exercise of judgment or discretion.

ministerial duty Obligation imposed by law upon a public officer, without opportunity for exercise of discretion or judgment.

ministerial officer Person holding a public office which requires obedience to orders of superiors without opportunity for exercise of independent judgment and discretion.

minister plenipotentiary [MIN is tuhr plen i poh TEN shee e ree] Diplomatic representative ranking below an ambassador, but having full power to act as a representative of his government.

minor Person below age of legal competence as defined by statute.

minority (1) Status of one below age of legal competence; (2) smaller amount, as, a minority vote upon some question.

minute book Journal in which official record of proceedings is kept, as, minute book of a court or corporation.

minutes Memoranda of a proceeding made for permanent record, as, minutes of a meeting or trial.

☆ **Miranda rights** The set of rights which a person accused or suspected of having committed a specific offense has during interrogation, and of which he or she must be informed prior to questioning, as stated by the U.S. Supreme Court in deciding Miranda v. Arizona and related cases.

misadventure Accident causing serious injury to a person without negligence, design or illegal conduct.

misapplication Improper or illegal use, as, misapplication of funds belonging to another.

misappropriation Embezzlement, application of another's property to illegal purposes.

misbranding Act of labelling an article falsely or in a manner intended to mislead.

misc. Miscellaneous.

miscarriage (1) Expulsion of embryo from a pregnant female at any time before birth; (2) error or failure, as, a miscarriage in administration of Justice.

miscegenation [mis uh juh NAY shuhn] Mixture of races, usually referring to marriage or sexual intercourse between white person and member of another race.

misconduct Intentional violation of an established rule of law or behavior.

misdelivery Erroneous delivery or delivery to an unauthorized person.

misdemeanant [mis duh MEE nuhnt] Person convicted of a misdemeanor.

misdemeanor [mis duh MEE nuhr] (1) Crime less than a felony; (2) crime not punishable by death or imprisonment in a state prison; (3) crime of lower grade as defined by statute.

☆ **misdemeanor** [mis duh MEE nuhr] An offense punishable by incarceration usually in a local confinement facility, for a period of which the upper limit is prescribed by statute in a given jurisdiction, typically limited to a year or less.

misdirection Error made by a court in instructing a jury on law of a case.

misfeasance [mis FEE zuhns] Improper or illegal performance of a lawful act.

misfortune Accidental adverse event.

misjoinder [mis JOYN duhr] Incorrect joining together of causes of action in one legal proceeding.

misleading Of such nature as to give an incorrect impression, deceiving.

misnomer [mis NOH muhr] Error in designation of person's name in a legal instrument or proceeding.

misprision [mis PRI zhuhn] (1) Contempt of court, contempt against sovereign or government, seditious or disloyal conduct;
(2) maladministration of public office; (3) failure by a citizen having knowledge of treason or other felony to reveal it to proper authorities;
(4) clerical error in a legal proceeding, that can be summarily corrected.

misprision of felony [mis PRI zhuhn uv FEL uh nee] Knowledge and concealment of commission of a felony, without participation.

misprision of treason [mis PRI zhuhn uv TREE zuhn] Knowledge and concealment of an act of treason without participation.

misrepresentation Untrue oral or written statement presented as fact.

mistake Unintentional error, erroneous belief, blunder.

mistress (1) Female head of a household; (2) female cohabiting habitually with a male to whom she is not married.

☆ **mistrial** [MIS trahy uhl] A trial which has been terminated and declared invalid by the court because of some circumstance which creates a substantial and uncorrectable prejudice to the conduct of a fair trial, or which makes it impossible to continue the trial in accordance with prescribed procedures.

mitigate To lessen, soften, alleviate, relieve.

mitigating circumstances Extenuating conditions, reasons which provide excuse or justification for some conduct or act.

☆ **mitigating circumstances** Circumstances surrounding the commission of a crime which do not in law justify or excuse the act, but which in fairness may be considered as reducing the blameworthiness of the defendant.

mitigation Reduction, diminution, abatement.

mitigation of damages Abatement or reduction of amount of damages offsetting that claimed in a legal action.

mittimus [MIT i muhs] Form of writ issued by a court, commanding designated officer to convey convicted person to prison for confinement therein, or to remove records from one court to another.

mixed Partaking of two or more varieties or classes.

☆ **M.O.** Modus operandi.

mob Assembly of many persons acting in a violent and disorderly manner and committing or threatening crimes against persons or property.

mobile Movable.

☆ **Model Penal Code** A generalized modern codification of that which is considered basic to criminal law, published by the American Law Institute in 1962.

moderator Chairman of a meeting.

modification Partial alteration, qualification.

☆ **modification of probation** A change in the terms and conditions of a probation order, making them more restrictive or less restrictive, as determined by a court.

modify (1) To restrict meaning; (2) to make more temperate.

modus operandi [MOH duhs op uh RAN dee] Method of procedure (frequently used as describing a criminal's characteristic pattern of unlawful conduct).

☆ **modus operandi** [MOH duhs op uh RAN dee] **(method of operation** or **M.O.)** A characteristic pattern of behavior repeated in a series of offenses that coincides with the pattern evidenced by a particular single person, or by a particular group of persons working together.

moiety [MOY uh tee] Half, one of two equal parts.

molest (1) To annoy, disturb, interfere; (2) to meddle by sexual misconduct.

monarchy Government ruled by one sovereign person.

money Circulating medium of exchange used as legal tender.

money bill Legislative enactment raising or appropriating funds for some purpose.

moneyed corporation One engaged in investment of money for profit.

money had and received Common law form of action for return of money.

money order Draft issued by post office or private firm, directing its branches or agents to pay amount specified in the order to the designated payee.

monogamy [mon OG uh mee] Status of marriage to one person at one time.

monograph Detailed written treatise on a particular subject.

monomania [mon oh MAY nee uh] Mental defect restricted to or concentrating on one subject matter.

monopoly Status of exclusive ownership or control of production, distribution or supply, in an entire field of business, to the exclusion of others.

month Usually defined by statute as a calendar month.

monument (1) Permanent object used as a reference point in surveying real property; (2) structure such as a stone erected over a grave as a memorial; (3) lasting evidence of great achievement.

moonshine Illegally made liquor.

moot (1) Controversial, unsettled; (2) deprived of practical significance, made academic.

moot court Mock court used by law students for practice.

moral Relating to conscience and principles of right conduct.

moral certainty That status of mind in which one has been convinced of some proposition beyond a reasonable doubt.

morality Conformity to accepted standards of conduct.

moral turpitude [MAW ruhl TUHR pi tood] Behavior that violates accepted moral standards of the community.

moratorium [maw ruh TAW ree uhm] Legally authorized period of delay in performance of legal obligations.

morbid (1) Affected or induced by disease; (2) characterized by feelings of gloom and depression; (3) grisly, gruesome.

more or less Approximately, substantially, to a varying degree.

moribund [MAW ruh bund] (1) Dormant; (2) approaching death.

moron (1) Mental defective whose mental age is between eight and twelve years; (2) feebleminded person.

mortal Deadly, fatal.

mortality table Statistical data based on experience showing rate of deaths over a period of years, by age groups.

mortgage [MAWR guhj] (1) Form of lien on real property as security for payment of a debt; (2) conditional conveyance of real property, subject to payment of a debt.

mortgagee [mawr guh JEE] One who lends money on the security of a mortgage.

mortgagor [MAWR guh juhr] Owner of property who places a mortgage on it as security for repayment of a loan.

mortis causa [MAWR tis KOU zuh] In contemplation of death.

most favored nation clause Provision often contained in international treaties by which parties agree that each shall enjoy, reciprocally, those specified benefits and privileges granted by the other to other nations.

motion Application to a court for an order, ruling or direction.

☆ **motion** An oral or written request made to a court at any time before, during, or after court proceedings, asking the court to make a specified finding, decision, or order.

motion in arrest of judgment Application by defense in a criminal case to prevent imposition of sentence, upon statutory grounds specified in the motion.

motive Inducement, cause, or reason why a thing is done.

☆ **motive** An inner stimulus that moves a person to act.

motorcycle Two-wheeled automotive vehicle in which the rider straddles the engine.

motor scooter Low two or three-wheeled automotive vehicle, smaller and less powerful than a motorcycle, and so designed that the rider does not straddle the engine.

motor vehicle Vehicle intended for highway travel and having its own motive power.

☆ **motor vehicle theft** *recommended statistical terminology* Unlawful taking, or attempted taking, of a self-propelled road vehicle owned by another, with the intent to deprive him of it permanently or temporarily.

motu proprio [MOH too PROH pree oh] Of one's own motion or impulse.

movable (moveable) Capable of being changed in place or chronology, not fixed, not stationary.

movant [MOO vuhnt] Person making a motion or application to a court.

move (1) To go forward, proceed, depart, actuate; (2) to propose action to a parliamentary body for their consideration; persuade; (3) to apply to a court, orally or in writing, for an order, ruling or direction.

moving papers Formal legal pleadings in support of a motion.

mulct [mulkt] -n. (1) Arbitrary exaction of money; -v. (2) to penalize by imposing a fine or forfeiture; (3) to defraud, swindle, obtain by duress.

multifarious [mul ti FA ree uhs] Having great variety.

☆ **multiple sentence** Two or more concurrent or consecutive sentences, or a combination of both types.

multiplicity State of being multiple or various.

multiplicity of action Series of similar legal actions grounded on the same subject matter.

municipal (1) Pertaining to a city; (2) relating to internal affairs as distinguished from foreign relations of a governmental body.

municipal bond Security issued by a local government as evidence of its debt.

municipal corporation Political unit such as a town, city or borough formed for purpose and having power of local self-government.

municipal ordinance Local law enacted by local government.

municipal security Evidence of debt such as a bond, which is issued by a local government as security for repayment of the debt.

muniments [MYOO ni muhnts] Documentary evidence which enables one to defend his title to property or maintain a claim for some right or privilege.

murder Unlawful killing of a human being by another, usually with intent to kill or in commission of a felony, as defined by statute.

☆ **murder** Intentionally causing the death of another person without extreme provocation or legal justification, or causing the death of another while committing or attempting to commit another crime.

must Is required, compelled, commanded, obliged to.

mutatis mutandis [myoo TOT is myoo TON dis] With necessary changes made.

mute -adj. Speechless, making no answer, maintaining silence; -n. person incapable of speaking.

mutilate To cut up, permanently alter or destroy.

mutiny Uprising against constituted authority, usually used in relation to military persons.

mutual Interchangeable, reciprocal, shared, given and received in equal amount, joint.

mutual enterprise Business endeavor whose members share equally in profits and losses.

mutual fund Investment company that invests funds of its shareholders in diversified securities of other corporations.

mutuality Quality of reciprocity, interchange, interdependence.

mutual savings bank Savings bank organized without stock, and whose earnings accrue to benefit of its depositors.

mutual wills Separate wills of two or more persons, made pursuant to agreement and containing similar or reciprocal testamentary provisions.

N

naked (1) Wanting in necessary conditions, lacking proven authority; (2) bare, unclothed.

name Identification or designation of individual, firm or corporation.

namely Expressly, specifically.

narrative Story, oral or written recital of a series of events.

natal [NAY tuhl] Pertaining to birth.

nation Territory having independent existence and government.

national -adj. Pertaining to a particular government; -n. one owing permanent allegiance to a nation without regard to his residence or citizenship status.

national bank Commercial bank organized under United States laws and operating under United States supervision.

national defense Entire Federal military establishment and all matters connected therewith.

national emergency State of national danger from any source, proclaimed by government authority.

nationality Legal and political status of an individual with respect to his allegiance to a nation and its protection afforded to him.

nationalization Process by which private property is vested in national government and former private owners are deprived of such property.

National Reporter System Collection of state and federal judicial opinions, and digests of those opinions, in a format developed by West Publishing Company.

native -adj. (1) Inherent, inborn, natural, indigenous; -n. (2) natural-born citizen, one born within a particular country; (3) person or thing indigenous to an area.

natural Determined by physical causes and conditions, as distinguished from legal causes and conditions.

natural-born citizen One born as a citizen or subject of a national government.

natural child Child born out of lawful wedlock.

naturalization Process by which an alien becomes a citizen of a country.

naturalize To confer citizenship upon an alien.

naturalized citizen One whose citizenship has been acquired by process of naturalization.

natural law Body of rules and principles for guidance of human conduct not founded on statutory law but arising from and conforming to man's intelligence and his mental, moral and physical makeup.

natural life Period of physical existence terminating in death.

natural person Human being as distinguished from a corporate or artificial person.

navigable waters Bodies of water united in a continuous channel that ships or vessels may pass.

N. B. (nota bene) Note well.

necessaries Services and articles actually needed by a person, such as food, clothing, shelter, medical care and furnishings, in reasonable accordance with one's station in life.

necessary Indispensable, essential.

necessity Indispensability, requirement.

need -n. (1) Necessary duty, obligation; (2) exigency; -v. (3) to be in want; (4) to be under necessity or obligation.

needless Without useful motive, unnecessary.

needy Indigent, poverty-stricken.

negative Denial, contradiction, refusal.

negative pregnant In pleading, a negative implying also an affirmative, as, a statement that the defendant did not strike the plaintiff's head with a hickory stick.

neglect Absence of care or attention, omission, failure, refusal or unwillingness to perform an act that can be done or that one is required to do.

negligence Failure to exercise care of a prudent man.

☆ **negligence** In legal usage, generally, a state of mind accompanying a person's conduct such that he or she is not aware, though a reasonable person should be aware, that there is a risk that the conduct might cause a particular harmful result.

negligence per se [NEG li juhns puhr say] Conduct which may be treated as careless without further proof, either because it is in violation of statute or so clearly opposed to dictates of common prudence that a reasonable person would not be guilty of it.

negligent Careless, lax, remiss.

☆ **negligent manslaughter** *(called "manslaughter by negligence")* In Uniform Crime Reports terminology, causing the death of another by recklessness or gross negligence.

negotiability Quality of being transferable.

negotiable Capable of having ownership transferred by endorsement or delivery.

negotiable instrument Written promise or order to pay specified sum on demand or at determined time, payable to order or to bearer so that ownership may be transferred by delivery or indorsement.

negotiate (1) To transact business, bargain or trade; (2) to meet and discuss in order to agree, compromise or settle a matter.

negotiation Course of conduct in seeking agreement on terms of a contract.

nepotism [NEP uh tiz uhm] Practice of appointing persons to positions or showing favoritism because they are relatives.

net Clear of all deductions such as charges, commissions, taxes and discounts.

net assets Excess value of resources over liabilities.

net estate Amount of gross estate remaining after deduction of proper items in settling estate.

net income Amount remaining after charges such as taxes have been made against gross income.

net proceeds Amount realized after proper deductions.

net weight Weight of an article excluding its wrapping and container.

net worth Amount remaining after liabilities have been deducted from assets.

neutral Impartial, not engaged on either side.

neutrality Status of impartiality as between opponents.

new Of fresh or recent origin, novel.

new and useful Conditions of having been previously unknown, and possessing practical utility, as requisites for the patentability of an invention.

newly discovered evidence Evidence obtained after verdict or judgment which could not in the exercise of due diligence have been obtained sooner but which could, if known, change the verdict or judgment.

new matter Allegation contained in a pleading which has not previously been alleged by either party.

☆ **new trial** In the broadest sense, any trial in which issues of fact and law are examined that have already been the subject of an earlier trial.

next Nearest, closest, immediately following, adjoining in a series.

next friend One appointed or admitted to act in legal capacity for benefit of another, such as an infant.

next of kin (1) Relative(s) sharing in an estate by statute of distribution; (2) person(s) in nearest degree of blood relationship to another person.

nexus [NEKS uhs] Connection, link.

nil [nil] Nothing.

nisi [NIS ee] Unless, not final, as, a decree nisi is one which remains operative unless party affected takes some action in a given time to procure its revocation or modification.

nisi prius [NIS ee PRAHY uhs] Court of original jurisdiction for jury trials.

no bill found Return or endorsement by a grand jury showing that after their consideration of a matter, they failed to vote an indictment.

☆ **nolle prosequi** [NOL ay PROS uh kwee] I. A formal entry upon the record of the court, indicating that the prosecutor declares that he or she will proceed no further in the action. II. *recommended statistical terminology* The terminating of adjudication of a criminal charge by the prosecutor's decision not to pursue the case, in some jurisdictions requiring the approval of the court.

nolo contendere [NOH loh kuhn TEN duh ruh] (I will not contest it) Plea by defendant in a criminal action that subjects him to punishment without admission of guilt, and permits his guilt to be challenged in a collateral proceeding.

☆ **nolo contendere** [NOH loh kuhn TEN duh ruh] *recommended statistical terminology* A defendant's formal answer in court to the charge(s) contained in a complaint, information, or indictment, stating that he or she will not contest the charge(s), but neither admits guilt nor claims innocence.

nol. pros. (nolle prosequi) Unwillingness to prosecute.

nominal Existing in name or form but not in reality or substance.

nominal damages Award of a token sum where no substantial injury is proven to have been sustained.

nominal defendant Person joined as defendant in an action not because of his liability but because action would be defective unless he were so joined.

nominal partner One who allows his name to be used as a partner of a business although he has no actual interest in the business.

nominal party Person having no actual interest in a legal action but joined because rules of pleading require his presence on the record.

nominal plaintiff Person whose name is used in prosecuting an action although he has no real interest in the subject matter.

nominate To designate for election or appointment.

nomination (1) Act of proposing person for an office; (2) appointment of person to an office.

nominee One proposed for an office, or designated to act for another.

non-age Status of legal minority.

non-assessable Not subject to further assessment, taxation or charge, as, non-assessable shares of stock in a corporation.

non-bailable Description of a criminal charge as one for which a person may not be released on bail, or a person so situated by statute because of previous criminal convictions.

non-cancelable (non-cancellable) Designation by which insurer is prevented from cancelling policy of insurance on which timely payment of premiums is made.

non compos mentis [nohn KOM puhs MEN tis] Not of sound mind, lacking mental capacity to act understandingly.

non-conforming use Use of real property allowed by a zoning board to continue although the area is not zoned for such use.

non-conformist One who refuses to comply with customs and conventions of others.

nondescript [non duh SKRIPT] Not capable of proper description.

nonfeasance [non FEE zuhns] Failure or neglect to perform a duty.

non-joinder [non JOYN duhr] Omission to include as a party to an action one who should be joined.

☆ **nonjury trial** *recommended statistical terminology* In criminal proceedings, a trial in which there is no jury, and in which a judicial officer determines all issues of fact and law in a case.

☆ **nonnegligent manslaughter** Intentionally causing the death of another, with provocation that a reasonable person would find extreme, without legal justification.

non obstante [nohn uhb STAN tay] Notwithstanding, an exception to a rule.

non obstante veredicto [nohn uhb STAN tay ver uh DI K toh] Notwithstanding the verdict, as a judgment directed for one party although the verdict was for his adversary, where the court believes that the party for whom verdict was rendered is not entitled, as a matter of law, to judgment thereon.

non-payment Neglect or refusal to pay a sum when due.

non-performance Neglect, failure, or refusal to do an act.

non-profit Not conducted or maintained for gain.

non seq. [nohn sek] (non sequitur) (it does not follow) A type of fallacy.

non sui juris [nohn SOO ee JOO ris] Without legal capacity to manage one's own affairs.

nonsuit Judgment against a plaintiff for failure to establish or prosecute his case.

no recourse Without right of the holder of an instrument to look to endorsers for payment.

normal According to established or average rule, principle or standard.

noscitur a sociis [NOH si toor o SOH see ees] (it is known from its associates) Meaning of doubtful words may be ascertained by referring to the meaning of other words associated with it.

notarial [noh TE ree uhl] Taken or performed by a notary public.

notary public Officer whose public function is to administer oaths and take acknowledgements in legal matters.

note Written instrument by which its maker promises to pay a specified sum to payee, bearer or to order at a specified time.

notes Memoranda or stenographic record made of a legal proceeding or similar matter.

not found Indorsement by a grand jury on its proceeding by which it reports failure to vote an indictment.

not guilty (1) Plea in criminal practice denying allegations of information, indictment or complaint and creating general issue; (2) verdict of acquittal in a criminal action.

☆ **not guilty by reason of insanity** *recommended statistical terminology* The plea of a defendant or the verdict of a jury or judge in a criminal proceeding, that the defendant is not guilty of the offense(s) charged because at the time the crime(s) was committed the defendant did not have the mental capacity to be held criminally responsible for his or her actions.

☆ **not guilty plea** *recommended statistical terminology* A defendant's formal answer in court to the charge(s) contained in a complaint, information, or indictment, claiming that he or she did not commit the offense(s) listed.

☆ **not guilty verdict** *recommended statistical terminology* In criminal proceedings, the decision by jury or judicial officer on the basis of the evidence presented at trial, that the defendant is not guilty of the offense(s) for which he or she has been tried.

notice Communicated knowledge of the existence of a fact or situation.

notice of appearance Written statement by an attorney showing his representation of a party in a legal proceeding.

notice of dishonor Notice given by the holder of a negotiable instrument to its maker and each endorser that payment has not been made in accordance with its terms.

notice of motion Written notice by a movant that a particular motion will be presented to a court on a designated date.

notice of protest Notice of dishonor given by a notary public when he has made demand for payment of an instrument, and it has not been paid or accepted for payment.

notice of trial Notice given by party to an action to the opposing party that he intends to bring the matter on for trial at the designated time.

notice to admit Procedure by which one party to an action calls upon his adversary to admit the existence and execution of a document, in order to narrow the issues and save expense of proof upon a trial.

notice to produce Written request in a legal action asking the opposing party to produce a particular document within its control at the trial, or be estopped from challenging testimony as to its contents.

notify To inform or make known, by words, writing or any means of communication.

notoriety State of being publicly known, usually in a derogatory sense.

notorious Universally recognized; widely and unfavorably known.

notorious possession Possession of real property, by one other than the owner, of such conspicuous nature as to be generally known and of which an owner may be presumed to have knowledge.

☆ **no true bill** *recommended statistical terminology* The decision by a grand jury that it will not return an indictment against the person(s) accused of a crime(s) on the basis of the allegations and evidence presented by the prosecutor.

novation [noh VAY shuhn] Substitution of a new contract for an old one, or substitution, with consent, of one of the parties to a contract.

now At the present time, under present conditions.

noxious Harmful, offensive, destructive, injurious.

nude (1) Naked, unclothed; (2) lacking some requisite.

nudum pactum [NOO duhm PAK tuhm] (nude pact) Agreement made without consideration, voluntary and unenforceable promise.

nugatory [NOO guh taw ree] Futile, invalid, worthless.

nuisance (1) That which annoys and disturbs one in possession of his property, or is injurious to health or offensive to the senses; (2) repeated invasion or disturbance of rights of others.

nuisance per se [NOO suhns puhr say] Condition which is a nuisance whenever it occurs regardless of location or surroundings.

null Of no validity or effect.

null and void Having no force, power or validity.

nullity Act or proceeding having no legal force or effect.

nullius filius [NUL ee uhs FIL ee uhs] (the child of nobody) An illegitimate child.

numbers Form of lottery in which player selects any three digit number and bets on his number winning, with determination of the winning number dependent upon which of several forms of the game is being played.

☆ **numbers game** An unlawful game of chance in which money is wagered on the occurrence of a chosen number and in which a winner is usually paid at odds.

nunc pro tunc [nuhngk proh tuhngk] (now for then) Presently considered as if occurring at an earlier date.

nuncupative [nun KYOO puh tiv] Oral, not written, as, a nuncupative will is one made without following statutory requirement that it be in writing.

nurture To feed, bring up, educate.

oath (1) Solemn pledge of faithful performance or truthfulness invoking
    responsibility to a supreme being; (2) any form of attestation by which one is
    bound in conscience to perform an act faithfully.

oath of allegiance Solemn pledge of fidelity to a government,
    administered generally to public officers, military personnel and
    aliens seeking naturalization.

obedience Compliance with a command, rule or duty.

obiter [OH bi tuhr] Incidentally, by the way.

obiter dictum [OH bi tuhr DIK tuhm] Expressed opinion of a court on a matter
    not necessary for its decision, and not actually bearing on the issues before
    the court.

object -n. (1) Aim, purpose, goal; (2) a thing; -v. (3) to oppose, argue against.

objection (1) Statement of disapproval; (2) adverse reason or argument.

objective -adj. Observable, perceptible, valid; -n. goal, object.

obligate To assume a duty or burden.

obligation (1) Legal or moral duty; (2) formal agreement to do a specified
    thing.

obligee [ob luh JEE] Peron in whose favor an obligation exists.

obligor [ob luh GAWR] Person under duty to perform an obligation.

obliteration Erasure or blotting out.

oblivious Forgetful, unaware.

obloquy [OB luh kwee] Censure, blame, reproach.

obnoxious Offensive, disagreeable, distasteful.

obscene Offensive to public morals and decency (see **obscenity**).

obscenity Matter whose dominant theme taken as a whole appeals to a prurient
    interest in sex, and which is patently offensive because it affronts
    contemporary community standards relating to the description or repre-
    sentation of sexual matters, and which is utterly without redeeming social
    value.

obscure Hard to understand, not clear, indistinct.

observe (1) To see, sense, view; (2) to celebrate or solemnize, as, to observe a
    marriage; (3) to comment on some subject.

obsession Inescapable and persistent idea.

obsolescence Condition of falling into disuse or deterioration.

obsolescent Going out of use.

obsolete No longer used, outmoded.

obstruct To hinder, impede, retard, block.

obstructing an officer Physical resistance made to a public officer in perform-
    ance of his duty.

obstructing justice Preventing or attempting to prevent regular course of judicial
    proceedings, as by hindering witnesses from appearing.

obstruction Hindrance, obstacle, barrier.

☆ **obstruction of justice** A class of offenses, sometimes so named in statutes,
    which at its broadest consists of all unlawful acts committed with intent to
    prevent or hinder the administration of justice, including law enforcement,
    judicial, and corrections functions.

obtain To acquire, secure possession of.

obvious Clear, evident, easily understood.

occasion -n. Opportunity, circumstance; -v. to cause, bring about.

occupancy Act of taking and holding possession.

occupant One having actual possession, as, the occupant of an apartment.

occupation (1) Possession and use; (2) business, employment, activity.

occupational disease Physical ailment contracted because of one's employment.

occupational hazard Risk of disease or injury by reason of one's employment.

occupy (1) To take or hold possession of; (2) to reside.

occur To happen, appear.

occurrence Event, happening, incident.

odd lot Any number of shares of stock less than that specified as standard trading unit on a stock exchange.

odium [OH dee uhm] Hatred, loathing, condemnation.

of Belonging to, connected with.

of counsel Attorney associated with and assisting attorney of record in a case.

of course As a matter of right, in regular conduct of business.

offender One who commits an offense, wrongdoer.

☆ **offender** *recommended statistical terminology* An adult who has been convicted of a criminal offense.

offense (1) Any violation of penal law; (2) breach of criminal law not amounting to a felony or misdemeanor; (3) resentment.

☆ **offense** Crime, delinquent act, status offense, infraction, and the like, and also civil (private) wrong, injury, or fault.

☆ **offenses against the family and children** In Uniform Crime Reports terminology, the name of the UCR category used to record and report arrests for offenses relating to desertion, abandonment, nonsupport, neglect or abuse of spouse or child, nonpayment of alimony, or other similar acts.

☆ **offenses known to police** In Uniform Crime Reports terminology, reported occurrences of offenses, which have been verified at the police level.

offensive Objectionable, disagreeable, annoying, obnoxious.

offensive weapon Dangerous instrument that may be adapted for attack.

offer -n. Proposal, endeavor; -v. to present for acceptance or rejection.

offer of compromise Proposal to settle a legal claim without a lawsuit and without admission of liability.

office (1) Place for regular transaction of business; (2) continuing public duty for employment.

officer Person having power and duty of exercising specified public functions.

official -adj. Pertaining to or done by an officer; -n. person having some specified authority.

official reports Judicial opinions printed as required by statute.

offset (1) Deduction, counterclaim; (2) method of printing.

offspring Children, issue.

of record Entered in an appropriate record.

of right As a matter of course.

okay (o.k.) Correct, all right, agreed.

oligarchy [OL i gahr kee] Form of government wherein all power is lodged in a few persons.

omission Neglect or failure of duty, lack of action.

omnibus [OM nuh buhs] For all, relating to many at one time.

omnibus bill [OM nuh buhs bil] Legislative enactment which includes several distinct and unrelated matters in one bill.

☆ **omnibus hearing** [OM nuh buhs HEE reeng] In criminal proceedings, a type of pretrial activity which occurs before the trial judge after an arraignment in which the defendant has pled not guilty.

on account In partial payment.

on all fours Similar in all respects.

on call On demand.

on default Upon failure or neglect of duty.

on demand Due on presentation without prior notice.

onerous [OH nuh ruhs] Burdensome, oppressive.

on information and belief Form of allegation when one does not have personal knowledge of the facts.

only Solely, exclusively, for no other purpose.

on or about Approximately, near, without substantial variation from.

on sight On presentation.

on the merits Based on substantive legal considerations, as distinguished from procedural defect or irregularity.

on the person In contact with body of a person or carried in his clothing.

onus [OH nuhs] Burden, charge, incumbrance.

onus probandi [OH nuhs proh BON dee] Burden of proof.

op. cit. [op sit] (opere citato) In the work quoted.

open -adj. Patent, visible, apparent; -v. to make available or accessible.

open account Debit and credit status between parties, with books open for further transactions.

open court Judicial proceeding at which public may freely be present.

opening (1) Beginning, commencement; (2) opportunity; (3) aperture.

opening statement Synopsis by counsel of his anticipated proof, made before taking of testimony, to advise jury and court of facts and issues in controversy.

open shop Place of employment hiring workers without regard to their union affiliation.

operate To produce an effect, perform a task.

operation Exertion of power or action, as, the operation of a business.

operation of law Determination of rights and liabilities by application of established rules of law without act of the parties.

operative -adj. Producing a force or effect; -n. private detective.

opere citato [OH puh ray sit OT oh] (op. cit.) In the work quoted.

opinion (1) Statement by judge or court of decision in a case, with exposition of the law and detailed reasoning; (2) statement prepared by an attorney for a client, giving attorney's understanding of the law applicable to given factual situation; (3) expression of view by an expert on subject matter of his expertise.

☆ **opinion** The official announcement of a decision of a court together with the reasons for that decision.

opinion evidence Inferences or conclusions stated by a witness as distinguished from facts known to him.

oppose To resist, contend against.

opposite Contrary, antagonistic.

opposite party Adversary, opponent.

opposition (1) Act of resisting; (2) status of antagonism; (3) creditor's refusal of consent to debtor's discharge in bankruptcy.

oppression (1) Act of cruelty, severity or excessive use of authority; (2) act of weighing down.

oppressor One who crushes or destroys.

opprobrium [up PROH bree uhm] Ignominy, infamy, shame.

optimum Best, most advantageous, greatest, most favorable.

option (1) Privilege, usually in nature of contract, giving its holder right to act within a given time on agreed terms, as, an option to purchase property whereby the seller is bound on exercise of the option;
(2) ability to choose between alternatives.

opus [OH puhs] Work, composition.

oral Spoken, by mouth.

ordain (1) To arrange, manage, regulate; (2) to prescribe, enact, command; (3) to invest with ministerial status.

order -n. (1) Mandate, command, rule, direction; (2) class or division;
(3) written direction of a court; -v. (4) to direct, rule, require.

orderly Regulated, systematic, neat.

ordinance Legislative enactment by a municipality.

ordinary Regular, usual, normal, average, common.

organic Fundamental, functional, inherent.

organic law Fundamental law or principles which define and establish organization of government.

organize To establish in systematic order.

☆ **organized crime** A complex pattern of activity which includes the commission of statutorily defined offenses, in particular the provision of illegal goods and services but also carefully planned and coordinated instances of offenses of the fraud, theft and extortion groups, and which is uniquely characterized by the planned use of both legitimate and criminal professional expertise, and the use for criminal purposes of organizational features of legitimate business, including availability of large capital resources, disciplined management, division of labor, and focus upon maximum profit; also, the persons engaged in such a pattern of activity.

original First in order, having its own authority, primary.

original jurisdiction Power and authority of a court to try a controversy at its inception.

☆ **original jurisdiction** The lawful authority of a court to hear or act upon a case from its beginning and to pass judgment on the law and the facts.

ostensible (1) Conspicuous, presentable; (2) appearing genuine but not so in fact.

ostensible agency Situation where one intentionally or from lack of ordinary care induces others to believe by implication or presumption that a third party is his agent, though in fact such relationship does not exist.

ostensible authority Such power as a principal intentionally or by want of ordinary care leads or permits a third person to believe is possessed by one as agent.

ostensible partner Person appearing to the world to be a partner of a business but in fact having no proprietary interest therein.

other Different, additional, further.

ought (1) Have a moral obligation or duty; (2) should.

oust To put out, eject, deprive of possession.

ouster Eviction, expulsion, putting out of possession.

outbuilding Small building separate from but appurtenant to a main building.

outcast Degraded and disgraced person, friendless person.

outlaw -n. Lawless person, fugitive; -v. to remove from legal jurisdiction.

outlawed Barred, as, outlawed by the statute of limitations.

outlawry Process of judicially declaring one outside protection of law, as in outlawry for treason.

outline (1) Exterior limit of an object, figure or boundary; (2) preliminary presentation of a proposed work.

out of court Without legal status to maintain an action.

output Product, something produced.

outrage Grave injury, serious wrong, gross insult.

outright Free from reserve or restraint, thoroughgoing.

outstanding (1) Remaining unpaid or undischarged; (2) prominent, conspicuous; (3) excellent.

over (1) Contingent limitation to take effect on failure of a prior estate, as, a gift over being one where a devise goes to another on failure of the original devisee to comply with some condition; (2) above.

overcome To counterbalance, conquer, surmount, as, to overcome a presumption by introduction of counterbalancing evidence.

overdraft Act of drawing out more money than one has on deposit in a bank, creating a loan with repayment implied.

overdraw To draw, as by check, upon one's deposited funds in an amount greater than is on deposit.

overdue Past maturity date for repayment.

overhead Administrative costs incurred in management, supervision or conduct of a business.

overrule To supersede, overcome, decide against.

overt Open, manifest, observable.

overt act Open act done in pursuance of criminal intent and bringing the doer nearer to commission of a crime.

overtime Time worked beyond set working hours.

owe To be bound to do something, as, to owe a debt or obligation.

owing Unpaid, indebted.

own To have legal title.

owner Proprietor, person in whom ownership or title is vested.

ownership Right of title, possession and disposal.

oyer and terminer [OY uhr and TUHR mi nuhr] (to hear and determine) Historical name of certain criminal courts having jurisdiction to hear and determine matters.

oyez [OY ez] (hear ye) Word used in securing attention to making of court proclamations.

P

p. Page.

pact Agreement, contract.

pad (1) To deceive by enlargement, as, to pad a payroll or expense account; (2) money paid as bribe or extortion; (3) (slang) apartment.

pain Bodily sensation of discomfort usually accompanying an injury.

pain and suffering Physical discomfort and mental distress.

pairing-off Practice in legislative bodies whereby two members on opposite sides of a given question agree mutually on their absence or restraint from voting on the question.

palm off To pass or dispose of something by fraud.

palpable Obvious, readily perceptible, distinct, evident.

pander (1) To procure females for prostitution; (2) to provide satisfaction for the desire of others.

panderer One who solicits for a prostitute.

panel (1) Group of persons selected for possible service as jurors during a term of court; (2) specially select group of persons whose purpose is to discuss specified topics.

par (1) Equality, accepted level; (2) equality between face value of securities and their actual selling price.

parallel Having the same direction or tendency.

parallel citation Identification of the same judicial opinion, appearing in two or more different series of opinions.

paramount Higher, superior, pre-eminent.

paramount title Ownership of real property senior and superior to that of another with which it is compared.

paranoia [pa ruh NOY uh] Mental condition characterized by delusions of persecution or of one's own greatness.

parcel -n. (1) Package; (2) specific tract of land; -v. (3) to divide property into separate portions.

parcener [PAHR suh nuhr] Joint heir.

pardon Executive act by which person convicted of crime is excused from punishment.

parens patriae [PA renz PO tree ahy] (parent of the country) The state in the capacity of guardian of persons under legal disability, or of those persons unable to protect themselves.

parent (1) Lawful father or mother of a child; (2) person standing in loco parentis; (3) group or source from which another entity is derived.

pari causa [PO ree KOU zuh] With equal right, equivalent in claim.

pari delicto [PO ree duh LIK toh] Equal in guilt, in equal fault.

pari materia [PO ree muh TEE ree uh] On the same subject.

parimutuel [pa ri MYOO choo uhl] Form of betting on races in which winners share total stakes less an amount for management.

pari passu [PO ree POS oo] By equal progress, without preference.

parish (1) In Louisiana, a territorial division of the state comparable to a county in other states; (2) area served by a church.

parity Equality.

park -n. Tract of land maintained for beauty and public recreation; -v. to allow a vehicle to remain unattended securely at the edge of a public way when not in use.

parking Act of leaving a vehicle unattended.

parkway Highway limited to passenger automobiles and bordered by landscaping.

parliamentary procedure Organized system of rules for regulation of meetings and legislative bodies.

parochial school Educational institution organized and maintained by a religious denomination.

parol [puh ROHL] Oral, by word of mouth.

parol evidence [puh ROHL EV i dens] Oral evidence, that given by word of mouth.

parol evidence rule [puh ROHL EV i dens rool] Rule providing that terms of a written agreement cannot be modified by parol evidence, in absence of fraud or mistake.

parole (1) Release of a person from a penal institution, prior to expiration of maximum period of imprisonment, conditioned upon his good behavior; (2) release of a person from custody, without bail, during pendency of a criminal action.

☆ **parole** The status of an offender conditionally released from a prison by discretion of a paroling authority prior to expiration of sentence, required to observe conditions of parole, and placed under the supervision of a parole agency.

☆ **parole agency** *recommended statistical terminology* A correctional agency, which may or may not include a paroling authority, and of which the principal functions are pre-release investigations and parole plan preparation for prospective parolees, and the supervision of adults having parole or other conditional release status.

☆ **parole officer** *recommended statistical terminology* An employee of a parole agency whose primary duties are the supervision of parolees or pre-parole investigation or planning.

☆ **parole revocation** *recommended statistical terminology* The administrative action of a paroling authority removing a person from parole status in response to a violation of lawfully required conditions of parole including the prohibition against commission of a new offense, and usually resulting in a return to prison.

☆ **parole supervision** *recommended statistical terminology* Guidance, treatment or regulation of the behavior of a convicted adult who is obliged to fulfill conditions of parole or other conditional release, authorized and required by statute, performed by a parole agency, and occurring after a period of prison confinement.

☆ **parole supervisory caseload** *recommended statistical terminology* The total number of clients registered with a parole agency or officer on a given date, or during a specified time period.

☆ **parole suspended** *recommended statistical terminology* The withdrawal by a paroling authority or parole agent of a person's effective parole status, usually accompanied by a return to confinement, pending a determination of whether parole should be revoked, or pending resolution of some problem that may require a temporary return to confinement.

☆ **parole violation** *recommended statistical terminology* An act or a failure to act by a parolee which does not conform to the conditions of parole.

parolee *recommended statistical terminology* A person who has been conditionally released by a paroling authority from a prison prior to the expiration of his or her sentence, and placed under the supervision of a parole agency, and who is required to observe conditions of parole.

parricide [PA ri sahyd] (1) Murder of one's father; (2) murder of close relative.

part -n. An integral portion of a whole; -v. to go away; become divided.

partial (1) Not complete or universal; (2) biased, favoring one side against another.

partial verdict Verdict which determines some of the issues in a case but not all.

particeps criminis [PAHR ti seps KRIM i nis] Accomplice in a crime.

participate To have a share of, experience in common with others.

participating stock Type of preferred stock that shares with common stock in distribution of dividends, in addition to preferred stock dividends payable at fixed rate.

particular Relating to a part only, separate, specific.

particularity Minute detail.

parties (1) Persons directly interested in act, proceeding, contract or conveyance; (2) major political organizations.

parties and privies [PAHR teez and PRIV eez] Those originally entering into an agreement (parties) and their successors in interest (privies).

parties in interest Any person having a pecuniary interest in the proceedings as, the creditors of a bankrupt debtor.

☆ **parties to offenses** All persons culpably concerned in the commission of a crime, whether they directly commit the act constituting the offense, or facilitate, solicit, encourage, aid or attempt to aid, or abet its commission; also, in some penal codes, persons who assist one who has committed a crime to avoid arrest, trial, conviction or punishment.

partition Division of real or personal property between co-owners.

partner Person who has joined with others as principals in conduct of a business.

partnership Status of two or more persons who join their resources in business, sharing both rights and obligations.

☆ **part-time temporary release** *recommended statistical terminology* The authorized temporary regular absence of a prisoner from a confinement facility, for periods of less than 24 hours, for purposes relating to such matters as employment or education.

party Person having a direct interest in a legal matter, transaction or proceeding.

party wall Wall built partly on land of each of two adjoining owners for their common benefit in support of construction of their respective buildings.

pass -n. (1) Authorization to come and go freely; -v. (2) to pronounce, as, to pass sentence; (3) to enact, as, to pass a new law; (4) to examine into and decide an issue, as, a court is said to pass upon a question before it; (5) to extend beyond, to proceed.

passage (1) Travel or movement from one place to another; (2) enactment of a bill by a legislative body.

passbook Record book issued by a bank to a depositor showing status of his account.

passenger (1) Person carried for hire or reward by a common carrier; (2) any person transported by another in a vehicle of any kind.

passim [PAS im] Everywhere, throughout.

passion Strong emotion such as rage, hatred, terror or love.

passive Inactive, permissive, submissive.

passport Document of protection and authority to travel issued by competent national authority to citizens or nationals.

patent -adj. Open, manifest, evident; -n. grant to an inventor, by government, securing exclusive right to make and sell his invention for specified period; -v. to record discovery and ownership of some new and useful article or process.

patentee Person to whom a patent is granted.

paterfamilias [po tuhr fuh MIL ee uhs] Male head of a household.

paternal Relating to a father.

paternity (1) State of being a father; (2) origination.

pathology Medical science of causes, symptoms and nature of diseases.

patricide Killing of one's father.

patrimony (1) Estate inherited from one's father; (2) one's inheritance from the past.

patron Customer, benefactor, sponsor.

patronage (1) Personal right of appointing persons to government jobs; (2) provision made by a benefactor for some purpose.

pauper (1) Person without resources except from charity; (2) very poor person.

pawn -n. Pledge, something deposited to ensure payment of a loan; -v. to pledge goods in bailment as security for a loan.

pawnbroker Person engaged in lending money on security of personal property held by him.

pawnor (pawner) Person borrowing money by depositing property as security.

pay -n. Compensation, wages; -v. to discharge a debt by payment of money.

payable Due, capable of being paid.

payee Person to whom an instrument such as a check is made payable.

payment Act of giving money in satisfaction of an obligation.

payor (payer) Person who should pay a bill or note.

peace officer Statutory designation for a person having specified law enforcement powers, including authority to make arrest.

peculation [pek yoo LAY shuhn] Misappropriation of funds in one's legal custody, embezzlement.

peculiar Particular, special.

pecuniary [puh KYOO nee e ree] Monetary.

peddler Itinerant vendor.

pedestrian Person travelling on foot.

pedigree (1) Family line, descent; (2) biographical information secured in criminal case from defendant after conviction.

peeping tom Person who spies on women undressing and couples embracing, caressing and kissing.

☆ **peeping tom** A popular name for a person who trespasses for the purpose of observing persons inside a dwelling.

peer (1) One having equal standing with another in attributes such as age, ability and social position; (2) member of British nobility.

penal [PEE nuhl] Punitive, relating to penalty.

penal bond [PEE nuhl bond] Written obligation to pay a sum as a penalty on happening or failure of some condition.

penal law [PEE nuhl law] Statutory code defining crimes and punishment for their commission.

penal servitude [PEE nuhl SUHR vi tood] Imprisonment at hard labor for crime.

penal sum [PEE nuhl sum] Amount specified in a penal bond to be paid as penalty upon happening or failure of specified contingency.

penalty (1) Punishment specified by statute for commission of a crime or offense; (2) amount forfeited as liquidated damages by agreement between parties conditioned upon some event or performance.

pendency [PEN duhn see] State of suspense.

pendens [PEN duhns] Pending, as, a lis pendens is a pending legal action.

pendente lite [pen DEN tay LEE tay] During litigation.

pending Unfinished, undetermined, imminent.

penetration (1) Insertion of male sex organ into that of female; (2) act of going through or entering.

penitentiary [pen i TEN shuh ree] Place of confinement, sometimes distinguished from prison as being more appropriate for rehabilitation of an inmate.

penology [pee NOL uh jee] Study of criminal punishment and penal institutions.

pension (1) Periodic payments to a retired employee, based upon services previously rendered; (2) that portion of retirement income paid for by an employer, to which is added annuity purchased by the employee.

pensioner Person supported by payment of pension.

peonage [PEE uh nuhj] Condition of enforced labor, involuntary servitude.

people (1) Body of inhabitants of a state or nation; (2) persons sharing some common attribute.

per [puhr] By means of, through, by way of.

per annum [puhr AN uhm] By the year, for the year.

per autre vie (pur autre vie) [puhr OH truh vee] For the life of another.

per capita [puhr CAP i tuh] To each person in equal amount.

per curiam [puhr KYOO ree uhm] (by the court) Brief and unanimous opinion or decision of a court, as distinguished from that of one of its judges.

☆ **per curiam opinion** An opinion issued by the court as a whole, without indication of individual authorship.

per diem [puhr DEE em] By the day.

peremptory [puh REMP tuh ree] Final, absolute, imperative, as, a peremptory challenge to a juror does not require any reason to be given.

peremptory challenge [puh REMP tuh ree CHAL uhnj] Exercise by one of parties to a jury trial of right to reject a prospective juror without giving any reason therefor.

perfect -adj. (1) Without flaw or defect, exact, expert; -v. (2) to complete, finish, as, to perfect an appeal; (3) to remove defects.

perfect condition State of being without defect or blemish.

perfecting an appeal The preparation and filing of all papers required to be filed for appellate consideration of a case, after a notice of appeal has been filed.

perform To execute or fulfill an obligation, function or act.

performam doni [puhr FAWR muhm DOH nee] In accordance with the terms of gift designated by its donor.

performance Fulfillment of a contract or obligation; accomplishment of some action.

performance bond Form of surety bond by which contractor gives security for faithful fulfillment of his contract.

peril Risk, hazard.

period Portion of time, interval.

periodical -adj. Repeating at fixed intervals; -n. publication appearing at regular intervals, as a magazine.

perish To die, come to an end, become ruined.

perishable Subject to decay.

perishable commodity Article which deteriorates rapidly, such as fresh fruit.

perjure [PUHR juhr] To make false statement under oath.

perjury [PUHR juhr ee] (1) Any false statement or testimony, given under oath, wilfully; (2) false statement or testimony, material to the issue, given under oath, wilfully.

☆ **perjury** The intentional making of a false statement as part of testimony by a sworn witness in a judicial proceeding on a matter material to the inquiry

permanent Fixed, lasting.

permanent alimony Alimony payment judicially ordered after decision of the marital controversy on the merits.

permission Authorization to act, consent to act.

permissive According discretion, optional.

permissive waste That form of waste resulting from failure of a tenant to maintain leased premises in good condition.

permit -n. License granted by proper authority to do an act for which permission is required, as, a permit to erect a building; -v. to allow, give leave, authorize.

perpetrate [PUHR puh trayt] (1) To commit, perform; (2) to be guilty of illegal or immoral act.

perpetrator [PUHR puh tray tuhr] Person who commits a crime, offense or immoral act.

☆ **perpetrator** The chief actor in the commission of a crime, that is, the person who directly commits the criminal act.

perpetual Continuous, unlimited, eternal, constant.

perpetual succession Continuous existence of a corporation.

perpetual trust Trust estate without time limitation.

perpetuate To preserve indefinitely.

perpetuity [puhr puh TOO i tee] Absence of limitation as to time.

perquisite [PUHR kwuh zit] Incidental privilege of an office, beyond its established salary.

per quod [puhr kwod] Whereby.

per se [puhr say] (1) By itself; (2) as such.

person (1) Legal entity possessing rights and duties; (2) human being.

☆ **person** In legal usage, a human being, or a group of human beings considered a legal unit, having the lawful capacity to defend rights, incur obligations, prosecute claims, or be prosecuted or adjudicated.

personal Relating or belonging to an individual.

personal action Civil legal action to enforce a debt or other legal obligation or right, against the person obligated, not involving rights in real property.

personal effects (1) Tangible movable property; (2) property such as is worn or carried on one's person.

personal injury Act adversely affecting one's mental and physical abilities.

personal liability Legal responsibility of one as an individual as distinguished from responsibility he may have in another capacity as a stockholder or director of a corporation.

personal property (1) All property other than real property; (2) movable and intangible property, chattels.

personal representative Person who acts for another in representing legal interests, such as an executor, administrator, receiver, guardian or committee.

personalty [PUHR suhn uhl tee] Movable things, personal property.

persona non grata [puhr SOH nuh nohn GRO tuh] Person not acceptable, as, a diplomatic representative may be persona non grata to the government to which he is accredited.

personate To represent one's self in a false capacity or identity.

personation Act of assuming a false capacity or identity.

per stirpes [puhr STUHR peez] Method of dividing estate by which a share is given to individuals constituting a group, rather than to individual persons, as, for example, a devise to B if he survives the testator; if not, then to his surviving children per stirpes.

persuade To induce by argument or appeal.

persuasion Act of influencing a particular determination or result.

persuasive authority Law or reasoning recognized by a particular court but which it is not required to follow.

pertinent Relevant, logically applicable.

per verba de futuro [puhr VUHR buh day fyoo CHOO roh] By words of future meaning.

per verba de praesenti [puhr VUHR buh day pruh ZEN tee] By words of present meaning.

petit [PET it] Small, minor, insignificant, as, petit larceny.

petition Formal written application, from one or more persons, requesting some action or relief, addressed to a court or other body in authority.

☆ **petition** A written request made to a court asking for the exercise of its judicial powers, or asking for permission to perform some act where the authorization of a court is required.

petitioner One on whose behalf an application such as a writ is presented to a court or other body in authority, for action or relief.

petition in bankruptcy Application filed by a debtor, or by his creditors, seeking an adjudication that debtor is bankrupt.

☆ **petition not sustained** *recommended statistical terminology* The finding by a juvenile court in an adjudicatory hearing that there is not sufficient evidence to sustain an allegation that a juvenile is a delinquent, status offender, or dependent.

petit jury [PET it JOO ree] Trial jury, usually composed of 6 to 12 persons, who determine issues in a legal action, as distinguished from grand jury usually composed of 23 persons.

☆ **petit jury** *recommended statistical terminology* A statutorily defined number of persons selected according to law and sworn to determine, in accordance with the law as instructed by the court, certain matters of fact based on evidence presented in a trial, and to render a verdict.

petit larceny [PET it LAHR suh nee] **(petty larceny)** [PET ee LAHR suh nee] Statutory form of larceny in which subject of larceny is less than amount specified in statute.

petty Small, minor.

pharmacist Person whose skill and knowledge in compounding and dispensing drugs and medicines on prescription is certified by appropriate regulatory body.

physical (1) Relating to the body; (2) material, existing in fact; (3) relating to natural science.

physical force Actual exertion or violence.

physical impossibility Act impossible of consummation.

physical incapacity Lack of bodily ability, as, physical incapacity to accomplish sexual intercourse.

physical injury Bodily harm.

picket -n. Person acting in behalf of an organization such as a labor union, who stations himself at entrance of premises seeking to persuade or influence others, as to refrain from entering, -v. to demonstrate by carrying placards or by other means in effort to persuade or influence conduct of others, at the place of controversy.

pick-lock (1) Instrument to open a lock without a key; (2) person who opens locks illegally, as a burglar.

pickpocket Person who removes property from person or clothing of another without his knowledge.

piece work Type of production of goods for which payment is made according to number of units produced.

pilfer To steal in small amounts.

pilferage Act of stealing in small amounts.

pimp Man who offers a female to others for purpose of prostitution and is supported from her earnings.

piracy (1) Robbery on the high seas; (2) unauthorized appropriation of another's work, as in copyright infringement.

pistol Short firearm, used in one hand, having barrel and chamber joined as one.

P. J. Presiding judge.

☆ **placement** The commitment or assignment of a person to a facility, or to any supervisory, care or treatment program, as the result of official or unofficial actions.

plagiarism [PLAY juh riz uhm] Use of another's literary or artistic work as being one's own.

plaintiff [PLAYN tif] Person who brings an action, party who complains or sues in an action.

☆ **plaintiff** A person who initiates a court action.

plan (1) Design, scheme, drawing; (2) method, procedure.

plat [plat] Plan, diagram or map showing subdivision of real property.

plea (1) Allegation of a party in a legal proceeding; (2) defendant's answer to plaintiff's complaint; (3) in criminal procedure, defendant's answer to a charge against him.

☆ **plea** In criminal proceedings, a defendant's formal answer in court to the charge contained in a complaint, information, or indictment, that he or she is guilty or not guilty of the offense charged, or does not contest the charge.

plea bargaining Process by which prosecution and defense work out a disposition of a criminal case on mutually acceptable terms, without a trial.

plead To argue, complain or answer in a legal action.

pleader One who drafts instruments in legal actions.

pleading System of making claims in legal actions, and defenses thereto, by formal written instruments which serve to present the issues and narrow the controversy.

pleadings Collective formal written allegations of plaintiff, and answers made thereto.

plea in abatement Plea by which an action is defeated or postponed because of some defect in form or substance not going to the merits.

plea in bar Defendant's answer which acts as a bar to plaintiff's cause of action.

plebiscite [PLEB i sahyt] Vote by entire body of voters upon an issue which is beyond powers of regular legislative body, such as choice of sovereignty.

pledge (1) Delivery of property by a debtor to his creditor for retention by the creditor as security until the debt is paid; (2) solemn promise.

pledgee Creditor, person to whom goods are delivered in pledge.

pledgor Debtor who places his goods with creditor as security for repayment of debt.

plenary [PLEN uh ree] Full, complete, without limitation, unqualified.

plenipotentiary [plen i poh TEN shee e ree] -adj. Absolute, having full power; -n. one having full power to act for another.

plottage (1) Area included in a plot of land; (2) additional value accorded to parcels of real estate by reason of their being contiguous.

plural Comprised of two or more.

plurality Excess of votes for a given candidate over those cast for another.

poaching Unauthorized hunting or fishing on another's land.

pocket veto Disapproval of pending legislation by failure of the executive to approve it within limited period fixed by statute.

point (1) Particular aspect of a legal question, as, a case in point; (2) principal element, as, the point of the matter.

police Part of executive branch of government whose particular concern is with preserving order, protecting safety, morals and property of community, and general law enforcement.

police action Military action without declaration of war against persons considered to be aggressors or violators of international peace and security.

police court Local court having jurisdiction over minor offenses and power to hold defendants to await further prosecution before higher courts.

police officer Member of uniformed or detective components of a police department or any other person designated by statute and having statutory law enforcement powers, including that of arrest.

police power Legislative power of state or its subdivisions to enact laws, within constitutional limits, to promote general health, safety, morals and welfare of the community.

policy (1) Group of principles which guide a government or other body in its conduct; (2) form of lottery in which winner has selected a sequence of numbers; (3) written insurance contract.

political Pertaining to administration of government.

political offense Violation of statutory law consisting of physical or other attack upon government to attain a political object.

political party Association of persons having similar beliefs as to government action, organized to achieve acceptance of their program and candidates.

political prisoner Person in prison because of a political offense.

politics Art of securing, organizing, administering and directing control of government.

poll -n. Act of voting, as, a poll of voters is the recording of each person's vote; -v. to receive one by one the votes of a group, as, to poll a jury or poll the electorate; -adj. without indentation, as, a deed poll is one cut in a straight line.

polling the jury Calling the names of jurors and asking each juror individually to state his verdict.

polls Places for voting.

poll tax Tax in a fixed amount placed on individual voter, without reference to his ability to pay, as a requirement for voting.

pollutant Substance which contaminates or makes another substance unclean.

pollute To defile, corrupt, taint, contaminate.

pollution (1) Act of making unclean; (2) defilement, corruption.

polyandry [pol ee AN dree] Status of one woman having several husbands at one time.

polygamy [puh LIG uh mee] Status of having several wives or husbands at the same time.

pool -n. (1) Association of persons or organizations joining resources and efforts in united action to achieve a common purpose; (2) in gambling total sum contributed by bettors, with winner taking entire pool; (3) small body of water; -v. (4) to join resources in a common effort.

pooling agreement Contract or informal accord of persons or organizations to join in concerted effort for a common purpose, usually in business activity.

pornographic Obscene, lewd, violating contemporary moral standards of the community.

pornography Material inherently obscene, or which without artistic merit violates accepted community standards of morality.

portion Part, share, limited amount or quantity.

positive (1) Absolute, express, explicit; (2) without doubt or reservation; (3) marked by agreement, as, a positive answer to a question is an affirmative one.

positive law Specifically enacted statute.

posse [POS ee] (properly called **posse comitatus**) Group of persons brought together to aid in keeping peace or apprehending criminals.

posse comitatus [POS ee kum i TOT uhs] (power of the county) Group of persons brought together to aid in keeping peace or apprehending criminals.

possess To occupy, control, have, be master of, own or maintain.

possession (1) Detention, control, exercise of power to exclusion of others, physical occupancy; (2) area subject to a government but not part of it.

possessor One who has custody, occupancy or control.

possessory Founded on possession.

possessory action Legal proceeding to obtain or recover actual possession of the subject-matter.

possibility An event whose occurrence is uncertain but physically feasible.

possible Feasible, capable of happening, practicable.

post -pref. (1) After, subsequent; -n. (2) mail system; (3) fixed military station; -v. (4) to bring to attention, as by placing a placard in a public place; (5) to transfer a bookkeeping entry to its proper place in the records, as, to post a ledger entry.

☆ **post-adjudicated** The status of a convicted adult, or of a juvenile who has been adjudged (judicially determined to be) a juvenile offender.

postage (1) Legal charge for mail service; (2) stamps showing payment of mail charge.

postal union International agreement for conduct and regulation of mails between countries.

☆ **postconviction remedy** *recommended statistical terminology* The procedure or set of procedures by which a person who has been convicted of a crime can challenge in court the lawfulness of a judgment of conviction or penalty or of a correctional agency action, and thus obtain relief in situations where this cannot be done by a direct appeal.

postdate To place a date on an instrument which is subsequent in time to the current date.

postdated check One bearing a future date in relation to date of its tender.

posterity One's descendants in direct line, to remotest degree.

post facto [pohst FAK toh] After the fact.

post hoc [pohst hok] After this, hereafter.

posthumous [POST yuh m uhs] After death.

posthumous child [POST yuh muhs chahyld] One born after death of a parent.

post litem motam [pohst LAHY tuhm MOH tuhm] After commencement of legal action.

postmark Impression by stamp put on mail by postal authorities to cancel stamps and indicate time and place of mailing.

post-mortem [pohst MAWR tuhm] After death.

postnuptial After marriage.

post office Government office for receipt and distribution of mail.

postpone To delay, defer, adjourn.

post road Route for transportation of mail.

postulate -n. An assumed proposition used as a basis for further reasoning; -v. to assume a proposition as a basis for further reasoning.

potable [POH tuh buhl] Drinkable, suitable for drinking.

potent Strong, powerful, capable of producing an effect.

potentate [POH tuhn tayt] Sovereign, monarch, ruler.

potential -adj. Possible but not yet existing; -n. possibility for future change or development.

pound -n. (1) Measure or unit of weight equal to 16 ounces; (2) English monetary unit; (3) place for detention of stray animals; -v. (4) to strike, beat.

pourparler [poor pahr LAY] Preliminary negotiation leading to a contract or agreement.

poverty Want or lack of material possessions, scarcity of supply.

power Ability, authority, right, control, prerogative.

power coupled with an interest Power to do an act, together with an interest in the subject matter of the power.

power of appointment Legal authority to name others in some matter, usually granted by will.

power of attorney Instrument authorizing one to act legally for another either generally or in a specified matter.

pp. Pages.

practicable Feasible, possible, capable of accomplishment.

practical (1) Relating to actual experience; (2) useful.

practice (practise) -n. (1) Habitual conduct, custom; (2) conduct of a profession; (3) form of legal proceedings; -v. (4) to train, drill for instruction or improvement; (5) to engage in a profession, as, to practice law.

practitioner One engaged in conduct of a profession, science or art.

pragmatic Practical, matter-of-fact.

pray To request, ask.

prayer (1) Request in a legal pleading for relief; (2) request to a court or legislature for its action.

preamble Introduction which precedes and explains purposes of a constitution or statute.

☆ **pre-arraignment lockup** *recommended statistical terminology* A confinement facility for arrested adults awaiting arraignment or consideration for pretrial release, in which the duration of stay is usually limited by statute to two days, or until the next session of the appropriate court.

precarious Hazardous, dependent on chance circumstances.

precatory [PREK uh taw ree] Referring to request, recommendation, wish or expectation which may not result in creation of legal right.

precaution Foresight to avoid misfortune.

precedence [PRES uh dens] (1) Order of preference employed on formal or ceremonial occasions; (2) priority or right of going before others or having superior importance.

precedent [PRES uh dent] Previously adjudged action or decision on same or similar point, serving as a rule or example for present guidance.

precedent condition [PRES uh dent kuhn DISH uhn] That which must occur or be performed before an estate can vest or be enlarged, or a contract can take effect.

preceding Previous in succession, going before.

precept (1) Written order issued by competent public authority to an officer commanding performance of some act; (2) principle employed as a general rule for action.

precinct (1) Geographical district of a city for police administration; (2) geographical political subdivision for purposes of election.

precise Exact, definite, absolute.

preclude To prevent, deter, stop.

preclusion Act of preventing.

predecessor Person going before, one who has been followed by another.

predicate Foundation upon which further action is based.

☆ **predisposition investigation** *recommended statistical terminology* An investigation undertaken by a probation agency or other designated authority at the request of a juvenile court, into the past behavior, family background and personality of a juvenile who has been adjudicated a delinquent, a status offender, or a dependent, in order to assist the court in determining the most appropriate disposition.

predominant (1) Greater than others in strength, influence or position; (2) controlling.

pre-empt To seize or take adversely as to others.

pre-emption Act of purchasing, appropriating, seizing or taking possession before others.

prefer (1) To give advantage to, as, to prefer one creditor as against another; (2) to bring a charge or complaint, as, to prefer a criminal charge against a person; (3) to favor one over another.

preference (1) Unjustified payment by a debtor to one creditor to the detriment of others, where all are entitled to equal treatment; (2) right of a creditor, having some particular status, to be paid before other creditors; (3) advancement of a case awaiting trial to a position on court calendar before others filed earlier; (4) choice above others.

preferential Favored above others.

preferential hiring Employment policy which requires hiring of union members if available, on condition that non-union persons may otherwise be hired, without their being required to join union.

preferred Having a privilege or advantage, favored.

preferred stock Ownership of a corporation represented by stock certificate and having a priority over common stock with respect to payment of dividends, and sometimes preferred also in distribution of assets.

prejudice (1) Bias or opinion not based upon independent judgment or fair appraisal of evidence; (2) preconceived adverse judgment; (3) attitude of irrational hostility usually directed against a race or group.

prejudicial error Substantial error in a legal proceeding materially affecting rights of one of the parties.

preliminary Introductory, preceding the main issue.

preliminary hearing *recommended statistical terminology* The proceeding before a judicial officer in which three matters must be decided: whether a crime was committed; whether the crime occurred within the territorial jurisdiction of the court; and whether there are reasonable grounds to believe that the defendant committed the crime.

preliminary injunction Writ issued by an equity court to restrain or prohibit specified conduct pending final determination of a controversy.

premeditate To plan, think, consider an act beforehand.

premeditation Act of planning or considering an act before doing it.

premier [pree MEER] -adj. First, principal; -n. prime minister of a government.

premise That which is assumed or upon which further consideration is based.

premises (1) A defined place, such as land, building or some part of a building; (2) statements or propositions previously presented, from which a conclusion may be drawn; (3) assumptions, presuppositions.

premium (1) Amount payable by an insured for a contract of insurance; (2) bonus, reward, prize.

preparation Preliminary arrangement of plans and material to accomplish a purpose.

prepare To make ready for some objective.

prepense [pruh PENS] Aforethought, planned, contrived.

preponderance [pruh PON duh ruhns] Superiority in influence or importance, as, a fair preponderance of evidence.

☆ **preponderance of the evidence** [pruh PON duh ruhns uv *th*ee EV i dens] The evidence offered in court to prove an alleged set of facts must be of better quality and amount, of greater weight, than the evidence in opposition.

prerogative Special privilege vested in a person, group, rank or office.

prescribe To direct, order, rule, impose with authority.

prescription (1) Manner of acquiring title based upon use and enjoyment for period prescribed by statute; (2) manner of acquiring title to incorporeal hereditament through long-established use; (3) manner of establishing rights by long assertion and use; (4) written direction for preparation and administration of drugs, medicine, device or treatment for illness, injury or physical incapacity.

presence (1) Status of being in a given place; (2) bearing and personal appearance of an individual.

present -adj. (1) Now existing, under consideration; -n. (2) gift, donation; -v. (3) to tender, as, a grand jury may present an indictment to a court, or a check may be presented to a bank for payment; (4) to introduce, offer.

☆ **presentence investigation** *recommended statistical terminology* An investigation undertaken by a probation agency or other designated authority at the request of a court, into the past behavior, family circumstances, and personality of an adult who has been convicted of a crime, in order to assist the court in determining the most appropriate sentence.

presentment [pruh ZENT muhnt] Report by a grand jury to a court concerning some matter they have investigated without voting an indictment.

☆ **presentment** Historically, written notice of an offense taken by a grand jury from their own knowledge or observation; in current usage, any of several presentations of alleged facts and charges to a court or a grand jury by a prosecutor.

presents [PREZ uhnts] The matter being considered, as in the phrase, "Know all men by these presents," meaning by the instrument then being considered.

preservation Conservation, safekeeping.

preserve To safeguard, prevent injury or decay, protect, maintain.

preside To take charge, control, conduct, regulate, govern.

president Chief executive officer.

presidential elector Person chosen by a state, in manner prescribed by law in that state, to cast a ballot for office of President and Vice-President of the United States, as a member of the Electoral College, wherein each state has electors in the total number of its senators and representatives in Congress.

☆ **presiding judge** The title of the judicial officer formally designated for some period as the chief judicial officer of a court.

presume (1) To assume without authority; (2) to anticipate, expect.

presumption Legal rule which requires that a particular inference must be drawn from ascertained facts, so that sufficient evidence would be required to overcome or rebut the presumption, as, for example, a presumption of innocence in a criminal proceeding.

presumption of fact Assumption which may logically be made as to some unknown matter, by inference drawn from known facts.

presumption of innocence Assumption favoring innocence of defendant in a criminal action, subject to rebuttal evidence which must be presented by prosecution in order to prove guilt of defendant beyond a reasonable doubt.

presumption of law Inference created by operation of law, based upon known facts, and requiring evidence to disprove such inference, as, a presumption of law that a person in recent and exclusive possession of stolen property is the thief.

presumptive Based on inference or probability.

pretended Alleged, falsely proposed.

pretense Misrepresentation, excuse.

pretermitted child [pree tuhr MIT uhd chahyld] Child of a testator omitted from his will.

pretext False reason, excuse.

☆ **pretrial conference** A meeting of the opposing parties in a case with the judicial officer prior to trial, for the purposes of stipulating those things which are agreed upon and thus narrowing the trial to the things that are in dispute, disclosing the required information about witnesses and evidence, making motions, and generally organizing the presentation of motions, witnesses and evidence.

☆ **pretrial detention** *recommended statistical terminology* Any period of confinement occurring between arrest or other holding to answer a charge, and the conclusion of prosecution.

☆ **pretrial discovery** In criminal proceedings, disclosure by the prosecution or the defense prior to trial of evidence or other information which is intended to be used in the trial.

☆ **pretrial release** *recommended statistical terminology* The release of an accused person from custody, for all or part of the time before or during prosecution, upon his or her promise to appear in court when required.

prevail To become effective, to triumph, persist.

prevailing party Successful party in a legal action.

prevailing price Market price in usual course of business.

prevent To prohibit, circumvent, hinder.

prevention Act of hindering, obstructing.

preventive justice Governmental action taken to prevent criminal behavior or reduce its occurrence.

previous Earlier, prior.

previous question Matter under consideration by a parliamentary body, so that a motion to move the previous question is designed to cut off debate and bring a vote on the matter being considered.

prima facie [PRAHY muh FAY shuh] At first sight, self-evident.

prima facie case [PRAHY muh FAY shuh kays] One where a valid cause of action has been established on plaintiff's case, which, if believed, would require rebutting evidence to disprove.

primary -adj. First; -n. election to determine which candidate of several will run as nominee of a particular political party.

primary authority Statute or judicial opinion which must be followed by a court in deciding cases.

primary evidence Firsthand evidence, best evidence.

prime -adj. (1) First, original, chief; -n. (2) most active period; -v. (3) to stimulate; (4) to instruct beforehand.

primogeniture [prahy muh JEN i chuhr] (1) Right of the eldest male descendant to inherit estate of his ancestor to the exclusion of all others; (2) status of being firstborn child of one's parents.

principal -adj. (1) Most important; -n. (2) executive head, as, principal of a school; (3) amount of a fund or debt, on which interest is paid or payable; (4) face amount of an insurance policy; (5) person who commits a crime, or aids and abets others in its commission; (6) person who employs others as agents to act in his behalf.

☆ **principal** The chief actor in a crime, or the chief actor and all persons actually or constructively present while it was being committed.

principal and agent Relationship between parties by which one as principal authorizes another, as agent, to act in his behalf.

principle Fundamental rule, comprehensive doctrine.

prior Preceding, earlier in sequence.

priority (1) Order of precedence before another, as, a first mortgage has priority over a second mortgage; (2) relative superiority of one subject matter in consideration of several.

prison Place of physical confinement provided by law, usually for persons convicted of a crime or offense.

☆ **prison** *recommended statistical terminology* A state or federal confinement facility having custodial authority over adults sentenced to confinement.

prison breaking Act of forcible escape by one confined in a prison.

☆ **prison commitment** *recommended statistical terminology* A sentence of commitment to the jurisdiction of a state or federal confinement facility system for adults, of which the custodial authority extends to persons sentenced to more than a year of confinement, for a term expressed in years or for life, or to await execution of a death sentence.

prisoner Person deprived of his liberty.

☆ **prisoner** I. A person in physical custody in a confinement facility, or in the personal physical custody of a criminal justice official while being transported to or between confinement facilities. II. *recommended statistical terminology* A person in physical custody in a state or federal confinement facility.

privacy Freedom from the companionship, oversight or observation of others.

private -adj. Personal, not generally known, restricted to an individual or group; alone; -n. lowest military rank.

private bill Legislative enactment concerning an individual or special group, as distinguished from one having general public applicability.

private law Body of law relating to rights and duties of individuals to each other.

private person Individual not holding public office.

☆ **private rehabilitation agency** *recommended statistical terminology* A private organization providing care and treatment services which may include housing, to convicted persons, juvenile offenders, or persons subject to judicial proceedings.

☆ **private security agency** *recommended statistical terminology* An independent or proprietary commercial organization whose activities include employee clearance investigations, maintaining the security of persons or property and/or performing the functions of detection and investigation of crime and criminals and apprehension of offenders.

private street Roadway owned by individuals or a group and reserved to their use.

privation [prahy VAY shuhn] Taking away, loss of something usually enjoyed.

privies [PRIV eez] Those having an interest in a legal subject matter so as to be bound by legal determinations concerning it, although not parties to the legal proceeding.

privilege Benefit, right or exemption enjoyed by one having a special position or office.

privileged Enjoying exemption from some obligation imposed on others.

privileged communication Giving or acquiring of information in the course of a confidential relationship such as attorney and client, clergyman and penitent, physician and patient, husband and wife, or others, which is exempt from any legal requirement as to compulsory disclosure.

privity [PRIV i tee] Relationship or connection between two or more parties in a common subject matter.

privy [PR IV ee] (1) Person who has an interest in or takes part in a matter with another; (2) person who has an interest in a relationship or legal status to which he was not a party.

pro For, favoring.

pro and con For and against.

probability Likelihood, preponderance in favor of an uncertain future event.

probable Appearing reasonable, convincing or capable of being proven.

probable cause Such known facts as would warrant action by a reasonable and prudent person.

☆ **probable cause** A set of facts and circumstances which would induce a reasonably intelligent and prudent person to believe that a particular person had committed a specific crime; reasonable grounds to make or believe an accusation.

☆ **probable cause hearing** *recommended statistical terminology* The proceeding before a judicial officer in which three matters must be decided: whether a crime was committed; whether the crime occurred within the territorial jurisdiction of the court; and whether there are reasonable grounds to believe that the defendant committed the crime.

probable consequence Result that is more likely than not to follow an act.

probate [PROH bayt] Process of proving before a legally authorized officer that an instrument submitted is in reality the last will and testament of a decedent.

probate court [PROH bayt kawrt] Court having jurisdiction over estates of deceased persons and sometimes over their minor children.

probate judge [PROH bayt juj] Judicial officer legally presiding in court having jurisdiction over estates of deceased persons and their minor children.

probate jurisdiction [PROH bayt joo ris DIK shuhn] Lawful exercise of power by a court over estates of deceased persons, guardianship of infants and related matters.

probation (1) Status in which person convicted of a crime is sentenced, conditionally, to observe prescribed conduct under the supervision of a probation officer, for a designated period while remaining at liberty; (2) trial period for evaluating individual performance.

☆ **probation** The conditional freedom granted by a judicial officer to an alleged or adjudged adult or juvenile offender, as long as the person meets certain conditions of behavior.

probationer Convicted person placed under supervision of a probation officer by sentence imposed by a court.

☆ **probationer** *recommended statistical terminology* A person who is placed on probation status and required by a court or probation agency to meet certain conditions of behavior, who may or may not be placed under the supervision of a probation agency.

probation officer Official assisting in administration of probation system and supervision of probationers, under applicable statutes and court direction.

☆ **probation officer** *recommended statistical terminology* An employee of a probation agency whose primary duties include one or more of the probation agency functions.

☆ **probation revocation** *recommended statistical terminology* A court order in response to a violation of conditions of probation, taking away a person's probationary status, and usually withdrawing the conditional freedom associated with the status.

☆ **probation termination** *recommended statistical terminology* The ending of the probation status of a given person by routine expiration of probationary period, by special early termination by court, or by revocation of probation.

☆ **probation violation** *recommended statistical terminology* An act or failure to act by a probationer which does not conform to the conditions of his probation.

probative [PROH buh tiv] Tending to prove, substantiating.

pro bono publico [proh BOH noh PUB lik oh] For the public good.

procedural Relating to method of enforcing legal rights and remedies.

procedure (1) Manner by which legal actions and matters are conducted; (2) established and accepted manner of performance.

proceed (1) To pursue an activity, continue; (2) to advance a legal action.

proceeding (1) Legal matter conducted before a judicial officer; (2) particular course of action; (3) conduct of business, such as at a meeting.

proceeds (1) Total amount received from a sale of property; (2) profit on a transaction; (3) net amount received.

process (1) Legal instrument used to secure compliance with orders of a court; (2) method or series of acts to produce a given result.

proclamation Formal public announcement.

procure (1) To obtain, win; (2) to persuade, cause, induce.

procurer (1) Pimp, one who secures customers for a prostitute; (2) one who obtains.

produce -n. (1) Product of natural growth in soil; (2) return, yield; -v. (3) to present, bring forward, originate, as, to produce evidence.

producer One who brings forth, presents.

producing Effective, operative.

producing cause That which is effective in achieving a result.

product Output.

production (1) Act of manufacture or origination; (2) act of bringing forth in court.

profane -adj. Irreverent, contemptuous of sacred things; -v. to treat a sacred matter with contempt and irreverence.

profanity Irreverence toward sacred matters, use of blasphemous language, cursing.

profess To declare publicly, follow, practice.

profession (1) Public declaration of intention; (2) intellectual occupation requiring skill and specialized knowledge.

professional -adj. (1) Conforming to accepted technical standards; -n. (2) person earning his livelihood in a particular occupation, as distinguished from an amateur; (3) person engaged in an intellectual occupation requiring a high degree of training and proficiency.

☆ **professional criminal** A popular name for a person who has made crime his or her livelihood, that is, a person who depends upon criminal activities for at least a substantial portion of his or her income, and who has developed special, related skills.

proffer To offer, propose.

profit (1) Excess of income over costs and expenses; (2) financial benefit received from management or sale of property.

profiteer One who secures excessive profit by trading in essential goods in an emergency.

pro forma [proh FAWR muh] As a matter of form.

progress -n. (1) Advance toward an objective; (2) progressive development; -v. (3) to go forward, advance.

progression Connected activity leading to an objective.

pro hac vice [proh hak VEE say] For this particular instance.

prohibit To prevent, forbid, preclude.

prohibited degree of consanguinity [proh HIB i tuhd duh GREE uv kon sang GWIN i tee] That degree of blood relationship within which persons may not legally marry.

prohibition Prevention, interdiction.

project -n. (1) Idea, enterprise, undertaking; -v. (2) to bring forward, imagine; (3) to protrude.

projection (1) Plan for future; (2) protruding part.

prolix [proh LIKS] Repetitious, long-winded.

prolong To extend in length or duration.

prolongation Extension, increase in duration.

promise -n. Agreement to perform an act; -v. to pledge performance.

promisee [prom i SEE] One to whom a pledge of performance is given.

promisor [PROM i sawr] Person making a pledge of performance.

promissory [PROM i saw ree] (1) Having the nature of a promise; (2) relating to future conduct.

promissory note [PROM i saw ree noht] Written and unconditional agreement to pay a specified sum of money at a future time.

promote To advance, put forward, encourage.

promoter One who advances and encourages a plan.

☆ **promotion of prostitution** The soliciting or aiding in any manner of another to engage in prostitution, or the soliciting or aiding of another to secure the services of a prostitute, or knowingly receiving any money or other thing of value which is the proceeds of prostitution.

prompt -adj. Immediate, rapid, without delay; -v. to suggest action or response.

promulgate To announce officially, make known publicly.

promulgation Act of making official and public announcement.

pronounce To make formal or official declaration, as, to pronounce sentence in a criminal case.

proof Matter by which certainty is logically established.

☆ **proof beyond a reasonable doubt** Proof that does not amount to absolute certainty but leaves no reasonable doubt that the defendant committed the alleged crime(s), that is, a standard of proof in which evidence offered in court to prove an alleged set of facts must preclude every reasonable hypothesis except that one which it supports, that of the defendant's guilt.

propagate To disseminate, cause to spread, transmit, extend.

proper Correct, appropriate, suitable, acceptable.

proper care Degree of attention to some subject matter employed by a prudent man in similar circumstances.

proper party One having an interest in some litigation so that his joinder in action would be necessary to conclude all aspects of the controversy without additional suit on the same subject matter.

property (1) Subject matter of ownership; (2) effect of an object or substance on other objects or substances.

proponent [pruh POH nuhnt] One who makes a proposal; one who offers a will for probate.

proportional representation System of voting designed to give maximum representation to all groups in relation to their actual numerical strength.

proportionate In comparative relation.

proposal Offer submitted for consideration.

proposition Plan submitted for consideration.

propound To offer for consideration or to propose, as, to propound a question for discussion or vote.

propria persona [PROH pree uh puhr SOH nuh] In one's own person.

proprietary Relating to ownership.

proprietor Owner.

propriety Appropriateness, conformity to accepted standards, suitability.

propter hoc [PROP tuhr hok] Because of this.

pro rata [proh RO tuh] According to proportion or share.

prorate To divide proportionately.

pro re nata [proh ray NO tuh] As the situation may arise.

proscribe To forbid, prohibit.

proscribed Forbidden, outlawed.

pro se [proh say] For himself.

prosecute (1) To proceed to final conclusion; (2) to conduct legal action against a defendant, as, to prosecute a criminal charge.

prosecuting attorney Attorney for government in criminal prosecutions.

prosecuting witness Person upon whose complaint and testimony a criminal prosecution is based.

prosecution (1) Carrying on of a legal proceeding to determine guilt or innocence, enforce a right or correct a wrong; (2) plaintiff in a criminal action.

☆ **prosecution agency** A federal, state, or local criminal justice agency or subunit of which the principal function is the prosecution of alleged offenders.

☆ **prosecution withheld** Prosecutor suspends proceedings conditional upon behavior of arrestee.

prosecutor Attorney whose duty is to present charges and maintain criminal actions against defendants.

☆ **prosecutor** *recommended statistical terminology* An attorney who is the elected or appointed chief of a prosecution agency, and whose official duty is to conduct criminal proceedings on behalf of the people against persons accused of committing criminal offenses; and any attorney deputized to assist the chief prosecutor.

☆ **prosecutorial screening decision** *recommended statistical terminology* The decision of a prosecutor to submit a charging document to a court, or to seek a grand jury indictment, or to decline to prosecute.

prosecutrix [pros uh KYOO triks] Female prosecutor.

prospective Future.

prospectus Document issued by a corporation describing its financial circumstances and inviting public participation by investment.

prostitute Person engaging in sexual relations for payment.

prostitution Sexual relationship based on payment.

☆ **prostitution** Offering or agreeing to engage in, or engaging in, a sex act with another in return for a fee.

☆ **prostitution and commercialized vice** In Uniform Crime Reports terminology, the name of the UCR category used to record and report arrests for offenses relating to the promotion or performance of sexual acts for a fee.

pro tanto [proh TON toh] To such extent.

protect To take care of, defend from harm.

protection Act of sheltering, defending.

protection order Form of order issued by a court having jurisdiction in domestic relations, placing under protection a person concerned with a proceeding therein, as a security measure.

protective Providing a safeguard or defense.

protectorate State which is protected in its international affairs by a stronger state, without further loss of its own sovereignty.

pro tem [proh tem] **(pro tempore)** [proh TEM puh ray] For the time being, temporarily.

protest (1) Formal declaration of disapproval or objection; (2) written statement by a notary that a described bill or note presented for payment or acceptance has not been honored, together with reasons therefor and demand for payment.

prothonotary [proh thoh NOH tuh ree] Principal clerk of certain courts.

protocol [PROH tuh kawl] Formal and recognized procedure for conduct of diplomatic and ceremonial affairs between nations.

prove To establish as true.

provide To supply, foresee, stipulate.

provided Subject to, modified by, conditioned upon.

provided by law Prescribed by statute.

province (1) Geographical portion of a country; (2) area or scope of jurisdiction, as, the province of a jury.

provision (1) State of advance preparation; (2) stipulation or proviso, made in advance.

provisional Temporary, conditional.

provisional government One having temporary status.

provisional remedy Temporary relief such as arrest, attachment or injunction, which may be secured by plaintiff in a civil action, to secure and protect his status during pendency of an action.

proviso [proh VAHY zoh] Limitation or exception in a grant, delegation of authority, contract or statute.

provocation Conduct which stimulates another to act in response.

provoke To arouse action or emotion.

provost-marshal [PROH vohst MAHR shuhl] Commander of military police at a military post, camp or station.

prox. [proks] (proximo) Of the following month.

proximate [PROK si muht] (1) Next, following, very near; (2) immediate, closest in connection.

proximate cause [PROK si muht kawz] Active cause nearest in effect or most immediately connected in producing a given result.

proximate damage [PROK si muht DAM uhj] Loss or injury which is brought on as the natural, direct and immediate effect of a given act.

proximately [PROK si muht lee] Directly, immediately, consequently.

proximate result [PROK si muht ree ZULT] Reasonably foreseeable effect of motivating acts.

proxy (1) Document giving authority to act as agent for another, usually in voting at stockholder's meetings; (2) person authorized to act for another.

prudence Reasonable care and caution in given circumstances.

prudent Cautious, careful, wise.

pseudonym [SOO doh nim] False or assumed name.

psychopath [SAHY koh path] Mentally ill person whose personality structure is poorly balanced or unstable.

psychosis [sahy KOH sis] Profound functional mental disorder in which an individual is often out of touch with reality.

psychotherapy [sahy koh THER uh pee] Method of treatment for mental or emotional disorders.

puberty Age of sexual maturity.

public -adj. Open to use by all, common, universal; -n. total number of inhabitants of an area or district, people as a whole.

☆ **public defender** I. An attorney employed by a government agency or subagency, or by a private organization under contract to a unit of government, for the purpose of providing defense services to indigents; also, occasionally, an attorney who has volunteered such service.

II. *recommended statistical terminology* The head of a government agency or subunit whose function is the representation in court of persons accused or convicted of a crime who are unable to hire private counsel, and any attorney employed by such an agency or subunit whose official duty is the performance of the indigent defense function.

☆ **public defender agency** *recommended statistical terminology* A federal, state, or local criminal justice agency or subunit of which the principal function is to represent in court persons accused or convicted of a crime(s) who are unable to hire private counsel.

publication (1) Act of making a matter generally known, as by public announcement; (2) act of legal notification; (3) act of issuing copies, as in the publication of a book.

publici juris [PUB li see JOO ris] Of public right, available to all.

publicity Widespread dissemination of information, as, publicity given to a speech.

publicly Openly, without concealment.

public policy Criteria by which government regulates its affairs for the good of the community.

☆ **public safety department** An agency organized at the state or local level of government incorporating at a minimum various law enforcement and emergency service functions.

public service corporation Incorporated body furnishing essential services, such as gas, electricity, telephone or transportation for the general public.

public utility Business organization having a monopoly granted by law and subject to regulation of its rates, service and facilities.

publish To circulate publicly, disclose, promulgate, utter.

publisher One who causes matter such as books and newspapers to be printed and circulated.

puffing Practice of increasing price or desirability of an article by making extravagant claims concerning it.

puisne [PWIZ nay] (1) Subordinate; (2) insignificant, petty; (3) later.

punish To impose a penalty, as, to punish one for violation of law.

punishable Amenable to the imposition of a penalty.

punishment Penalty provided by law for commission of crime or offense.

punitive [PYOO nuh tiv] Having the nature of a penalty.

punitive damages [PYOO nuh tiv DAM uh jiz] Monetary compensation awarded in excess of ordinary damages, as punishment for a gross wrong.

pur autre vie [poor OH truh vee] (for another's life) An estate limited by the duration of the life of a third person.

purchase Transfer of ownership by payment of money, as in purchase of land by payment of consideration therefor.

purchase money Money paid for property.

purchase money mortgage Mortgage executed by purchaser to seller or another, concurrently with transfer of title to property to him, as a loan to make payment for the property.

purchase price Amount agreed upon as consideration for sale of property.

purchaser One who acquires property by payment of consideration.

purchaser for value One obtaining title to property by payment of consideration, and without knowledge of any defects in title of the seller.

pure (1) Absolute, simple; (2) free from contamination or adulterant.

purge (1) To demonstrate innocence; (2) to atone for an offense, as, to purge one's self of contempt of court by submitting to the court's mandates.

purging contempt Exoneration from charge of contempt.

purloin [PUHR loyn] To steal, wrongfully appropriate.

purport [PUHR pawrt (n.), puhr PAWRT (v.)] -n. Intended meaning, substantial legal effect, intention, effect; -v. to intend, claim, profess.

purpose Intended result, design.

pursuant to In accordance with.

pursue (1) To carry out, as, to pursue a plan; (2) to follow another with intention of apprehension or harassment.

pursuer One who follows another to apprehend him.

pursuit (1) Chase, act of following another to apprehend him; (2) profession, employment or occupation.

pursuit of happiness In Constitutional meaning, the right to live in freedom, exercising unrestricted choice of legal occupation and having no burdens other than those imposed on all others similarly situated.

purvey [puhr VAY] To sell, provide.

purveyor [puhr VAY uhr] One who provides or procures.

purview [PUHR vyoo] Limit or scope, as, the purview of a statute.

put Speculative commodity transaction by which a party agrees to deliver subject matter of the contract at agreed price within period specified.

put and call System of speculative commodity transactions in which "put" is privilege of delivery or non-delivery of subject matter, and "call" is privilege of calling or not calling for it.

putative [PYOO tuh tiv] Supposed, commonly accepted.

putative father [PYOO tuh tiv FAH *th*uhr] Supposed or reputed father of a child.

putting in fear Causing anxiety in mind of a person as to his safety, thus constituting one of elements usually required in crime of robbery.

pyromania [pahy roh MAY nee uh] Compulsive desire to set fires.

Q

Q.B. Queen's Bench.

Q.C. Queen's Counsel.

Q.E.D. (quod erat demonstrandum) Which was to be proved or demonstrated.

qua [kwo] In the capacity of, considered as.

quack -adj. Marked by claim of ability unsupported by fact; -n. one claiming skill or qualification he does not possess.

quaere [KWEE ree] Query, question.

qualification (1) Possession of attributes needed for some status, such as the qualification of citizenship for voting; (2) restriction, limitation.

qualified Competent, eligible, fit.

qualified privilege In libel and slander, qualified (also known as conditional) privilege allows matter, if justified by facts, that would otherwise be libelous or slanderous, in the absence of actual malice or knowledge of falsity.

qualify (1) To follow required procedure to secure an office, appointment or status; (2) to modify, restrict.

quality Condition, character, kind.

quantum meruit [KWON tuhm ME roo it] (as much as he deserved) Commonlaw action for reasonable value of services, in the absence of agreement as to compensation.

quare [KWO ray] Wherefore, on what account.

quare clausum fregit [KWO ray KLOU zuhm FREG it] (wherefore he broke the close) Form of common-law action in trespass for damages due to unlawful entry on land.

quarrel Controversy, dispute, argument.

quarter sessions Designation of certain local courts whose sessions usually or historically are held four times in a year, and whose jurisdiction is in criminal cases and sometimes over administrative matters such as care of roads and bridges.

quash [kwosh] To annul, make void, abate.

quasi [KWAY zahy] (as if) Resembling another to which it is compared in some characteristics but not in others.

quasi contract [KWAY zahy KON trakt] Obligation enforced by law, although not in contract, in interests of justice and to prevent unjust enrichment of a party.

quasi in rem [KWAY zahy in rem] Referring to legal actions brought to affect property and make the property available to satisfy a claim against defendant.

quasi-judicial [KWAY zahy joo DISH uhl] Having a judicial character although not within the judicial system, such as holding hearings, investigating claims.

Queen's Bench English court.

quibble In discussion or argument, diversion from principal or real issue to some petty or irrelevant matter, which evades the actual point at issue.

quick (1) Prompt, rapid; (2) characterized by presence of life.

quid pro quo [kwid proh kwoh] (something for something) Term denoting the giving of something in exchange for something else, as between parties to a contract.

quiet -adj. Free from disturbance, calm, settled; -n. repose; -v. to pacify, make calm.

quiet enjoyment Status of peaceful and undisturbed possession of premises by tenant.

quit -adj. Clear, free; -v. to leave, surrender, depart, discharge, cease.

quitclaim Release of a claim.

quitclaim deed Conveyance passing any right, title or interest which grantor may have in property.

quod vide [kwod VEE day] (which see) Referring to some designated source; usually abbreviated q.v.

quorum [KWAW ruhm] (1) Majority of entire body; (2) number of persons of an organized body required to be present for valid transaction of business as in stockholder's meetings.

quota Proportionate share, quantity or number allowed.

quotation (1) Statement of current price or offer for an article or security; (2) exact excerpt of language, as, a quotation from a statute or judicial decision.

quotient Mathematical result obtained by dividing one number by another.

quotient verdict Determination by jury of damages to be awarded by totalling amounts suggested by each juror and dividing total by number of jurors.

quo warranto [kwo wuh RON toh] Legal proceeding to test an official's right to a public office, the right to a franchise, or right to hold office in a corporation.

q. v. (quod vide) Which see.

R

racket Organized illegal enterprise, fraudulent scheme.

racketeer One engaged in illegal enterprise such as extortion, fraud or unlawful interference with business.

radical -adj. Drastic, extreme; -n. one seeking extreme and immediate change of existing social or political structure.

raffle Form of lottery in which chances to win a prize are sold, and the winner is drawn at random from this group.

railroad -n. (1) Permanent roadway having steel rails on which wheeled cars are operated; (2) entire transportation system including passenger and freight traffic carried by rail and in buses or trucks as part of the system; -v. (3) to secure approval of a matter without due consideration; (4) to secure quick and unjustified conviction of an accused person.

railway In law, same as railroad (see -n. above).

raise an issue To advance a ground of controversy for decision or resolution.

raise a presumption To create an inference requiring evidence to rebut.

range -n. (1) Tract of land for grazing livestock; (2) land division on a map; -v. (3) to extend in direction, rove; (4) to arrange in line.

rank Order of standing or precedence in relation to others.

ransom Amount paid or requested to secure release of a person from captivity.

rape (1) Sexual penetration of a female without her consent, by means of force, intimidation or deception; (2) sexual penetration of a female deemed incapable of consent, as defined by statute.

☆ **rape** Unlawful sexual intercourse with a female, by force or without legal or factual consent.

ratable (1) Proportional; (2) subject to tax.

rate (1) Established portion or amount according to scale or standard; (2) quantity measured in relation to some other quantity.

ratification Approval of a prior act, confirmation.

ratify To give approval, confirm, sanction.

ratio decidendi [RO shee oh des i DEN dee] Reason for decision.

ratio legis [RO shee oh LEG is] Reason for a law.

rationale Justification, controlling explanation.

ravish (1) To rape, have sexual intercourse with a female by force and against her will; (2) to carry away by force.

raw material Matter from which a further product is made.

raze To tear down, make level with the ground, destroy.

re [ray] Regarding, in the matter of.

ready Prepared, fit for immediate action.

ready and willing Prepared, fit for immediate action.

ready, willing and able Prepared, capable and desirous of proceeding.

real (1) Existing in fact; (2) relating to land; (3) genuine.

real estate Land, buildings, improvements thereto and natural assets such as crops.

real evidence Things offered as evidence for examination and consideration by court and jury.

real property Land and buildings erected thereon, as compared to
  personal property.

realize (1) To acquire funds or profit from a transaction, as, to realize
  a profit on an investment; (2) to convert property into money; (3) to understand clearly.

realty Land and buildings.

reargument Renewed presentation and consideration of a matter
  previously considered.

reason (1) Motivating cause; (2) ground for some action, explanation;
  (3) process of orderly and rational thought.

reasonable (1) Appropriate in the circumstances; (2) moderate;
  (3) fair, equitable.

reasonable care That degree of caution which would be exercised by person of
  ordinary prudence, in similar circumstances.

reasonable doubt (1) That state of mind which after careful and impartial
  consideration of all the evidence falls short of moral certainty of guilt;
  (2) uncertainty as to guilt, for which a reason can be given after considering all
  the evidence.

rebate Retroactive credit or refund.

rebei Person who opposes authority or established custom.

rebellion Organized and violent resistance to established government.

rebut (1) To contradict, offer opposing evidence; (2) to defeat, challenge,
  repulse.

rebuttable presumption Inference or assumption established by law but subject
  to defeat by appropriate evidence.

rebuttal (1) Contrary evidence; (2) stage of legal proceeding in which a
  party may offer additional testimony, contradicting or opposing that offered by
  opponent.

rebutter [ree BUT uhr] Defendant's answer to plaintiff's surrejoinder.

recall (1) Procedure for removal from office of a public official by popular vote,
  based upon petition filed by required number of qualified voters;
  (2) remembrance, recollection; (3) act of summoning back, as, the recall of an
  ambassador.

recant (1) To withdraw a statement made publicly; (2) to take back, retract, admit
  one's error.

recapitalization Fiscal procedure by which a corporation reorganizes
  its financial structure with respect to amount of its securities
  outstanding, their value, yield and preference as to payment, or
  other matters.

recapture (1) Act of taking into custody that which was previously in custody; (2)
  recovery; (3) seizure by government of profits in excess of fixed amount.

receipt (1) Act of receiving; (2) writing which acknowledges payment
  or delivery.

receive To accept, take, hold, greet, acquire.

receiver (1) Person appointed by a court to take charge of property, such as a
  business, and conserve, maintain and operate it pending the disposition of a
  legal proceeding; (2) person appointed pursuant to statute to terminate or
  conserve some enterprise while further proceedings are pending; (3) in
  criminal law, person who knowingly takes stolen property from a thief.

receiver pendente lite [ree SEE vuhr pen DEN tay LEE tay] Person appointed to take charge of property while some litigation about it is pending.

receivership (1) Status of bankruptcy, as where court appoints receiver as trustee to manage affairs of the bankrupt, while proceeding is pending; (2) status of business or property being administered by receiver; (3) status of one appointed as a receiver.

receiving stolen goods Acceptance of property by one who knows it has been secured by theft, or who in exercise of reasonable prudence should know that property was illegally obtained.

recess Brief suspension of business for a court or legislative body.

☆ **recidivism** [ree SID uh vi zuhm] The repetition of criminal behavior.

recidivist [ree SID uh vist] Habitual criminal, repeater.

☆ **recidivist** A person who has been convicted of one or more crimes, and who is alleged or found to have subsequently committed another crime or series of crimes.

reciprocal Mutual, related inversely, corresponding to each other.

reciprocal wills Testamentary dispositions made by several persons, each one disposing of his estate in favor of the others.

reciprocity (1) Mutuality, even exchange; (2) mutual recognition by two jurisdictions of the validity of privileges granted by either to its citizens, such as admission to practice law.

recital Formal statement of facts in a legal instrument, usually commencing with the word "whereas".

recite To set forth formally in a legal instrument.

reckless driving Such operation of a motor vehicle as to demonstrate deliberate or negligent lack of care.

recklessly With awareness of and conscious disregard for a substantial and unjustifiable risk, which risk is of such nature and degree that its disregard constitutes a gross deviation from the standard of conduct that a reasonable person would observe in the situation.

recklessness Conduct characterized by disregard of danger or consequences.

reclaim (1) To secure return of some matter; (2) to reform, as, to reclaim one from criminal behavior; (3) to obtain something of value from waste.

recognition Acknowledgement, confirmation, acceptance.

recognizance [re KOG ni zuhns] Obligation entered into before a court to do a specified act or incur a penalty.

recognize (1) To acknowledge, admit as true or valid; (2) take notice of.

recognized (1) Publicly known; (2) bound by an obligation (recognizance).

recommend To advise, urge.

recompense -n. Repayment in money or in kind; -v. to remunerate, return in kind.

reconcile (1) To bring differing persons or ideas into agreement; (2) to harmonize, bring about mutual acceptance.

reconciliation (1) Securing of agreement between differing persons or ideas; (2) act of harmonizing or bringing into agreement.

reconstruct To rebuild, reorganize, reassemble.

reconstruction (1) Act of constituting again that which was formerly in existence; (2) period following U. S. Civil War, in which the states which had seceded from the national government were restored to previous status.

record -n. Public or private memorandum made as permanent evidence of an act, transaction or event; -v. to preserve memoranda in permanent form, for reference, or to give notice to all interested parties.

recorder (1) Official having responsibility for enrollment of documents in permanent form; (2) local judicial officer, having jurisdiction similar to that of a magistrate.

recoup [ree KOOP] To retain, secure the return of, set off.

recoupment [ree KOOP muhnt] Action of one withholding some portion of a payment due, as recovery on his own claim.

recourse (1) Act of looking to another for payment, satisfaction or help. (2) right to demand payment, from maker or endorser of negotiable instrument.

recover (1) To secure return, as by repurchase or payment of amount pledged; proceedings.

recovery (1) Right to something obtained by reason of judgment in a legal action; (2) return of property previously held, restoration of usual condition.

recrimination Accusation by an accused against his accuser.

rectification Correction.

rectify To correct, make good.

recurrent Repeated from time to time.

recuse [ree KYOOZ] (1) To disqualify oneself as a judge in a particular case; (2) to object or except to a judge, usually based on his interest or partiality.

redact [ree DAKT] (1) To edit, revise, select for publication; (2) to compose in writing, prepare a draft.

redaction [ree DAK shuhn] Act of editing, revising or adapting for publication.

redeem (1) To secure return, as by repurchase or payment of amount pledged; (2) to release from blame, atone for.

redeemable Subject to return upon payment of debt or fulfillment of condition.

redemption (1) Act of buying back; (2) act of regaining property or legal title, by satisfying an obligation.

red-handed In the act of committing a wrong.

red tape Expression for unnecessary complexity of certain legal or governmental procedures resulting in duplication of records, prolonged delay and wasted energy.

reduce To make smaller, condense, diminish.

reductio ad absurdum [ree DUK tee oh ad ab SUHR duhm] (reduction to the absurd) Process of opposing some proposition by demonstrating the absurdity of following it to a logical conclusion.

reduction (1) Diminution, act of making smaller; (2) transformation into a different form.

redundant Repetitious, superfluous.

re-enact (1) To effectuate again, as, to re-enact a repealed statute; (2) to perform again.

re-entry (1) Resumption of former possession or occupancy, (2) entry by grantor on granted premises pursuant to a right reserved, for failure of tenant to perform specified conditions.

re-examination (1) Renewed questioning by a party of his witness, limited to matters elicited on cross-examination; (2) re-direct examination.

refer To direct to, make reference to.

referee Officer having power conferred by a court to examine a controversy, take testimony, determine facts, and make a report and recommendation to the court.

referee in bankruptcy Officer appointed by bankruptcy court to take charge of administrative and preliminary matters in a proceeding in bankruptcy, subject to review and determination by the court.

reference (1) One who gives information concerning another's character, business standing or personal attributes to a third party; (2) source used as a guide; (3) act of forwarding a matter for further action, decision or information.

reference statutes Laws which incorporate other laws by adopting them and making them applicable to the subject matter.

referendum (1) Popular vote by the electorate on proposed or approved legislation; (2) right of electorate by vote to reject a law passed by its legislative body.

refinance To reorganize the conditions upon which a debt is based, either by making a new loan, or extending the existing loan on revised terms.

refine (1) To make more pure; (2) to improve, perfect.

reform To correct, improve.

reformation Act of changing, correcting or improving.

reformatory Penal institution for persons considered amenable to improvement of their character.

refresh To renew, replenish, revive.

refund -n. (1) Return of payment; -v. (2) to give back; (3) to incur a new obligation in order to apply the proceeds in payment of an existing debt.

refund annuity contract Agreement by which an insurer agrees to make monthly payments in a specified amount, during the insured's life, with the further provision that any balance in his account at his death shall be paid to some person designated by the insured.

refunding bond Formal certificate acknowledging indebtedness, issued to secure funds to pay off an outstanding indebtedness.

refusal Rejection, denial.

refuse To deny, reject, decline to accept.

regard -n. (1) Esteem, care, respect; -v. (2) to notice, pay attention to; (3) to have relation to.

regime [ray ZHEEM] (1) Form of government or administration; (2) usual pattern of action.

register -n. (1) Formal, official record of specified matters; (2) officer having responsibility for keeping specified records and documents, -v. (3) to secure entry in a formal or official record; (4) to enroll on a list, as, to register bonds for their replacement in case of loss or theft.

register of deeds Officer having authority and duty to file and maintain records of ownership and other matters relating to real property.

registered (1) Entered in a formal record; (2) formally or officially qualified.

registered bond Bond whose ownership is recorded on the bond and on records of the issuing organization.

registered mail Postal matter whose receipt, delivery and transmission is recorded and insured by the postal system, upon payment of additional fee.

registered trademark Trademark whose ownership is recorded in U.S. Patent Office or in one of the states wherein such registration is provided.

registered voter One whose qualification to vote has been established and recorded.

registrant One who enrolls himself or something to obtain a specific right, title or status.

registrar [REJ is trahr] An official having specified responsibility in maintaining files and records.

registration Act of enrolling, as, registration for voting.

registry (1) Act of recording, enrollment; (2) place where records are kept; (3) book in which records are kept; (4) nationality of a vessel as entered in records.

regular (1) Formed or controlled according to established procedure, law or principles; (2) normal, typical.

regular course of business Habitual, usual, normal conduct of trade or business activity.

regularly (1) At periodic intervals; (2) in a lawful manner.

regular on its face Apparently valid, and containing nothing to indicate any defect or irregularity.

regulation (1) Process of controlling; (2) rule established for guidance of conduct in some specified activity.

rehabilitate To reconstitute, reconstruct, renovate, restore to former or normal condition, as, to rehabilitate a building or rehabilitate a witness.

rehabilitation Restoration to former or normal condition.

rehearing Review of previous consideration given to a matter, by the same tribunal, by permitting further argument upon the same pleadings.

reimburse To pay back, indemnify.

reinstate To restore to former condition.

reinsurance Contract by which an insurer transfers to another all or some part of the risk upon which he as original insurer is primarily liable.

rejoin [ree JOYN] To answer, in legal pleading, to plaintiff's second pleading (replication).

rejoinder [ree JOYN duhr] Second pleading by defendant, as an answer to plaintiff's second pleading.

relate (1) To tell, recite, describe; (2) to connect, refer, apply retroactively.

related Connected, having similar properties or common ancestry.

relation (1) Connection; (2) status with respect to others by consanguinity or other connection, such as master and servant; (3) recital, narrative.

relative -adj. (1) Comparative, pertaining to others; (2) connected; -n. (3) person connected to another by consanguinity or affinity; (4) thing connected with or dependent on another thing.

relator [ree LAY tuhr] Person upon whose narrative or in whose behalf a proceeding is founded, as in habeas corpus.

release -n. (1) Termination of a claim made by one party against another, discharge from responsibility; -v. (2) to relinquish custody, set free, give permission; (3) to give up a legal claim or right.

☆ **release on own recognizance** *recommended statistical terminology*
A pretrial release in which the defendant signs a promise to appear but does not pledge anything of value to be forfeited upon nonappearance.

☆ **release to third party** *recommended statistical terminology* A pretrial release without financial guarantee in which a person or organization other than the defendant assumes responsibility for returning the defendant to court when required.

relegate To set aside, banish.

relevance Pertinence, applicability.

relevant (1) Having applicability to the subject matter under consideration; (2) pertinent, applicable, germane.

reliable Trustworthy, dependable.

relief (1) Legal remedy; (2) public financial support for indigent persons; (3) removal of burden, pain or danger.

relieve (1) To give help; (2) to lighten, free from a burden; (3) to remove one from a duty or assignment.

religious Pertaining to a body of spiritual and moral principles and beliefs.

religious corporation Artificial legal person formed for and advancing beliefs and activities of a particular denominational religious group.

religious freedom Right of spiritual worship according to conscience in any form consonant with public order, including right to espouse views such as atheism.

religious society Organized group formed for spiritual worship and allied activities.

relinquish To release, cease, desist from, surrender.

relinquishment Act of giving up, abandoning.

relocate To remove to another place.

relocation Act of establishment in a new place.

rely (1) To be grounded upon, depend; (2) to trust, have confidence.

rem, action in [rem, AK shuhn in] Legal proceeding against property.

remainder (1) Estate, created by will, determined by that which is left after payment of specific bequests; (2) estate in property to take effect at a specified time in the future or upon happening of a specified event, such as death of a tenant for life; (3) book sold by publisher at a reduced price after its regular sale has become unprofitable.

remainderman [ree MAYN duhr man] One entitled to remainder of an estate.

remand [ree MAND] -n. (1) Act or instrument by which a case or person is returned to place of origination; -v. (2) to send back; (3) to commit to custody, as, to deprive a person of his liberty in a criminal proceeding; (4) to return a case from one court or tribunal to another.

☆ **remand** To send back. When, for example, the judgment in a case is appealed and a higher court returns the case to a lower court for retrial or other reconsideration, it is said to be remanded.

remedial Corrective, providing a remedy.

remedial statute Legislative enactment to provide redress or compensation for unjust loss brought about by governmental action.

remedy (1) Enforcement of a right; (2) object of a legal action; (3) means of curing a disease or restoring health; (4) correction of evil.

remise [ree MAHYZ] (1) To give, grant; (2) to surrender, as in a deed.

remise, release and quitclaim [ree MAHYZ, ree LEES and KWIT klaym]
Term used, usually in a quitclaim deed, to convey all rights to another.

remiss (1) Derelict in performance of duty, negligent; (2) lazy, careless.

remission (1) Forgiveness, cancellation of a debt, claim or penalty; (2) temporary diminution of symptoms of a disease.

remit (1) To remand, transmit, send; (2) to waive, relinquish, release.

remittance (1) Funds sent from one person or place to another; (2) instrument by which funds are sent.

remittee One to whom funds are sent.

remitter (1) Person sending funds to another; (2) action by which a legal matter is sent to another court.

remittitur [ruh MIT i tuhr] (1) Legal process by which an appellate court transmits to the court below the records and proceedings before it, together with its decision, for such further action and entry of judgment as is required by the decision of the appellate court; (2) reduction through court action of a verdict for damages considered to be excessive.

rem, judgment in [rem, JUJ muhnt in] Court mandate which determines result in an action against property.

remote (1) Distant, far apart, separated; (2) far-fetched, not proximate.

remote cause Far removed circumstance leading to an event through one or more other acts or circumstances.

removal (1) Transfer of pending legal action to another court; (2) act of taking away.

removal of cause Transfer of a pending legal action to another court.

removal of cloud in title Action taken to establish marketable title to property, where some defect appears in such title.

remunerate [ree MYOO nuh rayt] To pay, compensate.

remuneration [ree myoo nuh RAY shuhn] Payment, compensation.

render (1) To give, deliver, surrender; (2) to pay; (3) to administer, as, to render justice to all.

renew (1) To restore to original condition; (2) to repeat, resume, replace.

renewal (1) Act of restoring to original condition; (2) act of extending for additional period, as, the renewal of a lease.

renounce To abandon, repudiate, resign, disclaim.

rent -n (1) Payment to an owner for use of his property, usually real estate; -v. (2) to pay owner for use of property; to accept payment for use of property.

rental Compensation paid to an owner for use of his property.

rent insurance Contract by which owner of rented property is compensated for loss of income due to severe damage or destruction of the rented property.

rent-roll Total income derived or available from rental of premises.

rents, issues and profits Net profit derived from ownership of property.

renunciation Rejection, relinquishment, repudiation.

reopen To resume some subject that has previously been concluded.

reorganization (1) Act of reconstituting, rehabilitating; (2) in regard to an insolvent corporation, procedure taken to rearrange its financial affairs by forming a new corporation which continues the business and endeavors to pay creditors.

reorganize To reconstitute, change.

repair To restore to previous good condition.

reparation   Financial payment to redress a wrong or give satisfaction for some injury.

repatriate   To cause the return of one to his country of citizenship or origin.

repatriation   Act of return to country of citizenship or origin.

repay   To return payment, compensate, recompense.

repeal   Withdrawal, abrogation, revocation, as, repeal of a statute.

repeat   To occur again, perform again, say again, divulge, reiterate.

repetition   Renewed occurrence of something.

replead   To substitute a second pleading for its predecessor.

replete   Full, complete.

replevin   [ruh PLEV in] Common law action to recover goods wrongfully taken or withheld.

replevy   [ruh PLEV ee] To recover goods by action in replevin.

replicant   [REP li kuhnt] **(repliant)** [ree PLAHY uhnt] (1) In common-law pleading, one who files a replication or reply; (2) plaintiff who files a pleading in opposition to defendant's plea or answer.

replication   [rep li KAY shuhn] Plaintiff's pleading as a reply to answer made by defendant, used to deny defendant's plea or answer and its legal sufficiency.

reply   -n Something said or done in response; -v to answer, as in argument.

report   (1) Formal account of a matter; (2) findings submitted, as by a master or referee appointed by a court; (3) notification.

reporter   (1) One who compiles court decisions or legislative proceedings for information and guidance in subsequent matters; (2) one who records, by any means, verbatim account of legal proceedings and makes written transcript therefrom.

repository   (1) Place where articles, such as historical documents, are kept; (2) depository, storehouse.

represent   (1) To assert as true; (2) to act for another, as, an attorney represents his client; (3) to serve in a legislative body; (4) to portray, depict, show.

representation   (1) Presentation of some matter as being true, given as basis for negotiation, agreement, contract or favorable action; (5) status of attorney acting for client; (3) appearance in behalf of others.

representative   (1) One who acts for another or a group; (2) sample, specimen; (2) member of lower house of U.S. Congress or similar state legislative body.

reprieve   Act of executive clemency by which execution of a sentence is suspended for a given period.

☆ **reprieve**   An executive act temporarily suspending the execution of a sentence, usually a death sentence. A reprieve differs from other suspensions of sentence not only in that it almost always applies to temporary withdrawing of a death sentence, but also in that it is usually an act of clemency intended to provide the prisoner with time to secure amelioration of the sentence.

reprimand   Censure, formal disapproval.

reprisal   Action taken in retaliation for some other action.

republic   (1) Political entity characterized by equality of its members and usually having a president as chief of state; (2) form of government in which citizens elect their leaders, and are governed according to law.

republican government   Political administration of a country by democratically elected leaders, governing according to law.

republication Re-establishment of that which has previously been revoked, as a will.

repudiate (1) To reject that which was previously accepted; (2) to disown, renounce, disclaim.

repudiation Rejection, refusal of an obligation.

repugnant Offensive, contrary, inconsistent, opposed.

reputable [REP yuh tuh buhl] Widely accepted, respectable.

reputation (1) Opinion held by others concerning a person; (2) public esteem in which one is held.

repute Opinion, fame.

reputed Accepted, believed, thought.

request -n. Expression of desire; -v. to ask for.

require To claim, demand, need.

requirement Mandatory condition, necessity, essential need.

requisition Formal demand, application made with authority.

res [rayz] Thing, matter, subject.

resale Sale of goods by their purchaser.

rescind [ree SIND] To withdraw, revoke, cancel.

rescission [ree SISH uhn] Annulment, abrogation, cancellation.

res controversa [rayz kon truh VUHR suh] Matter in controversy.

rescue Removal from danger or detention.

reservation (1) In a legal instrument, the setting aside or withholding of some right or interest which would otherwise be transferred; (2) land area allocated by national government to a specific use, such as a military reservation; (3) limitation, condition, exception.

reserve -n. Something set aside or held back, as a fund; -v. to withhold, set aside for later use, defer.

reserved power Political authority described in a constitution as being incapable of delegation to any other body.

resettle To review a judicial order for purpose of making some modification.

resettlement Act of reviewing an order previously granted and agreeing upon its modification.

res fungibiles [rayz fun juh BIL ays] Things not having a special identity, so that they may be mixed with other similar goods or replaced in like kind, such as sugar or grain.

res gestae [rayz JES tahy] (body of the thing) In law of evidence, an exception to hearsay rule,permitting in evidence spontaneous acts and declarations that are concomitant with an act being considered and which explain its character and quality.

reside To live, dwell.

residence Dwelling place, place where one actually lives.

resident Person living in a given place.

☆ **residential commitment** *recommended statistical terminology* A sentence of commitment to a correctional facility for adults, in which the offender is required to reside at night, but from which he or she is regularly permitted to depart during the day, unaccompanied by any official.

☆ **residential facility** *recommended statistical terminology* A correctional facility from which residents are regularly permitted to depart, unaccompanied by any official, for the purpose of daily use of community resources such as schools or treatment programs, and seeking or holding employment.

residual -adj. Pertaining to a remaining part; -n. disability continuing after recovery from physical ailment.

residuary [ree ZID yoo e ree] Pertaining to remaining part.

residuary bequest [ree ZID yoo e ree bee KWEST] Disposition by will of that portion of an estate not included in specific bequests.

residuary clause [ree ZID yoo e ree klawz] That part of a will which disposes of property remaining after specific bequests have been filled.

residuary estate [ree ZID yoo e ree es TAYT] That portion of a testator's property remaining after provision for administration costs and specific bequests .

residuary legatee [ree ZID yoo e ree leg uh TEE] Beneficiary of a will with respect to property remaining after specific bequests and costs of administration.

residue [REZ i dyoo] (1) Remaining portion; (2) portion of a testator's estate remaining after costs of administration, payment of debts, statutory allowances for widow and children and payment of specific bequests.

resign To relinquish a position voluntarily.

resignation (1) Act of voluntary relinquishment of a position or office; (2) formal notice of relinquishment of a position or office.

res ipsa loquitur [rayz IP suh LOK wi tuhr] (the things speaks for itself) Doctrine applicable to matters so clear as to require no additional proof.

resist To oppose, contest.

resistance Act of opposing or contesting.

resisting an officer Obstructing and opposing a public official, such as a police officer, in performance of his duty.

☆ **resisting an officer** Resisting or obstructing a law enforcement officer in the performance of an official duty.

res judicata [rayz joo di KO tuh] (1) Doctrine that an issue decided between two parties is binding thereafter on parties and their privies; (2) doctrine that judicial decision is binding upon all concerned with same subject.

res nova [rayz NOH vuh] New matter, matter not previously decided.

res nullius [rayz NUL ee uhs] (1) Property Of nobody; (2) abandoned property.

resolution (1) Formal expression of view by a group or official body; (2) formal instrument showing action taken by a corporate board of directors; (3) determination.

resolve (1) To determine, settle; (2) to make a resolution.

resort -n. (1) Place for rest and recreation, as, a summer resort; (2) source of help; -v. (3) to make use of, to seek aid.

resort, court of last Tribunal from whose determination no appeal may be taken.

resourceful Possessed of ingenuity in coping with unexpected developments.

resources (1) Money, assets, property; (2) sources of revenue; (3) means available in case of need.

respective Relating to particular persons or things.

respite [RES pit] Delay, reprieve, postponement.

respond To answer, reply.

respondeat superior [ruh SPON day ot soo PEE ree uhr] (let the master answer) Principle that the master is liable for wrongs committed by his servant.

respondent [ree SPON duhnt] (1) One who answers; (2) one who answers appeal by his adversary; appellee.

☆ **respondent** Generally, the person who formally answers the allegations stated in a petition which has been filled in a court; in criminal proceedings, the one who contends against an appeal.

responsibility Duty, obligation, legal liability, accountability.

responsible Liable, answerable, accountable.

rest -n (1) Repose, relaxation, freedom from duty: -v (2) to repose, trust, rely; (3) to indicate completion of presentation of one's evidence in a Judicial proceeding.

restitution Act of restoring that which has been taken unlawfully, act of making good for some loss, damage or injury.

☆ **restitution** *recommended statistical terminology* A court requirement that an alleged or convicted offender pay money or provide services to the victim of the crime or provide services to the community.

restrain To limit, confine, hold back, enjoin, prevent.

restraining order Preliminary judicial order prohibiting specified conduct pending decision on an injunction.

restraint Obstruction, confinement, restriction.

restraint of trade Agreement by contract or combination to cause a monopoly, interfere with competition, maintain artificial prices, and obstruct normal free commerce and trade.

restraint on alienation Restriction on ability to convey property.

restrict To circumscribe, limit, confine.

restriction Limitation, qualification.

restrictive Limiting, confining.

restrictive covenant Agreement between contracting parties binding all successors in interest to the specified limitation; usually in relation to use of real property, limiting nature of use or restricting occupancy to members of a designated group.

restrictive endorsement Statement placed on a negotiable instrument by an endorser,before affixing his signature, which limits the further negotiability of the instrument as set forth in the endorsement.

result -n Conclusion, effect, outcome, decision; -v to arise or give rise to as a consequence or conclusion.

resume To continue after interruption.

resumption Continuance after interruption.

retail Sale of goods or commodities direct to ultimate consumer.

retailer Merchant who sells goods to ultimate consumers.

retain To keep, hold back, employ.

☆ **retained counsel** A defense attorney selected and compensated by the defendant or offender, or by other private person(s).

retainer (1) Engagement by client of an attorney for continuing legal services; (2) fee paid to an attorney for continuing legal services;
(3) document expressing authority given by client to an attorney for performance of continuing legal services.

retaliate To return like for like, evil for evil.

retaliation Return of like for like, evil for evil.

retire To withdraw from use, service or action.

retract To take back, draw back.

retraction Act of taking back, withdrawal.

retreat Voluntary withdrawal from hazard or difficulty.

retribution Giving or receiving of reward or punishment.

retroactive Having effectiveness in prior time.

retrospective Having reference to past events.

return -n. (1) Official endorsement made on a writ or other legal order, showing action taken; (2) report of election results; (3) formal document on prescribed forms, showing income or other tax due, with supporting data; (4) yield, profit, earnings, result; -v. (5) to go back, revert, bring to former status.

returnable Required by law to be presented or disposed of at a given time and place.

return day Date fixed for a party to answer some legal process.

revenue Income, profit, amount of yield.

reversal Action of a higher body, such as an appellate court, in negating action or judgment of body subordinate to it.

reverse (1) To overturn a judicial decision; (2) to change to opposing view or direction.

☆ **reversed** The determination by an appellate court which sets aside a judgment of a trial court.

reversion (1) Estate remaining to grantor by operation of law after other estates are terminated or completed; (2) return to former condition or type.

revert To return to, go back.

review To reconsider, re-examine.

revise To change, correct, improve.

revised statutes Body of statutory law codified, collected and arranged in order.

revision Change, re-examination.

revival Bringing to renewed attention or extended life.

revive To bring to life again, recover strength.

revocable [REV uh kuh buhl] Capable of being withdrawn.

revocation [rev uh KAY shuhn] Act of withdrawal, taking back, repeal.

revoke To take back, rescind, cancel.

revolt Uprising against constituted authority.

revolution (1) Violent overthrow of established government; (2) fundamental change in thought or action; (3) rotation.

reward Payment or benefit offered for doing an act or rendering a service.

rider Addition to a legal instrument, physically affixed to it and modifying its terms.

rig (1) To manipulate prices by artificial means; (2) to put into position for use.

rigging the market Creation of artificial demand for some security or commodity by causing its market price to rise through unusual and contrived trading.

right (1) Capacity, interest, entitlement to some claim, property or status; (2) legal entitlement; (3) natural condition; (4) moral justice.

right of action State of facts entitling one to pursue a legal proceeding.

right of assembly Constitutional guarantee for people to come together for any purpose not expressly forbidden by law.

right of asylum Principle of international law by which one is protected at a place such as the embassy of a foreign country or residence of a foreign sovereign.

right of confrontation Principle of law embodied in constitutions and statutes by which an accused person is entitled to face his accusers and cross-examine them.

right of entry Legal entitlement to enter upon land, as in the case of a landlord entering leased premises to make repairs.

right of privacy Legal entitlement of an individual to live without the companionship, oversight or observation of others.

right of property Legal entitlement and status of an individual to own real or personal property.

right of redemption Legal entitlement conferred by statute upon a mortgagor to avoid foreclosure or recover property upon payment of the debt and costs.

right of support Legal entitlement of owner of land to have it supported by adjoining land.

right of visitation Right of non-custodial parent after separation or divorce to companionship of child or children of the marriage for limited time as determined by mutual agreement or court decree.

right of way Legal entitlement of persons to passage over a given route.

rights (1) Collective body of legal entitlement; (2) options accorded to security owners to acquire additional securities at advantageous terms.

☆ **rights of defendant** Those powers and privileges which are constitutionally guaranteed to every defendant.

rigor mortis [RIG uhr MAWR tis] Stiffening of muscle tissues of the body after death.

ring Combination of persons, usually for an illegal purpose.

riot Violent disturbance of public peace and order usually by three or more persons.

☆ **riot** The coming together of a group of persons who engage in violent and tumultuous conduct, thereby causing or creating a serious, imminent risk of causing injury to persons or property, or public alarm.

riparian [rahy PAY ree uhn] Relating to edge of a river, stream, or other body of water.

riparian owner [rahy PAY ree uhn OH nuhr] One owning land bordering on a river, stream or other body of water.

riparian right [rahy PAY ree uhn rahyt] Legal status accruing to riparian owner, to have access to bathing, navigation, domestic use and wharfing.

risk Hazard, danger, contingency.

river Large natural flowing stream.

road (1) Highway for public passage; (2) space between curbs.

roadbed Physical surface and grade of highway.

rob To steal property from another by threat or use of physical force as defined by statute.

robber One who steals property from another by threat or use of physical force.

robbery The stealing of property from another by threat or use of physical force.

☆ **robbery** *recommended statistical terminology, Uniform Crime Report usage* The unlawful taking or attempted taking of property that is in the immediate possession of another, by force or the threat of force.

rod Unit of length equal to 16–1/2 feet.

rogatory letters [ROG uh taw ree LET uhrz] Written request issued by a court or judge to a foreign court, requesting that testimony of a witness residing therein be taken in accordance with request and forwarded to the requesting court for its use in a pending proceeding.

roll List, schedule, record of legal proceedings, formal record.

rolling stock Wheeled vehicles of a railroad or motor carrier.

room (1) Enclosed space for occupancy; (2) opportunity for something.

roomer Lodger, one who rents an enclosed space in a dwelling for his own occupancy.

☆ **ROR** Release on own recognizance.

roster List, table of organization, schedule of members.

route Designated course for travel or passage.

royalties Payment to an owner made for use of his property, such as to an author for publication of copies of his work.

R. S. Revised statutes.

rule -n. (1) Promulgated standard to regulate specified actions; (2) written order of a court regulating its practice; (3) generally valid statement; -v. (4) to command, control, guide, decide a legal question.

rule against perpetuities [rool uh GENST puhr puh TOO i teez] Commonlaw legal requirement that interest given in property must vest within 21-year period after termination of specified lives in being when the interest is created, plus period of gestation for one conceived but unborn and entitled to the estate.

rule in Shelley's case Ancient principle of inheritance holding that an estate given to 'A' for life with remainder to his heirs gives 'A' title in fee simple which he may convey in his lifetime.

rule nisi [rool NIS ee] Legal direction which will become final in given period unless good cause be shown to contrary.

rule of court Procedural requirement promulgated by a court for guidance of litigants.

run -n. (1) Sustained and heavy demand by customers or creditors, as, a run on a bank or on the stock market; -v. (2) to have continuing legal validity, as, to run with the land; (3) to operate in legal consequence, as, the statute of limitations runs from inception of a right to a cause of action; (4) to conduct a business or enterprise; (5) to seek election as a candidate; (6) to continue in effect, as, an agreement having a limited period to run.

☆ **runaway** *recommended statistical terminology* A juvenile who has been adjudicated by a judicial officer of a juvenile court, as having committed the status offense of leaving the custody and home of his or her parents, guardians or custodians without permission and failing to return within a reasonable length of time.

running account Debits and credits occurring between parties on a continuing basis.

running of the statute of limitations Passage of time limited for legal action to commence or be barred.

running with the land Effect of a limitation on real property which binds all purchasers, assignees and successors in interest.

S

S. C. Supreme Court.

Sabbath (1) Sunday; (2) day prescribed for rest and religious observance by a religious group.

sabotage [SAB uh tahzh] Malicious destruction of property and interference with normal operations, with intent to damage or interfere with an enterprise.

sadism [SAY diz uhm] (1) Pleasure derived from physical or mental suffering inflicted on others; (2) sexual or other gratification obtained by the infliction of beatings, mistreatment and humiliation on others.

safe -adj. Secure, protected, harmless; -n. place for protecting valuables.

safe-conduct Privilege granted by a country to an enemy or alien for travel, as specified, within its borders, with assurance of personal safety.

safeguard To protect.

safety island Area in a roadway set aside for protection of pedestrians or to guide movement of traffic.

said Aforementioned.

salable (saleable) In condition suitable to be sold, marketable.

salary Periodic monetary compensation for services rendered.

sale (1) Contract for transfer of title to property from one person to another for an agreed consideration; (2) disposal of goods at bargain prices.

salvage (1) Securing and preservation of property following its exposure to hazard or injury, as by fire or shipwreck; (2) compensation paid for rescuing a ship, its cargo or persons on board from danger.

salvor One who provides service in preservation of property after its exposure to danger, as in case of shipwreck.

same (1) Identical, equal; (2) of like kind or species; (3) resembling in relevant details.

sample Small quantity presented as being representative of the whole.

sanction (1) Authorization, encouragement; (2) penalty imposed for noncompliance; (3) solemn ratification or acceptance.

sanctuary (1) Place affording protection and refuge; (2) place consecrated to religious worship.

sane Rational, mentally sound, able to distinguish right from wrong.

sanity Soundness of mind, ability to distinguish right from wrong.

satisfaction (1) Discharge of a legal obligation or claim by making payment; (2) legal instrument showing discharge of an obligation; (3) means of enjoyment, gratification; (4) compensation for loss or injury.

satisfaction piece Formal written acknowledgement that a mortgage or judgment has been paid, and authorizing the recording of its discharge.

satisfactory Acceptable, conforming to expectation or requirement, convincing.

satisfy (1) To conform to requirements, fulfill; (2) to convince, please; (3) to meet a financial obligation.

save (1) To reserve, accumulate; (2) to rescue from danger.

saving Act of economizing; preserving from danger.

saving clause Restriction set forth in a statute or instrument to reserve a legal position which might otherwise be affected, or providing that if part is held invalid, the remaining part shall not be affected.

saving the statute of limitations Action taken to enforce a legal right which would otherwise be barred by passage of time specified by statute.

savings and loan association Cooperative banking institution receiving its capital in savings shares and investing its funds in mortgages.

savings bank Financial institution receiving interest-bearing savings deposits and making legally approved investments including mortgage loans.

scab (1) One who works in place of a striking employee; (2) one who works for less than union wages.

scandal (1) Situation that violates morality or propriety; (2) allegation in a pleading of matter that detracts from dignity of the court, is contrary to good manners or is slanderous.

scandalous matter (1) Slanderous of defamatory language in a pleading; (2) language offensive to morality or propriety.

schedule (1) Formal statement of matters set forth in detail, usually in tabular form, such as schedule of assets and liabilities of a bankrupt; (2) detailed plan for future procedure.

scheme (1) Plan, program, design; (2) unethical or illegal project.

schizophrenia [skits oh FREE nee uh] Mental condition characterized by loss of contact with reality, disintegration of the personality, hallucinations and delusions.

scienter [see EN tuhr] -adj. Knowingly, wilfully; -n. such knowledge on the part of one doing an act as to make him legally responsible for its consequences.

scilicet [SIL i set] That is to say, namely; usually abbreviated as ss.

scintilla [sin TIL uh] Minute particle.

scire facias [SKEE ray FO kee uhs] Common law form of judicial writ, comparable to order to show cause.

scope Limit, boundary, range of consideration, opportunity for action.

scrip (1) Currency issued for temporary use; (2) certificate showing that holder is entitled to some specified payment or benefit.

scurrilous [SKUHR uh luhs] Vulgar, evil, abusive.

seal Mark made for authentication of an instrument, usually by physical impression on paper or other surface, through use of a die with raised letters.

sealed (1) Fastened so as to require mutilation of container in order to open; (2) bearing a raised impression for authenticity.

sealed instrument Legal document containing, in addition to required signature, raised impression made by use of die, to provide additional authenticity.

sealed verdict Finding of a jury in determination of a matter submitted to them, delivered to court officials for safekeeping in absence of judge, and placed in a closed envelope until court is again in session, at which time it is opened by the court in the presence of the jury.

search -n. (1) Physical examination of person or premises; (2) critical survey; -v. (3) to explore, examine thoroughly.

☆ **search** The examination or inspection of a location, vehicle, or person by a law enforcement officer or other person authorized to do so, for the purpose of locating objects relating to or believed to relate to criminal activities, or wanted persons.

search warrant Order in writing, issued by a competent judicial officer, directed to a peace officer, commanding a search for specified property at a given location, and a return to be made on the warrant as required by law.

☆ **search warrant** *recommended statistical terminology* A document issued by a judicial officer which directs a law enforcement officer to conduct a search at a specific location, for specified property or persons relating to a crime(s), to seize the property or persons if found, and to account for the results of the search to the issuing judicial officer.

seasonable Timely, opportune.

seasonal employment Occupation available only at particular periods during a year, such as picking fruit.

second -adj. (1) Ranking next to the first; -n. (2) one-sixtieth part of a minute; (3) damaged or defective article of merchandise; (4) in parliamentary procedure, required act of endorsement of a motion; (5) one who assists another, as, a second in a duel.

secondary (1) Next below first in value; (2) inferior, subordinate.

secondary boycott In labor relations, union activity seeking to discourage trade with a company dealing in goods or services of a struck company, to secure compliance with union demands.

secondary evidence Next best proof available when the best proof cannot be presented.

secondary liability Legal obligation occurring on default of one primarily responsible.

Secret Service Branch of United States Treasury Dept. charged with protection of national currency and protection of President, Vice-President and their families.

sect (1) Group of persons holding particular religious belief as part of a larger group; (2) group of persons adhering to particular doctrines.

sectarian (1) Pertaining to a group having a common religious belief; (2) limited in character or scope.

section (1) Subdivision, as, a section of a statute; (2) division, portion, part.

secular (1) Pertaining to worldly affairs, as distinguished from religious matters; (2) relating to the state of the laity, as distinguished from the clergy.

secure -adj. (1) Safe, confident, solid; -v. (2) to obtain; (3) to guarantee; (4) to guard.

secured creditor One to whom a debt is due, and who holds some assurance of repayment, such as a mortgage.

securities Stocks, bonds, notes, or other certificates showing right to property.

security (1) Protection, safety; (2) something deposited as assurance of payment or performance; (3) measures taken against sabotage or espionage.

Security Council Executive agency of United Nations.

security deposit Sum deposited by tenant with landlord to assure tenant's faithful performance of lease.

security for costs Undertaking required by a court, usually of a non-resident plaintiff, to cover payment of costs in case of adverse decision or judgment.

sedition [suh DISH uhn] (1) Offense of inciting action to overthrow existing government; (2) insurrection against or resistance to lawful authority.

seduce (1) To persuade another into having sexual intercourse; (2) to persuade a female of previous chaste character to have sexual intercourse; (3) to induce, coax, entice into disobedience or disloyalty.

seduction Sexual intercourse with a female of previous chaste character, or with another, brought about by false representations or other means of persuasion.

seisin [SEE zin] Possession of real or personal property.

seize To take legal possession; to put in possession; to confiscate, capture, arrest, take possession of.

seizure Act of taking possession by force or legal authority.

☆ **seizure** The taking into custody of law, by a law enforcement officer or other person authorized to do so, of objects relating to or believed to relate to criminal activity.

select -adj. (1) Chosen from a group; (2) superior, choice; -v. (3) to make a choice, to pick out from a group.

self-defense Plea offered in justification of acts done to protect one's person, property, or family from injury.

☆ **self-defense** The protection of oneself or one's property from unlawful injury or the immediate risk of unlawful injury; the justification for an act which would otherwise constitute an offense, that the person who committed it reasonably believed that the act was necessary to protect self or property from immediate danger.

self-executing Effective and operative without further action or on happening of some event.

self-serving (1) Gratuitously favoring one's self; (2) objection to introduction in evidence of a statement made to serve one's own interests.

seller One who offers or transfers his property to another in contract of sale.

selling long Practice of selling securities or commodities at current market price, in expectation of later replacing them at a lower price.

selling short Practice of selling securities or commodities which one does not own by borrowing the securities to make delivery in the expectation of replacing them at a lower price at a later time.

senile State of impairment of mental ability by reason of age.

senile dementia [SEE nahyl duh MEN shee uh] Mental disorder by reason of advanced age, and manifested by loss of memory, confusion and irrational ideas.

senility State of impairment of mental capacity by reason of age.

senior Elder, in greater precedence of time as compared with another, ranking above another.

seniority (1) Ranking superior to others; (2) status recognized in labor relations by which privilege such as selection of vacation period is first accorded to oldest employee in point of service.

sense Meaning, understanding, substance.

sentence Judgement imposed by a court upon a defendant, after his conviction in a criminal prosecution, which specifies the punishment determined by the court.

☆ **sentence** I. The penalty imposed by a court upon a person convicted of a crime. II. The court judgment specifying the penalty imposed upon a person convicted of a crime. III. Any disposition of a defendant resulting from a conviction, including the court decision to suspend execution of a sentence.

sentences running concurrently Status whereby a defendant serving different sentences on different cases or charges receives credit for time served on each at same time.

sentences running consecutively Status whereby a defendant convicted in separate cases or charges and receiving several sentences must complete one sentence before commencing another.

☆ **sentencing hearing** *recommended statistical terminology* In criminal proceedings, a hearing during which the court or jury considers relevant information, such as evidence concerning aggravating or mitigating circumstances, for the purpose of determining a sentencing disposition for a person convicted of an offense(s).

☆ **sentencing postponed** *recommended statistical terminology* The delay for an unspecified period of time, or to a remote date, of the court's pronouncement of any other sentencing disposition for a person convicted of an offense, in order to place the defendant in some status contingent on good behavior in the expectation that a penalty need never be pronounced or executed.

separable Able to be divided or separated.

separate Distinct, not connected to others, detached.

separate but equal Previously followed doctrine referring to segregation of whites and blacks by providing individual facilities for each group, as in schooling, but endeavoring to achieve similar facilities for each.

separate estate Status of individual ownership of property by one of several persons who are otherwise joined as in a business partnership or in marriage.

separate maintenance Financial provision made for support of wife and children when living apart from husband.

separate trial In case of two or more persons jointly charged with crime, individual proceeding as to each, apart from the other, to determine guilt or innocence.

separation Cessation of cohabitation of husband and wife.

separation a mensa et thoro [sep uh RAY shuhn o MEN suh et THAW roh] Physical estrangement from bed and board.

separation order Judicial order recognizing status of husband and wife living apart, and specifying conditions, including support for wife and children.

seq. [sek] (sequel) The following.

sequelae [SEE kwuh lahy] Results, events following.

sequester [see KWES tuhr] To separate, set apart, hold aside for safekeeping or awaiting some determination.

sequestration [see kwes TRAY shuhn] (1) Act of separating or keeping apart; (2) act of separating property from its owner until a demand is satisfied or some action completed.

sequestrator [SEE kwes tray tuhr] One holding property or setting it aside for others, pending determination of some matter.

serial bond One of an issue of bonds which mature at different dates.

seriatim [see ree OT im] In order, one by one.

serious Grave, important, solemn.

☆ **serious misdemeanor** A class of misdemeanors having more severe penalties than other misdemeanors, or procedurally distinct; sometimes a statutory name for a type of misdemeanor having a maximum penalty much greater than the customary maximum one year incarceration for misdemeanors.

servant One employed by another, and whose performance and conduct while so employed is directed by the employer.

serve (1) To aid in furtherance of some objective, to be of use; (2) to effectuate actual or constructive delivery of legal process, such as summons or subpoena; (3) to hold an office or act in some capacity.

service (1) Labor performed for an employer, who directs its manner of performance; (2) actual or constructive delivery of legal process, such as summons or subpoena; (3) labor producing an intangible product, or to repair something.

servient [SUHR vee uhnt] Burdened with duty or obligation, as, to be servient to an easement.

servitude Status of being bound in some duty, obligation or subjection to another.

session Period during which a body, such as a court or legislature, is transacting its business, which may be considered as a period during a given day, or as the entire time interval from inception to final adjournment.

session laws Published laws of a particular state, arranged by order of enactment within a legislative session rather than by subject matter.

set aside To revoke, annul, vacate, discard.

set down (1) To determine a later date for proceeding in a matter; (2) to record.

setoff Debtor's equitable right to reduce his debt by amount owed him in unrelated transaction between the parties.

set out To describe, allege, recite.

settle (1) To agree, determine; (2) to establish in residence; (3) to conclude a lawsuit by agreement of the parties, usually by compromise.

settlement Agreement, adjustment of opposing views, payment of accounts between parties.

settler One who takes up residence in a new location.

settlor [SET luhr] One who creates a trust or makes a marriage settlement.

sever To separate, divide, keep apart.

severable [SEV ruh buhl] Capable of being separated into parts independent of each other.

several Individual, separate, independent.

severally Individually, separately, one at a time.

severalty [SEV ruhl tee] Separate status, distinctness.

severalty, estate in [SEV ruhl tee, es TAYT in] Ownership by one without joint ownership by any other person.

severance [SEV ruhns] Separation, division, destruction of unity of interest.

☆ **severance** In criminal proceedings the separation, for purposes of pleading and/or trial, of multiple defendants named in a single charging document, or of multiple charges against a particular defendant listed in a single charging document.

severe Harsh, grave, strict.

☆ **sex offenses** I. In current statistical usage, the name of a broad category of varying content, usually consisting of all offenses having a sexual element except forcible rape and commercial sex offenses. II. *tentatively recommended major national category for prosecution, courts and corrections statistics* All unlawful sexual intercourse, unlawful sexual contact, and other unlawful behavior intended to result in sexual gratification or profit from sexual activity.

sexual Pertaining to male and female sexes and reproductive organs.

☆ **sexual assault** All sexual intercourse and contact offenses involving force, plus statutory rape.

sexual intercourse Penetration of female sexual organ by the male.

sham False, counterfeit, deceitful.

share -n. (1) Portion, proportional part; (2) one equal portion of capital stock of a corporation; -v. (3) to partake or use with others; (4) to divide in portions.

share and share alike In equal amounts, per capita, as tenants in common.

share certificate Instrument issued by a corporation as evidence of title to unit of its capital stock.

shareholder Person owning portion of capital stock of a corporation or portion of other property.

Shelley's case, rule in Ancient principle of inheritance holding that an estate given to 'A' for life with remainder to his heirs gives 'A' title in fee simple which he may convey in his lifetime.

shelter (1) Protection; (2) home, residence.

Shepard's Citations The publications of Shepard's Citations, Inc. which enable a researcher to trace the subsequent history of a reported judicial opinion.

sheriff County officer, usually charged with duties in aid of the courts, such as service of process, summoning jurors, custody of prisoners and maintenance of courtroom security; in some jurisdictions, serves in police capacity.

sheriff's sale Sale of property, pursuant to judicial order, conducted by sheriff in his official capacity.

shifting Passing from one to another.

shifting the burden of proof Transferring affirmative obligation for presentation of evidence to establish one's case, from the party previously having that responsibility, to his adversary.

shifting use Limitation of use applied to an estate so that the interest will shift or transfer itself from one beneficiary to another upon the happening of a specified contingency, as, for example, an estate for the use of 'A', limited so that on the marriage of 'B', the estate shall then be for the use of 'C'.

ship -n. Vessel used in navigation; -v. to transport from one place to another, by any means.

shipment (1) Delivery of goods to a carrier for transfer from one place to another; (2) subject matter of delivery of goods, cargo, consignment.

shipper One who sends goods for delivery to another.

shipping articles Agreement in writing between master of a vessel and crew members, setting forth terms and conditions of employment.

shipwreck Destruction or loss of a vessel at sea, as by forces of nature.

shock (1) Sudden disturbance of mental faculties; (2) violent blow, concussion; (3) profound bodily depression, produced by injury or mental disturbance.

shoot (1) To propel an object from a weapon, usually a firearm; (2) to wound with a propelled missile.

shopbook rule Rule of evidence by which an original record kept in usual course of business may be received in evidence upon proper authentication.

shopkeeper One who sells commodities in his retail establishment.

shop right Employer's entitlement to use in his own business, without royalty, his employee's invention if developed in the course of employer's business.

shore Land adjacent to water.

short (1) Brief, quick; (2) inadequate, insufficient; (3) in trading on an exchange, having less of a commodity or security than one needs to meet his requirements.

short rate Descriptive term for computation of insurance premium for period less than full period of coverage, whereby the charge made is greater than the pro rata share of the premium for the period elapsed.

shotgun Any smooth-bore weapon primarily designed to expel shot by explosion of gunpowder.

show -n. Exhibition, performance; -v. to prove, allege, reveal, demonstrate, explain, exhibit.

show cause order Judicial order, addressed to a party, requiring him to appear and present reasons and objections to the court against issuance of a proposed order.

shutdown Stoppage of work.

shyster [SHAHY stuhr] Unscrupulous lawyer.

sic [sik] (so, thus) Intended to appear as is.

sic passim [sik PAS im] (so throughout) Able to be found at various places in a text.

sidewalk Part of public street reserved for use of pedestrians.

sight Vision, observation, appearance.

sight draft Order for payment of funds, to be honored upon presentation.

sign -n. (1) Bodily motion conveying some meaning; (2) signal, token, symptom, mark; (3) lettered board, conspicuously displayed, conveying information; -v. (4) to affix one's mark or signature on a paper in approval, ratification or for identification.

signal (1) Means of transmitting information; (2) token, indication.

signatory [SIG nuh taw ree] Party to a signed agreement, signer with others.

signature (1) Mark made by an individual on paper to show his approval of contents; (2) name of a person, written by him on a paper to show his approval or to identify himself.

signify (1) To show, express, make known; (2) to imply, intimate.

silence Absence of sound or noise.

silence, estoppel by [SAHY lens, e STOP uhl bahy] Agreement inferred from failure of one to speak.

similar Resembling, comparable, like.

similiter [sim IL i tuhr] Likewise, in like manner.

simple (1) Plain, unassuming modest; (2) uneducated, stupid, foolish; (3) gullible, naive; (4) basic, fundamental; (5) easy.

simple assault Unlawful physical contact without aggravated circumstances; usually used in reference to misdemeanor crime of assault.

☆ **simple assault** Unlawful intentional inflicting of less than serious bodily injury without a deadly or dangerous weapon, or attempt or threat to inflict bodily injury without a deadly or dangerous weapon.

simulate (1) To pretend; (2) to assume false character or status.

simulated sale Pretended transaction to transfer title to property, which is in reality not a sale but a device to make property unavailable to creditors of the seller.

simulation Misrepresentation, pretense, imitation.

simultaneous Occurring identically in time, concurrent.

since After, before the present time.

sinecure [SAHY nuh kyoor] An employment in which compensation is paid but little or no duties are performed.

sine die [SIN ay DEE ay] Without date, indefinitely.

sine numero [SIN ay NOO muh roh] Without limit.

sine prole [SIN ay PROH lay] Without issue.

sine qua non [SIN ay kwo nohn] (without which not) Indispensable condition, essential.

single -adj. (1) Unmarried; (2) consisting of one, individual; -n. (3) separate individual or unit.

singular (1) Relating to one, individual; (2) unusual, extraordinary.

sinking fund Sum of money accumulated and set aside to pay off a debt at its maturity.

sister Female person having same father and mother as another.

sister-in-law (1) Sister of one's spouse, wife of one's brother; (2) wife of one's spouse's brother.

site (1) Land space for a building; (2) specific location.

sitting Session of a court or legislature.

situate To place in position, locate.

situation (1) Aggregate of conditions and circumstances, state of affairs; (2) employment.

situs [SAHY tuhs] (1) Location, position; (2) place deemed to have jurisdiction.

situs delicti [SAHY tuhs duh LIK tahy] Location of a crime.

skill Practical ability combined with knowledge of subject matter, competence.

slacker (1) Person who avoids duty; (2) person who avoids military service in wartime.

slander Oral defamation by public utterance of false and malicious statements concerning another, to his damage.

☆ **slander** Defamation by spoken communication.

slander of title False and malicious statement adversely affecting and damaging a person's title to property.

slanderous per se [SLAN duh ruhs puhr say] False words spoken concerning a person which impute his commission of a crime involving moral turpitude, existence of a loathsome disease or which tend to his prejudice in a trade or profession or with respect to inheritance.

slave Person wholly subject to control of another.

slavery Bondage, servitude, subjection.

slay To kill.

slight Trivial, superficial, frail.

slip law A legislative enactment separately published after its passage.

slip op. (slip opinion) Individual court decision published separately shortly after it has been made.

slot machine Mechanical apparatus in which a player deposits money and, by chance, may receive money or property in return, according to action of the apparatus.

slung shot Small dense mass fixed on a flexible handle or strap, for use as a weapon.

slush fund Sum of money available for corrupt purpose.

smart money Damages awarded beyond actual damage, by way of punishment and example.

smuggling (1) Import or export of anything in violation of customs laws; (2) intentional bringing in or taking out, contrary to law, of persons or property, to or from a country of place.

☆ **smuggling** Unlawful movement of goods across a national frontier or state boundary, or into or out of a correctional facility.

so Therefore, then.

sober (1) Serious, thoughtful; (2) temperate, free from effects of intoxicants; (3) containing less than 0.05 percent of alcohol in one's blood.

socialism Social and political system in which means of production and distribution of goods and services are owned and controlled by the state.

society Voluntary association of persons united for some common purpose.

sodomy [SOD uh mee] Carnal intercourse between persons of the same sex, or with an animal, or unnatural carnal intercourse with a person of the opposite sex.

☆ **sodomy** Unlawful physical contact between the genitals of one person and the mouth or anus of another person, or with the mouth, anus or genitals of an animal.

sojourn To stay temporarily.

sold Having title transferred by contract of sale.

sole Single, alone, solitary.

solemn (1) Serious; (2) formal; (3) in proper form.

solemnity Formality, ceremonious observance.

solemnize To observe, with legal or formal ceremony.

solicit (1) To apply for, request, plead; (2) to entice, lure, accost.

solicitation Act of requesting, importuning.

☆ **solicitation** Unlawful intentional asking in any manner of another person(s) to commit a crime.

solicitor Law officer of a political subdivision or government department.

solicitor general Legal officer of United States, assisting Attorney General by representation of government in Supreme Court.

solitary Alone, single.

solitary confinement Isolation of a prisoner from company of others.

solution (1) Explanation; (2) liquid containing dissolved matter.

solvency Ability to pay one's debts.

solvent Able to pay one's debts.

son Immediate male descendant of a parent.

son-in-law One's daughter's husband.

sound -adj. (1) Free from defect, healthy; (2) reliable, safe; (3) legal, valid; (4) level-headed; -n. (5) that which is heard; -v. (6) to be founded, as, to sound in damages; (7) to make known, put into words, proclaim.

sounding in damages Founded upon monetary recovery for injury or loss, rather than relief such as recovery of possession or specific performance.

source Cause, origin, place from which taken.

sovereign [SOV ruhn] (1) Supreme ruler of a country; (2) one having supreme authority.

sovereign power [SOV ruhn POU uhr] Supreme authority of government.

sovereign state [SOV ruhn stayt] Political unit not subject to any other jurisdiction.

sovereignty [SOV ruhn tee] (1) Supreme political power; (2) independence.

speaker Title of presiding officer of legislative body, such as in United States House of Representatives.

special Unusual, unique, noteworthy, designed for particular purpose.

special damages Monetary payment for injury or loss, based upon particular proof which must be established.

specialist (1) In stock exchange parlance, broker who trades in limited group of stocks; (2) one who confines his activities to a limited area, thereby acquiring greater proficiency.

special jury Panel of jurors possessed of better education or greater intelligence than usual, to consider complicated or important issues.

special master Person appointed by a court to take testimony in a case and make findings of fact, or perform other designated service in court's behalf.

special sessions Designation of certain inferior courts of criminal jurisdiction, usually presided over by panel of judges.

specialty Legal instrument containing a seal.

special verdict Determination by jury as to facts only, leaving judgment on such facts to the court.

specie [SPEE shee] (1) Monetary coins in kind; (2) in identical form.

specific Definite, exact, precise, explicit.

specification (1) Description of charge or accusation, as in case of one accused of a military offense; (2) statement describing a matter in particular detail, as, for example, specification forming part of a construction contract, or details of a patent.

specific performance Equitable remedy for breach of contract whereby defendant may be compelled to carry out his contractual obligation rather than pay damages for breach of contract, in an instance where payment of damages would be an inadequate remedy.

specify To set forth in detail, to be precise.

specimen Sample of the whole.

speculation (1) Conjecture, guess; (2) financial transaction of unusual risk directed to anticipated profit from price fluctuations.

speculative (1) Hazardous, involving high risk; (2) conjectural, theoretical.

speedy Rapid, swift.

speedy trial In a criminal case, determination of the charge, by trial, with reasonable diligence under all the circumstances.

☆ **speedy trial** The right of the defendant to have a prompt trial, as guaranteed by the Sixth Amendment of the U.S. Constitution: "In all criminal prosecutions, the accused shall enjoy the right to a speedy and public trial..."

spend To expend, disburse, consume.

spendthrift One who spends money recklessly.

spendthrift trust Fund created for benefit of a person but secured against reckless spending and attachment by creditors.

spinster Woman who has never married.

spite fence Partition enclosing land, having no useful purpose but to annoy by unreasonably closing off light, air and view.

☆ **split sentence** A sentence explicitly requiring the convicted person to serve a period of confinement in a local, state or federal facility followed by a period of probation.

splitting a cause of action Maintenance of a legal action directed only to part of several grounds upon which the action may be maintained.

spoliation [spoh lee AY shuhn] Destruction, injury, as, the spoliation of evidence.
sponsor One who vouches for or assumes responsibility for a person or thing.
spontaneous combustion Fire occurring without originating flame, but merely from internal heat.
spontaneous exclamation Unplanned statement made concurrently with or immediately following an event and therefore admissible as part of the explanation of the happening.
sporting house Brothel, house of prostitution.
spouse Husband or wife.
spurious [SPYOO ree uhs] False, counterfeit, not authentic.
spy Person who secretly obtains information and conveys this to his principals.
squatter One occupying land of another without legal authority.
squib [skwib] A concise statement of a judicial opinion or point of law.
squire (short form of "esquire") (1) Country gentleman, large landowner; (2) justice of the peace, lawyer, judge.
ss. (scilicet) Namely, to wit.
stab To wound by thrusting with a sharp object.
stake Sum of money representing a wager, usually held by a third person for delivery to the winner.
stakeholder One holding money deposited with him by two or more persons, the sum being paid to one or more of the persons involved depending on some contingency, such as result of a wager or outcome of litigation.
standard Recognized and established practice, model, example or specification.
standard mortgage clause Provision in fire insurance policy that in case of loss, payment shall be made to mortgagee, whose interest shall not be affected by any action of the mortgagor.
standard of weight or measure Established specimen and authority for extent and quantity of anything, used as a basis for official comparison.
standing (1) Legal capacity and position to maintain an action; (2) person's social or business position in his community.
standing by (1) Available for use if needed; (2) present, near at hand.
standing mute Silence on part of a person required to plead to a criminal charge or allegation.
standing orders Rules having permanent effect.
staple -adj. (1) Standard, principal; -n. (2) wire fastener having two prongs inserted through papers or other material and then folded over; (3) commodity, such as sugar, which has widespread use, is produced in large quantities, and enjoys constant demand.
Star Chamber Ancient English court long since abolished, known for its secret, oppressive and irresponsible proceedings.
stare decisis [STO ray duh SAHY sis] Legal doctrine that the judicial decision of an issue constitutes a principle to be applied to later proceedings on similar issues.
star pagination System used in unofficial editions of judicial opinions to identify corresponding volume and page number of the same opinion in official edition.
state -n. (1) Political entity occupying definite territory over which it exercises sovereign control in behalf of the population; (2) political body forming component part of a federal union, such as in United States; (3) condition, nature, status; -v. (4) to assert, declare, announce.
stated Fixed, established.

stated account Record of debits and credits between parties, which has been agreed upon by both as being correct.

stated meeting Formal coming together of a group at a specified time and place, pursuant to its regulations or by-laws.

stated term Regular court or legislative session, held at specified time for transaction of regular business.

stated times At specified intervals.

statement (1) Allegation of fact, made orally or in writing; (2) periodic tabulation of debits and credits sent to a customer by a bank or business establishment; (3) in a legal pleading, preliminary showing of facts upon which the action is based.

statement of facts Presentation of existing conditions.

☆ **state's attorney** *recommended statistical terminology* An attorney who is the elected or appointed chief of a prosecution agency, and whose official duty is to conduct criminal proceedings on behalf of the people against persons accused of committing criminal offenses; and any attorney deputized to assist the chief prosecutor.

state's evidence Testimony given in behalf of prosecution in a criminal proceeding, usually referring to testimony by an accomplice to the crime.

status (1) Relative legal condition, standing; (2) position in relation to others.

☆ **status offender** *recommended statistical terminology* A juvenile who has been adjudged by a judicial officer of a juvenile court to have committed a status offense.

☆ **status offense** *recommended statistical terminology* An act or conduct which is declared by statute to be an offense, but only when committed or engaged in by a juvenile, and which can be adjudicated only by a juvenile court.

status quo [STAT uhs kwoh] (state in which) Existing state of affairs.

statute Legislative enactment, a law.

statute of frauds Legislation of common law origin requiring certain documents to be in writing and signed by the party to be charged, thereby minimizing opportunity for fraud or perjury.

statute of limitations Legislative enactment limiting time within which specified actions or prosecutions must be instituted.

statutory [STACH uh taw ree] Enacted by legislation.

statutory crime [STACH uh taw ree krahym] Violation of penal law as enacted by legislature, but not having common-law origin.

statutory lien [STACH uh taw ree leen] Charge on property to satisfy a debt, provided by legislation but not otherwise.

statutory rape [STACH uh taw ree rayp] Sexual intercourse with a willing or unwilling female whose age is less than the statutory age of consent.

☆ **statutory rape** Sexual intercourse with a female without force or threat of force, when female has consented in fact, but is below age of consent specified in state law.

statutory tenant [STACH uh taw ree TEN uhnt] One in possession of land of another, whose term has expired but is enabled to remain in same status by payment of rent, pursuant to emergency legislation such as rent control laws.

stay -n. (1) Delay, by judicial or executive order; (2) delay, postponement; -v. (3) to delay or suspend the effect or progress of judicial or executive proceedings; (4) to delay, pause; (5) to remain.

stay of execution Temporary delay in carrying out judgment of a court.

☆ **stay of execution** The stopping by a court of the carrying out or implementation of a judgment, that is, of a court order previously issued.

stay of proceedings Temporary delay in business of a court relating to a particular action.

steal To take personal property of another for one's own use and without consent of the owner.

stealth (1) Theft; (2) furtiveness.

steerer One who directs persons, usually to some illegal or immoral activity.

stepchild An offspring by a previous marriage of one's spouse.

sterile (1) Barren, lacking in creativity; (2) free from living organisms; (3) lacking capacity to reproduce, impotent.

stet [stet] (let it stand) Direction to nullify a previous order, often used as proofreader's instruction to printer.

stickup (colloquial) Robbery.

still -adj. (1) Quiet, stationary; -n. (2) apparatus for separation of alcohol; (3) silence; -v. (4) to stop or settle something.

stillborn Born dead or in such an early stage of fetal development as to be incapable of living.

stipend [STAHY pend] Sum fixed as periodic payment for services, or a regular allowance for living expenses.

stipulate To agree formally with one's adversary in a legal proceeding on some matter forming part of the proceedings or record.

stipulation Formal agreement between legal adversaries governing some aspect of their proceeding.

stock (1) Inventory, goods offered for sale, supply; (2) corporate capital, represented by proportionate shares; (3) original from which others have descended.

stockbroker Person trading for others in corporate securities.

stock certificate Written instrument issued by a corporation to show ownership of designated part of its capital.

stock company Corporation, often referring to insurance business, whose capital has been obtained by sale of stock, as distinguished from a mutual company which is owned by its insureds.

stock dividend Distribution of profit by a corporation to its shareholders in form of issuance of shares of its stock in a designated ratio to stock ownership.

stock exchange Association of persons who maintain a market for trading in securities.

stock in trade Inventory kept for sale.**stockholder** One who owns capital stock in a corporation.

stockholder One who owns capital stock in a corporation.

stockholder's derivative suit Legal action maintained by stockholder of a corporation, in his own name, to seek redress of a wrong to the corporation, for which the corporation has failed to act.

stockholder's liability Obligation of stockholder to pay full par value for his stock, or in certain cases, obligation to pay debts of the corporation.

stockholder's representative action Legal action maintained by a stockholder with respect to some corporate act, seeking redress for himself and all other persons similarly situated.

☆ **stolen property; buying, receiving, possessing** In Uniform Crime Reports terminology, the name of the UCR category used to record and report arrests for offenses of knowingly buying, receiving, possessing, or attempting to buy, receive, or possess, stolen property.

☆ **stolen property offenses** *tentatively recommended national category for prosecution, courts and corrections statistics* The unlawful receiving, buying, distributing, selling, transporting, concealing, or possessing of the property of another by a person who knows that the property has been unlawfully obtained from the owner or other lawful possessor.

stop -n. (1) Cessation, end; (2) impediment, obstacle; (3) act of bringing to a halt; (4) device to impede movement; -v. (5) to intercept, plug, obstruct; (6) to cease or change a course of conduct; (7) to deduct or withhold, as, payment on a check.

☆ **stop and frisk** The detaining of a person by a law enforcement officer for the purpose of investigation, accompanied by a superficial examination by the officer of the person's body surface or clothing to discover weapons, contraband, or other objects relating to criminal activity.

stop order Direction of a customer to his broker that when price of his security reaches a given level the broker shall trade in customer's behalf on best terms then available.

stop sign Posted traffic direction requiring vehicles to cease movement before entering or crossing an intersection.

stowaway One who conceals himself to obtain free transportation.

straddle To favor two opposing sides, as, for example, to direct buying and selling transactions at same time in same stock.

straight-line depreciation Accounting basis for computing loss due to passage of time or to deterioration over a given span of time, and allocating for each equal time period an equal percentage charge for such loss.

stranded (1) Left at some place without transportation or funds; (2) run aground.

stranger (1) Person unknown to another; (2) person dealing with another without previous relationship.

stratagem [STRAT uh jem] Trick to gain one's end.

stray -n. That which has departed from group or accustomed route; -v. to wander from a group or from an accustomed route or practice.

street Road, thoroughfare, public way.

☆ **street crime** A class of offenses, sometimes defined with some degree of formality as those which occur in public locations, are visible and assaultive, and thus constitute a group of crimes which are a special risk to the public and a special target of law enforcement preventive efforts and prosecutorial attention.

☆ **street time** Time spent on conditional release. If parole or other conditional release is revoked, and the person reconfined, all or part of this time may become "dead time" in calculations of time served under correctional jurisdiction, according to administrative or court decision.

strict Exact, precise, governed by rules which permit no deviation.

strictissimi juris [strik TIS i mee JOO ris] (of the strictest right) Of precise legal interpretation.

strictly Rigorously, closely, exactly adhering to requirement.

strictly construed Manner of interpretation of statute by which its terms will be held to represent legislative intent without latitude for judicial construction, expansion or limitation.

strike Concerted stoppage of work by employees as a means to enforce compliance by employer with their demands, or to protest against conditions imposed by employer.

strikebreaker One who replaces a workman who has joined with others in ceasing work in order to obtain changes in working conditions.

strike off (1) To print; (2) to remove from a roll, as, to strike off a juror who is not qualified to serve.

strip -n. Narrow area; -v. to remove, deprive, divest, bare.

struck (1) Hit, wounded; (2) affected by temporary organized work stoppage.

struck jury Special jury, chosen by parties striking off names from those called, until 12 jurors remain.

structure (1) Building, construction; (2) form, composition.

style Distinctive manner, form, mode.

sua sponte [SOO uh SPON tay] Voluntarily, upon its own motion or will.

sub judice [sub JOO di see] Under judicial consideration, not yet determined.

subcontract Legal agreement made between one of parties to a prime or previous contract, and a stranger, whereby stranger agrees to perform for the prime contractor some or all of the work to be done under the prime or previous contract.

subcontractor One who enters into a legal agreement to perform some act, for a person who has previously contracted to perform such act under a prime contract.

subdivide To separate into smaller parts, as, to subdivide unimproved land.

subdivision (1) Process of reduction into smaller parts; (2) tract of land divided into lots.

subject -n. (1) Topic, matter of concern; (2) person owing allegiance to a country or ruler; -v. (3) to make liable, put under control, subjugate.

subjection Subordination, condition of being under obligation or control.

subject matter Topic of consideration, thing in dispute, right claimed by one party as against another.

subject to Governed by, provided, subordinate to.

sublease Agreement by which a tenant conveys to a third person some portion or all of the estate he has leased, for a period shorter than his own, and retaining some interest under his original lease.

sublet To convey to another the rights of one holding as a tenant.

submission (1) Act of yielding to some authority; (2) referral of a controversy or issue for determination or consideration.

submit (1) To yield; (2) to present for determination, refer; (3) to offer, supply.

sub nom. [sub nom] **(sub nomine)** [sub NOM i nay] Under the name of.

subordinate (1) Having lower position or rank in relation to another; (2) coming under control of higher authority.

suborn [sub AWRN] To procure by secret or improper means the performance of an illegal or immoral act.

subornation of perjury [sub awr NAY shuhn uv PUHR juh ree] Act of procuring another to commit perjury.

suborner [sub AWR nuhr] One who procures another to perform an illegal or immoral act, such as perjury.

subpoena [suh PEE nuh] Legal process which commands a witness to appear and testify, at specified time and place.

☆ **subpoena** *recommended statistical terminology* A written order issued by a judicial officer, prosecutor, defense attorney or grand jury, requiring a specified person to appear in a designated court at a specified time in order to testify in a case under the jurisdiction of that court, or to bring material to be used as evidence to that court.

subpoena ad testificandum [suh PEE nuh ad tes ti fi KON duhm] Legal process requiring one to appear and testify.

subpoena duces tecum [suh PEE nuh DOO suhs TAY kuhm] Legal process requiring one to appear as a witness, and bring with him specified books and records in his possession.

subrogation [sub ruh GAY shuhn] (1) Substitution of one person to stand in place of another in respect to legal rights, claims and debts; (2) succession by an insurer to rights of its insured against party causing loss, after payment by the insurer of the loss.

subrogee [sub ruh JEE] One who succeeds to the rights of another through subrogation.

subscribe (1) To write underneath; (2) to agree to join or contribute, as in subscribing money for some purpose.

subscriber (1) One who signs a paper; (2) one who agrees to purchase stock of a corporation on its original issue; (3) one who purchases delivery of a periodic publication for a given period, such as a year; (4) one who favors or supports something.

subscribing witness One who signs his own name to an instrument which he has seen executed.

subscription (1) Act of placing one's signature on a written instrument; (2) matter added at the end of a document; (3) amount obtained from persons who share in a program or offering.

subsequent Later, following, succeeding.

subsidiary That which is a part of or inferior to something else.

subsidy Grant of money or property to further some purpose.

subsistence (1) Support, livelihood; (2) food and shelter required to live; (3) payment for living expenses while away from home; (4) existence.

substance (1) Material component; (2) essential nature, gist.

substantial (1) Valuable, important; (2) real, solid, material.

substantial compliance Such conformity with requirements as is material and faithful such that any omission or defect would be minor.

substantially Essentially, without major variation.

substantial performance Compliance in essential details, without important omission or defect.

substantial right Legal right as to a matter of substance, as distinguished from one of form.

substantiate To verify, establish the existence of, make firm.

substantive (1) Essential, relating to substance rather than form or procedure; (2) real, firm, solid.

substantive evidence Testimony offered to prove a fact, rather than to discredit a witness.

substantive law Body of law regulating rights and duties as opposed to adjective law which sets forth procedural steps to enforce rights and duties.

substitute -n. That which takes the place of another or is available to do so; -v. to exchange for another.

substituted executor Designated personal representative of testator, to function as such in event that first named executor does not serve.

substituted service Delivery of legal process upon a defendant by other than personal service, as authorized by statute, and including, for example, by publication in a newspaper.

substitution Change of one person or thing in place of another.

subtenant One who leases part or all of leased premises from the original lessee for a term less than that of the original lessee.

subterfuge [SUB tuhr fyooj] Deception, stratagem.

succession (1) Transfer of title to property by law of descent and distribution; (2) transfer of an office or status from a predecessor; (3) act of following in order, becoming entitled to rights and position of another.

successive Following in order, consecutive.

successor One who follows in place of another.

sudden Unforeseen, happening unexpectedly.

sudden heat of passion Unforeseen spasm of rage or anger, arising directly from some provocation and giving immediate cause for retaliation.

sue To commence or maintain a legal action.

sue out To apply for, as, to sue out a writ.

suffer (1) To feel pain or discomfort; (2) to endure, permit, allow.

sufferance [SUF ruhns] (1) Consent implied from failure to enforce an adverse right; (2) patient endurance.

sufficient Adequate, necessary for some purpose, enough.

sufficient cause Adequate reason in the particular situation as judicially determined.

suffrage [SUF ruhj] Act or right of voting.

suggestion Presentation of an idea for consideration.

suicide Intentional death of a person produced by his own act.

suicide clause Provision in life insurance policy limiting liability of company to return of net premiums paid if insured kills himself within specified period after inception of coverage.

sui generis [soo ee JEN uh ris] Unique, of its own kind or class.

sui juris [soo ee JOO ris] (of his own right) Having legal capacity to act for one's self and enjoy all civil rights.

suit Legal action or proceeding.

suitable Appropriate in the circumstances, qualified.

summarily Without delay, briefly, quickly performed.

summary -adj. Brief, concise; -n. synopsis resume, restatement.

summary judgment Decision of court entered on the pleadings without a trial when it appears to the court that no triable issue is shown.

summary proceeding (1) Statutory action to evict tenant; (2) prompt and simple disposition of a legal matter.

summon (1) To serve a summons, by which defendant is notified that legal action against him has been commenced in a court and informing him of time and place to appear and answer; (2) to call.

summons Signed notice for a person to appear in court at a specified time to answer a legal action against him.

☆ **summons** *recommended statistical terminology* In criminal proceedings, a written order issued by a judicial officer requiring a person accused of a criminal offense to appear in a designated court at a specified time to answer the charge(s).

summons and complaint Notice to appear and answer in a pending action, together with formal pleading setting forth basis of the action, and providing a basis for default judgment if no answer is entered.

sum up To review evidence for the jury by counsel for each side, together with their making reasonable inferences, deductions and conclusions.

superficial Trivial, extending only on the surface, external.

superintend To direct, regulate, manage.

superintendent (1) One who has charge of something, as, a manager; (2) custodian of a building.

superior -adj. Of higher grade or degree; -n. one who is above another in rank or position or surpasses another in some attribute.

supernumerary [soo puhr NOO muh re ree] Person in excess of number authorized or required.

supersede (1) To replace, set aside in behalf of another, override; (2) to postpone, discontinue, annul.

supersedeas [SOO puhr SEE dee uhs] Common law writ in nature of stay of proceedings or writ of prohibition.

supervene To take place after or during some other event, so as to alter the existing situation.

supervise To control, direct, inspect.

supervision Act of direction, inspection and evaluation.

☆ **supervision** Authorized and required guidance, treatment, and/or regulation of the behavior of a person who is subject to adjudication or who has been adjudicated to be an offender, performed by a correctional agency.

☆ **supervisory custody (corrections)** Responsibility for supervision of a probationer, parolee or other member of a non-incarcerated correctional case-load.

supp. Supplement.

supplemental Additional.

supplemental affidavit [sup luh MEN tuhl a fi DAY vit] Sworn writing made to add to information contained in a previous sworn writing.

supplemental pleading Additional pleading submitted to add new facts or correct a defect in a previous pleading.

supplementary Additional.

supplementary proceedings Further inquiry, under court jurisdiction, after entry of judgment, to determine means for enforcing the judgment against judgment debtor.

supply -n. (1) Available or needed quantity; -v. (2) to add required information; (3) to provide that which is needed or desired.

support -n. (1) Means of livelihood; (2) assistance; -v. (3) to provide funds for living expenses; (4) to advocate; (5) to provide means, maintain, sustain; (6) to provide verification.

supp. pro. [sup proh] Supplementary proceedings.

suppress To prohibit, prevent from coming forward, put down, keep from public knowledge, as, to suppress evidence obtained illegally.

suppression Act of prohibiting, preventing from coming forward, concealing from public knowledge.

☆ **suppression hearing** A hearing to determine whether or not the court will prohibit specified statements, documents, or objects from being introduced into evidence in a trial.

supra [SOO pruh] (above, upon) Referring to previous place in the text.

Supreme Court (1) In Federal practice, the highest court; (2) in New York State, the highest court of original jurisdiction for both civil and criminal matters.

surcharge Additional cost, charge in excess of usual or normal amount.

surety [SHOOR uh tee] One who assumes obligation and is primarily liable for another's payment of debts or performance of duty.

surety company [SHOOR uh tee KUM puh nee] Commercial enterprise which, for a fee, obligates itself for another's payment of debts and performance of duty.

suretyship [SHOOR uh tee ship] Status of person who assumes obligation and is primarily liable for another's payment of debts and performance of duty.

surface Exterior.

surmise [suhr MAHYZ] Conjecture, suspicion, guess.

surname Family name.

surplus (1) Excess, remainder, residue, unused part; (2) amount by which corporate net worth exceeds value of capital stock; (3) amount by which receipts exceed disbursements.

surplusage [SUHR pluh suhj] Irrelevant, redundant or unnecessary matter such as may be contained in a legal pleading.

surprise Unexpected situation.

surrebutter [su ruh BUT uhr] Plaintiff's answer to defendant's rebutter.

surrejoinder [su ruh JOYN duhr] Plaintiff's answer to defendant's rejoinder.

surrender To yield, restore, give up.

surreptitious Stealthy, concealed, furtive.

surrogate [SU ruh guht] Judicial officer who has jurisdiction over settlement of estates of deceased persons and sometimes over minors and incompetents.

surrogate's court [SU ruh guhts kawrt] Probate court, presided over by surrogate, having jurisdiction over settlement of estates of deceased persons and sometimes over minors and incompetents.

surround To enclose on all sides, encircle.

surveillance [suhr VAY luhns] Supervision, close observation.

survey -n. (1) Plan drawn to scale showing a measured area of land; (2) comprehensive and critical examination of some condition; -v. (3) to determine exact measurement of land, buildings and related dimensions; (4) to investigate and determine the condition of something.

surveyor (1) One who measures land and makes scale diagram of his findings; (2) customs official who determines amount and value of goods passing through a port.

survive To remain alive after another's death or after some event.

surviving Remaining alive after another's death or after some event.

survivor One who outlives another, or outlives some event.

survivorship (1) State of one remaining alive after another; (2) in a group of two or more persons having joint interests in property, the right of those remaining alive to receive the share of those who die.

suspect -n. Person being considered as perpetrator of a crime; -v. to distrust, have doubts about.

☆ **suspect** An adult or juvenile considered by a criminal justice agency to be one who may have committed a specific criminal offense, but who has not been arrested or charged.

suspend To interrupt, delay, temporarily discontinue or withdraw.

suspended sentence Imposition of judgment as being one indefinitely postponed, contingent upon good behavior.

☆ **suspended sentence** I. The court decision to delay imposing or executing a penalty for a specified or unspecified period, also called "sentence withheld." II. *recommended statistical terminology* A court disposition of a convicted person pronouncing a penalty of a fine or commitment to confinement, but unconditionally discharging the defendant or holding execution of the penalty in abeyance upon good behavior.

suspense (1) State of dormancy, temporary cessation; (2) anxiety, apprehension.

suspension (1) Temporary delay, interruption; (2) temporary removal from an office or position, as a penalty.

suspicion (1) Lack of trust on some matter without basis of proof; (2) apprehension or imagination of an adverse event without proof or on slight evidence.

☆ **suspicion** Opinion based on slight evidence, upon facts or circumstances which are somewhat less than reasonable grounds to believe something.

suspicious (1) Questionable, suspected; (2) questioning, suspecting.

sustain To bear, maintain, support, prolong, uphold.

swear (1) To take an oath; (2) to solemnly assert as true; (3) to emphatically promise; (4) to pledge.

swindle -n. Act of obtaining money by fraud or deceit; -v. to obtain money by fraud or deceit.

☆ **swindle** Intentional false representation to obtain money or any other thing of value, where deception is accomplished through the victim's belief in the validity of some statement or object presented by the offender.

swindler One who obtains something of value by fraud or deceit.

sworn Bound by formal oath.

syllabus [SIL uh buhs] In United States Supreme Court opinions, a summary of the opinion, written by the Court's Reporter of Decisions.

symbol Characteristic mark, representation, conventional sign.

symbolic Conveying meaning by representation rather than specific objects.

syndicate (1) Combination of persons or firms to carry out some enterprise; (2) a loose organization of racketeers for purposes of organized crime.

synonymous Expressing the same idea.

synopsis Brief summary, abstract.

system Orderly arrangement, methodical combination.

T

table -n. Columnar or systematic arrangement of data; -v. to withdraw from consideration, as, to table a motion.

tacit [TAS it] Implied, inferred, without being expressed.

tail -adj. Limited, abridged, as, an estate tail; -v. to follow someone to observe his actions.

tail, estate in Ownership of property by inheritance in a direct line which terminates upon failure of issue.

taint (1) To affect with some undesirable quality; (2) corrupt, stain.

take (1) To seize, gain possession of, procure; (2) to acquire or receive, as, to take title to property; (3) to accept, as, to take an oath.

take back To revoke, retract.

take care of To support, look after, discharge responsibility for.

take effect To come into operation.

take over To assume control from another.

taking Seizure, act of exercising control.

talesman [TAYLZ man] (1) Juror; (2) person called as part of an additional panel from which jury may be chosen.

tally Account, score.

tamper (1) To interfere, meddle; (2) to negotiate or influence improperly.

tangible Real, material, having physical existence.

tangible property Physical subject matter of ownership.

tare [tayr] (1) Allowance for weight of container in which merchandise is packed; (2) weight of container or of vehicle in which it is shipped.

tariff (1) Tax imposed on import or export of goods; (2) schedule of import or export taxes; (3) published schedule of rates charged by a common carrier or public utility.

tavern Establishment serving alcoholic beverages.

tax -n. (1) Charge imposed upon persons or property by public authority for its support; -v. (2) to levy a charge for support of government; (3) to make judicial determination of an amount, as, to tax costs in an action.

taxable Subject to collection of charge by government, or charge by court against a party.

taxable year Annual period used by taxpayer for accounting purposes.

taxation (1) Imposition of a charge by government for its support; (2) judicial determination of an amount, as, taxation of bill of costs.

tax deed Document showing title to real property of one acquiring such property at sale for non-payment of taxes.

taxicab Passenger-carrying vehicle and driver, available for public use at a cost to passenger.

tearing of will Revocation of written testamentary disposition by act of mutilation.

technical (1) In accordance with strict legal interpretation; (2) relating to specialized scientific or mechanical knowledge; (3) complicated, specialized.

teller (1) Bank employee who deals with customers in receiving or paying out money; (2) person appointed to count votes.

temperance Moderation, restraint, sobriety.

temperate Moderate, reasonable, self-controlled.

temporal [TEM puh ruhl] (1) Pertaining to lay, as distinguished from religious affairs; (2) pertaining to earthly time as opposed to eternity or heavenly time.

temporarily For a limited period, briefly.

temporary Transitory, pertaining to a restricted period.

tenancy [TEN uhn see] (1) Legal interest in property; (2) temporary possession of another's property pursuant to agreement.

tenancy by the entirety [TEN uhn see bahy *thee* en TAHY ruh tee] Joint ownership of real property by husband and wife, survivor to become sole owner.

tenancy in common [TEN uhn see in KOM uhn] Shared ownership of property by two or more persons with the interest of each tenant in common passing to his distributees on his death.

tenancy, joint [TEN uhn see, joynt] Interest of two or more persons in property, arising by the same conveyance, commencing at the same time and constituting one united possession, with survivorship extending to the last survivor.

tenancy, several [TEN uhn see, SEV ruhl] Separate property ownership.

tenant (1) One having legal possession of property (usually real property) of another; (2) one having a legal possessory interest in real property of another.

tenant at will One having legal possession of property (usually real property) of another, duration being at owner's discretion, with no pre-determined limitation or agreement as to time.

tenant for life One having a legal possession of property (usually real property) of another, for a period of time measured by the length of his own life.

tenant for years One having legal possession of property (usually real property) of another, for a specified number of years.

tenant from year to year One having legal possession of property (usually real property) of another, continuing in such status without agreement or lease following the expiration of a prior period of years.

tend To lean, incline, favor.

tender (1) An offer, as of money or service; (2) unconditioned offer of performance, to avoid a penalty or forfeiture.

tenement Dwelling, usually multiple apartments.

tenor General meaning, intent, trend.

tenure Holding of a right, status or privilege.

term (1) Defined or limited period, duration; (2) time set for a court to sit; (3) word or group of words having precise meaning.

terminable Able to be ended.

terminate To end.

terminus [TUHR min uhs] Limit, boundary, end.

terms Conditions, as, the terms of a contract.

terra firma [TE ruh FUHR muh] Solid land.

terra incognita [TE ruh in COG nit uh] Unknown or unexplored country or field of study.

terra nullius [TE ruh NUL ee uhs] Territory not owned by any nation.

territory (1) Geographical area under jurisdiction of a government; (2) land area of great extent; (3) independent portion of country prior to becoming a state; (4) defined geographic area, as, a salesman's territory.

terror Extreme fear, apprehension of great harm.

test -n. Examination, criterion; -v. to examine, analyze, validate.

test action Lawsuit selected from a group of several based on similar grounds, and serving as a guide, by agreement of all parties, to the disposition of all actions.

testacy [TES tuh see] State of person who dies leaving a valid will.

testament Written instrument by which a person provides for the disposition of his property after his death.

testamentary [tes tuh MEN tuh ree] Pertaining to a will.

testamentary capacity [tes tuh MEN tuh ree kuh PAS i tee] Such competent mental condition as is required to make a will.

testamentary guardian [tes tuh MEN tuh ree GAHR dee uhn] Person appointed by will to have legal custody of minor children or other persons incapable of managing their own affairs.

testamentary trust [tes tuh MEN tuh ree trust] Equitable estate in property, created by will.

testate [TES tayt] Leaving a will.

testator [TES tay tuhr] One who executes a will.

testatrix [TES tuh triks] Female who makes a will.

test case Legal action likely to serve as a guide to disposition of a number of cases based on similar facts or legal issues.

testify To give evidence as a witness under oath.

testimonial (1) Something offered as proof; (2) endorsement of a person, product or service.

testimonium clause Final clause of an instrument, usually beginning "in witness whereof" and showing date, signature and witnesses, if any.

testimony (1) Evidence by a witness, given under oath; (2) outward sign, proof.

text (1) Body of printed matter; (2) original language of a literary work; (3) principal source of information or authority.

theft (1) Larceny, stealing; (2) taking of property from another without his consent, with intent to deprive him of it and appropriate it to one's own use.

☆ **theft** Generally, any taking of the property of another with intent to permanently deprive the rightful owner of possession; in the broadest legal usage the name of the group of offenses having this feature: larceny, fraud, embezzlement, false pretenses, robbery and extortion.

theft by false pretenses Larceny by trick or device, so that the victim's consent is usually obtained by the trick or device.

then (1) In that event; (2) at that time; (3) next in order, shortly after.

then and there (1) At the specified time and place; (2) immediately.

thence (1) From that place; (2) from that fact.

theory (1) Idea advanced as a guide to action; (2) working hypothesis, supposition.

theory of case Basis of liability or defense.

there (1) In that place; (2) at that time.

thereabout Approximately, near.

thereafter After the specified time, from then on.

thereby By such means.

therefore Consequently, in conclusion.

therein In that place.

thereto To that.

thereupon (1) Immediately after, without delay; (2) on account of that.

thief One who steals.

things (1) Objects of property, possessions, (2) state of affairs.

think (1) To believe, consider, intend, remember; (2) to apply mental exertion in some matter.

third degree Application of mental or physical abuse to a prisoner in order to obtain incriminating statements from him.

third party (1) Person who is not a party to a legal action or matter; (2) one other than the principals in a legal matter.

third party beneficiary One who is to benefit from a contract made between two others.

thoroughfare Street for passage of traffic.

threat Declaration of intention to hurt or damage another.

☆ **threat** The declaration by words or actions of an unlawful intent to do some injury to another, together with an apparent ability to do so.

three-mile limit Marine boundary of that off-shore area of a state over which the state asserts jurisdiction.

through (1) Because of, by means of; (2) from the nearest to the furthest extreme of, as, to travel through a place.

throw To hurl, propel.

throwback Reversion to an earlier state.

throw out To discard, reject, get rid of.

thrust -n. (1) Drive, lunge; (2) movement or action in a given direction; -v. (3) to push, drive, exert force upon.

thus (1) In this manner; (2) because of this.

ticket (1) Document issued as evidence of some right; (2) tag, label, summons; (3) evidence of a right such as passage or admission; (4) list of candidates of a given political party.

tide Rise and fall of body of water, caused by action of gravity of sun and moon upon the earth.

tie -n. (1) Equality of number or amount; (2) unifying force; -v. (3) to restrain, bind; (4) to equal.

time Duration, interval, period for performance of some action.

time immemorial (1) Indefinite past period of history; (2) past period beyond memory of living persons.

☆ **time served** Generally, time spent in confinement in relation to conviction and sentencing for a given offense(s), calculated in accord with the rules and conventions specific to a given jurisdiction; also, total time served under correctional agency jurisdiction.

tip (1) Gratuity, gift of money for performance of service; (2) item of confidential information.

tipstaff [TIP staf] Court officer, bailiff.

tithe [tahyth] One-tenth portion of one's income given regularly and voluntarily for religious purposes.

title (1) Name, heading, caption; (2) right of ownership, valid reason or justification; (3) portion of a legislative enactment usually including sections and articles; (4) designation accorded to nobility, rank, office, or as a matter of deference.

title insurance Contract by which holder of interest in real property is made secure as to possible loss arising by defects found in chain of interest in the property.

together Joined, in unity with, simultaneously.

token (1) Mark of something, outward indication; (2) coin or device made for specialized use, such as subway token or credit identification token.

tolerate To accept or endure without approval.

toleration Acceptance without approval.

toll -n. (1) Payment for passage, as, a toll paid on a toll bridge or toll road; (2) charge for use of public utility facilities, such as long-distance telephone call toll charge; -v. (3) to defeat, bar or remove, as, to toll the statute of limitations.

tolling the statute Showing of facts which removes the statute of limitations as a bar to prosecution of an action.

ton Measure of weight in U.S. equal to 2,000 pounds.

tonnage (1) Capacity for carrying freight, which on American vessels is estimated from the physical dimensions of the hold; (2) total weight in tons.

tontine [ton TEEN] Financial plan in the nature of insurance whereby payments and benefits are shared by a group with provision that on death or default of any member, his share is distributed among the remaining members, ultimately going to the last survivor or to those survivors living at an agreed date.

took Acquired possession of.

tool Instrument for manual use in performing work.

tools of a trade Implements commonly used in pursuit of one's vocation.

Torrens title [TAH ruhns TAHY tuhl] Indicia of ownership of real property under system by which a court or other government agency on appropriate proceedings issues a certificate showing title to the property (named for Sir Robert Torrens).

tort [tawrt] Wrongful act or breach of legal duty resulting in damage, not founded on contract.

tort-feasor [tawrt FEE zuhr] One who commits a wrongful act or breach of a legal duty not founded on contract, resulting in damage.

tortious [TAWR shuhs] Having nature of a tort, injurious, wrongful.

torture Infliction of great pain, torment or agony.

total -adj. Whole, complete, absolute; -n. sum, aggregate, amount.

total dependency Complete need for subsistence and care provided by another.

total disability Complete incapacity to pursue a useful occupation.

totalitarian Dictatorial, despotic, authoritarian.

totality (1) Sum; (2) quality of completeness.

total loss Complete destruction of value.

Totten trust [TOT uhn trust] Property right created by one's deposit of money or property in a fund, in his own name as trustee for the benefit of another, title passing on death, delivery or some unequivocal act.

touch To contact physically.

tour (1) Trip, journey; (2) period of duty assignment; (3) one's turn in a schedule.

tout [tout] (1) One who seeks to influence another in placing a wager; (2) one who solicits patronage.

toward In the direction of.

to wit That is to say, namely.

town Geographical and political subdivision, usually of a county.

toxemia [tok SEE mee uh] Poisoning.

toxic Poisonous.

toxicology Study of poisons.

trace -n. (1) Minute particle; (2) evidence of something formerly present; -v. (3) to follow, detect; (4) to copy.

tract Land area.

trade (1) Commerce, business, occupation, employment, craft; (2) group of persons engaged in a particular occupation or industry; (3) exchange of property usually without money.

trade acceptance Draft for payment of purchase price of goods, drawn by seller on the purchaser and accepted by the purchaser for payment.

trade discount Percentage deduction from list price given by vendors to their customers engaged in trade or in resale of the merchandise.

trade fixtures Articles such as shelving and machinery placed in premises by occupant to carry on his business, and which are removable without material damage to the premises.

trademark Distinctive word, letter, mark, sound or emblem or combination thereof, used by a maker or seller for product or service identification and authenticity.

trade name Distinctive designation used as title of a business.

trade secret Product or method known only to owner of a business or his designated agents, and used commercially in the business.

trade union Combination of workers in a particular occupation, organized to advance their working conditions by collective efforts, as, for example, a carpenters' union, as distinguished from union which organizes its members by industry.

trader (1) One who buys and sells, for himself or for others; (2) merchant, dealer.

tradesman (1) Shopkeeper, merchant; (2) skilled workman.

trading Doing business, buying and selling.

trading corporation Incorporated commercial body engaging in buying and selling merchandise.

trading stamps Paste-bearing coupons or stamps, similar to postage stamps, given by some merchants to their patrons in proportion to the patrons' purchases, said stamps being redeemable for selected articles.

tradition (1) Inherited or established use and practice; (2) inherited body of principles serving as a guide.

traffic (1) Business, commerce; (2) movement, as flow of vehicles, pedestrians, or other forms of transportation.

☆ **traffic offenses** I. A group of offenses usually informally categorized as such, and usually consisting of those infractions and very minor misdemeanors relating to the operation of self-propelled surface motor vehicles which are excluded from most information systems relating to criminal and correctional proceedings. II. *tentatively recommended national category for prosecution, courts and corrections statistics* Motor vehicle violations requiring appearance in court, other than "hit and run" and "driving under the influence."

trailer Vehicle designed to be attached to and pulled by another vehicle.

train (1) Connected group of railway cars; (2) orderly succession.

traitor (1) One who betrays; (2) one who commits treason.

transact To do business, to negotiate.

transaction (1) Act, usually commercial; (2) activity involving two parties reciprocally.

transactional immunity The form of freedom from conviction or imposition of any penalty or forfeiture applying to an entire transaction, matter or thing about which evidence is given.

transcript (1) Copy of an original; (2) official copy of court proceedings or other legal matter.

transcription (1) Act of copying; (2) changing into typewritten form from source material.

transfer -n. (1) Conveyance of right, title or interest in property from one person to another; (2) ticket valid for continued passage on a connecting common carrier; (3) removal from one location to another; -v. (4) to convey right, title or interest in property from one person to another; (5) to pass something from one to another; (6) to move to another location.

transferable (1) Able to be conveyed from one person or place to another; (2) negotiable.

transferee One to whom a transfer or conveyance is made.

transference Substitution of one for another.

transfer in contemplation of death Conveyance of property to another in one's lifetime, in imminent apprehension of impending death which does thereafter occur.

transferor (transferror, transferer, transferrer) (1) One who makes a transfer; (2) one who conveys right, title or interest in property to another.

transfer tax Financial imposition made by government to produce revenue for its support, upon specified change of ownership, such as in security trading.

transgression Violation of law or duty.

transient -adj. Of short duration; -n. traveller.

transit -n. Movement, journey; -v. to go over or pass through.

transitory (1) Temporary; (2) passing from one place to another.

transitory action Legal proceeding that may be brought in any court where jurisdiction of defendant may be had.

translation (1) Reproduction in one language of something originally written or spoken in another; (2) change to another form or appearance.

transmission Act of sending or emitting.

transportation Process of moving people or things from one place to another.

transshipment Shipment by a carrier other than the original carrier of a consignment of goods.

trap -n. Device for catching person or animal; -v. to confine, entangle.

trauma [TROU muh] Wound, blow, injury.

traumatic [trou MAT ik] Caused by a wound, blow or injury.

travel -n. Journey, trip, passage; -v. to go from one place to another.

traveler's check Draft payable on demand drawn by an issuer upon
itself or designated representative, subject only to validation by signature of its
original holder for comparison with same signature affixed at time of issuance.

traverse [truh VUHRS] -n. Pleading which makes formal denial of allegations of
adversary; -v. to deny, answer, go against, oppose.

treason Crime committed by one owing allegiance to a country, consisting of overt
acts of adherence to an enemy or giving aid and comfort to an enemy.

treasurer Fiscal officer of an organization or institution.

treasure-trove Articles of value, whose ownership is unknown, found hidden in
some private place or in the earth.

treasury securities Stocks and bonds of a corporation, once issued
but purchased by corporate funds and held for future use as an asset
of the corporation.

treasury stock Fully paid corporate stock, issued and later acquired by the
issuing corporation, and now held as an asset of the corporation.

treatment (1) Means taken to diagnose, treat and cure injury or disease;
(2) conduct in dealing with someone or something.

treaty Formal agreement between two or more countries, usually consisting of a
document signed by their authorized representatives.

trespass -n. (1) Unauthorized entry upon property of another; (2) unlawful and
violent invasion of rights of another; (3) offense, transgression;
-v. (4) to enter on land of another without authority; (5) to err,
invade, infringe.

trespasser One who enters upon property of another without authority.

trial (1) Judicial examination of a legal issue between adversaries, according to
prescribed procedure; (2) procedure to determine a question by examination
of proof.

☆ **trial** I. The examination in a court of the issues of fact and law in a
case, for the purpose of reaching a judgment. II. *recommended
statistical terminology* In criminal proceedings, the examination
in a court of the issues of fact and law in a case, for the purpose
of reaching a judgment of conviction or acquittal of the
defendant(s).

trial by jury Examination of a legal issue between adversaries, according to
prescribed procedure, and with a presiding judge submitting certain issues to
a selected panel of citizens for their verdict.

☆ **trial court** *recommended statistical terminology* A court of which the primary
function is to hear and decide cases.

☆ **trial de novo** [TRAHY uhl day NOH voh] A new trial conducted in a court of
record as an appeal of the result of a trial in a lower court not of record.

☆ **trial Judge** A judicial offficer who is authorized to conduct jury and nonjury trials,
and who may or may not be authorized to hear appellate cases; or the judicial
officer who conducts a particular trial.

☆ **trial Jury** *recommended statistical terminology* A statutorily defined
number of persons selected according to law and sworn to determine,
in accordance with the law as instructed by the court, certain matters of fact
based on evidence presented in a trial, and to render a verdict.

tribunal [trahy BYOO nuhl] Body having judicial functions, such as a court.

tributary One that is subject to or subordinate to another.

tribute (1) Sum paid by one ruler or nation to another as evidence of submission or to secure protection; (2) exorbitant payment of money induced by coercion; (3) deserved praise.

trier [TRAHY uhr] One who examines a matter and renders a decision.

trip -n. (1) Journey; (2) error, misstep; -v. (3) to stumble; (4) to make a mistake.

trivial Slight, minor

trover [TROH vuhr] Common law action for damages caused by wrongful detention of or interference with one's goods.

troy weight System of measure of weight in which twelve ounces equals one pound.

truce Temporary suspension of hostilities.

true (1) Correct, accurate, conforming to fact; (2) straight, exact; (3) legitimate, proper, valid.

true bill (1) Indictment; (2) indorsement made by a grand jury and signed by their foreman upon an indictment which they vote and present to a court.

true verdict Free, voluntary and informed determination of a jury upon an issue submitted to them.

trust -n. (1) Property right held by one person for benefit of another; (2) reliance, belief, credit; (3) business combination usually intended to reduce competition; -v. (4) to rely on, believe, credit.

trustee (1) One holding legal title to property, which he administers for the benefit of another; (2) member of a board which administers funds and controls policies of an organization, such as a school or hospital; (3) one entrusted with supervision of something, in a fiduciary capacity.

trust receipt Agreement between debtor and creditor by which creditor surrenders possession of collateral to the debtor but retains its title, on condition that the collateral will be held in trust for the creditor, or if sold, the proceeds will be paid to satisfy the indebtedness.

☆ **trusty** An inmate of a jail or prison who has been entrusted with some custodial responsibilities, or who performs other services assisting in the operation of the facility.

truth (1) Consistency between thought and reality; (2) actuality, honesty.

try (1) To examine an issue by judicial process; (2) to experiment, test; (3) attempt, endeavor

tumult Noisy disturbance, commotion.

turnkey Prison officer, jailer.

turnpike (1) Public road upon which a toll is or may be charged; (2) main road.

turpitude [TUHR pi tood] (1) Inherently base or vile conduct, depravity; (2) conduct contrary to justice, honesty or morality.

tyranny (1) Cruel and oppressive government; (2) unjust domination; (3) government with absolute power in one person.

tyrant (1) Unjust, arbitrary, despotic ruler; (2) person who acts arbitrarily or oppressively.

U

ubiquitous [yoo BIK wi tuhs] Present in many places or everywhere at one time.

ubiquity [yoo BIK wi tee] Presence in many places or everywhere at one time.

ubi supra [oo bee SOO pruh] (where above) Where above stated.

☆ **UCR** An abbreviation for the Federal Bureau of Investigation's "Uniform Crime Reporting" program.

ukase [yoo KAYS] Official edict or decree.

ult. [ult] (ultimo) In the previous month.

ulterior Concealed, hidden.

ultima ratio [UL ti muh RO shee oh] Last argument or recourse.

ultimate (1) Final, extreme; (2) last in sequence.

ultimate fact Fundamental data essential to determination of an issue.

ultimatum [ul ti MAY tuhm] Final demand.

ultimo [UL ti moh] In the previous month.

ultra [UL truh] -adj. Extreme, going beyond others; -pref. beyond, outside of.

ultra mare [UL truh MO ray] Beyond the sea.

ultra vires [UL truh VEE rays] Beyond legal power or authority.

umpire One having authority to render a decision.

unanimity State of agreement by all concerned.

unanimous Having the agreement of all.

☆ **unarmed robbery** Unlawful taking of property in the immediate possession of another by use or threatened use of force without a deadly or dangerous weapon or attempting the above act.

una voce [oo nuh VOH chay] (one voice) Unanimously.

unavoidable Inevitable, incapable of being prevented.

uncertain Vague, indefinite, indeterminate, doubtful.

uncertainty Vagueness, obscurity, lack of precise meaning, doubt.

unconditional Without restriction or qualification, absolute.

☆ **unconditional release** The final release of an offender from the jurisdiction of a correctional agency; also, a final release from the jurisdiction of a court.

unconscionable Harshly offensive to conscience, unfair, outrageous.

undefended (1) Not appearing, defaulting in appearance or answer; (2) without legal assistance.

under (1) Beneath, below; (2) subordinate, inferior to.

under control With such regulation as is appropriate in the circumstances.

under-lease (underlease) Sub-lease for period less than that remaining unexpired.

undersigned Subscriber, person whose signature appears at end of an instrument.

understand To comprehend, realize, have knowledge of.

understanding (1) Agreement, meeting of minds; (2) comprehension.

understood Agreed, settled.

undertake To engage in, assume performance of something, accept responsibility for.

undertaking (1) Enterprise; (2) promise, agreement; (3) agreement by which security is pledged for required appearance of person on bail.

underwrite (1) To insure, guarantee, pledge support for; (2) to assume a risk as an insurer; (3) to become responsible for purchase of an entire issue of securities.

underwriter (1) One who insures another, guarantor; (2) one who, by himself or with others, agrees to purchase an entire issue of securities.

undisputed Not contested, not challenged.

undivided (1) Intact; (2) held under one title by joint tenants or tenants in common.

undue influence (1) Improper or wrongful persuasion; (2) influence exercised over another so as to prevent free exercise of his will.

unearned income Money received as a return from ownership of property rather than as payment for services or labor.

unequivocal Clear, plain, certain of meaning, explicit.

unexpired Not yet run out.

unfair (1) Unjust, not equitable; (2) excessive.

unfair competition Illegal, dishonest or fraudulent business rivalry.

unfair labor practice Procedure followed by employer or employee which violates civil statute administered by a labor relations board.

unfaithful Dishonest, untrustworthy.

unfinished business Matters carried forward from one meeting or session to another.

unfit Not qualified for particular purpose, incapable.

unforeseen Unexpected.

unified Joined into one, integrated, consolidated.

uniform -adj. (1) Equally applicable; (2) without variation or deviation; -n. (3) distinctive attire worn by members of a group.

Uniform System of Citation A manual published and distributed by the Harvard Law Review Association for standardized use of citations and abbreviations in court papers, generally referred to as the "Blue Book".

unify To bring together into one, consolidate, integrate.

unilateral One-sided, ex parte.

unimproved (1) In its natural state; (2) as to land, without buildings or cultivation.

union (1) Joinder, association of several into one; (2) labor organization.

union shop Place of employment in which new employees must join recognized labor organization as condition of continued employment.

unit One of anything; quantity used as a standard of measurement.

unite To join, connect, combine.

united in interest Joined in and affected by same subject matter.

United Nations International organization composed of Security Council, General Assembly and other agencies.

United States Magistrate Official of Federal judicial system with power in cases, usually criminal in nature, similar to that of justice of the peace.

unity (1) Character of an estate held in joint tenancy, comprising joinder of interest, title, time and possession; (2) state of harmony, accord; (3) state of being one, quality of constituting a whole.

unity of interest In case of joint tenants, property right arising by the same conveyance as to each joint tenant.

unity of possession In joint tenancy, enjoyment of undivided rights in the whole.

unity of time In joint tenancy, vesting of interests of all at the same time.

unity of title In joint tenancy, single instrument showing ownership of all tenants.

universal (1) Worldwide, encountered everywhere; (2) pertaining to all.

unjust Unfair.

unjust enrichment Acquisition of profit or benefit which equitably or legally belongs to another so that restitution would be proper.

unlawful assembly Planned meeting of three or more persons which disturbs public peace.

unlawful entry Act of entering a building without authority with intent to commit a crime under circumstances not amounting to burglary.

unlawfully Illegally.

unlimited Without restriction, undefined.

unmarketable title Indicia of ownership which a prudent man would reject.

unnatural act Sodomy, buggery, sexual act defined by statute as abnormal or unnatural.

unnecessary Not required, useless.

unofficial reports Judicial opinions published without statutory requirement for their publication.

unreasonable (1) Exorbitant, excessive, unconscionable; (2) foolish, unwise.

unsafe Dangerous, unreliable.

unsound (1) Unhealthy, diseased; (2) false, invalid.

until Up to a given time.

unusual (1) Rare, remarkable, unique; (2) different, peculiar.

unwritten law (1) Body of law not enacted in statutory form; common law; (2) custom of acquitting one who kills to avenge seduction of or adultery with a member of his family.

upkeep Maintenance.

upland (1) High land away from the sea; (2) land area above flood level.

upset price Minimum amount set as sale price at an auction.

urban Pertaining to a city.

usage Custom, practice, prevailing procedure, usual behavior.

U. S. C. United States Code.

use -n. (1) Exercise or employment of something; (2) usual procedure; (3) legal enjoyment of property; (4) ability, purpose, function; -v. (5) to employ, exercise, utilize.

useful (1) Beneficial, advantageous; (2) serviceable.

use immunity The form of freedom from conviction or imposition of any penalty or forfeiture applying only to evidence given by a witness, but not barring conviction, penalty or forfeiture for the transaction if that can be obtained without the evidence for which use immunity has been given.

user (1) One who utilizes; (2) act of utilization; (3) legal right arising by utilization of another's property over long period.

usual Customary, habitual.

usufruct [YOO suh frukt] Right of enjoyment of something owned by another.

usurious [yoo ZOO ree uhs] Relating to payment of interest in excess of legal
rate.

usurp [yoo SUHRP] To seize without right.

usurpation [yoo suhr PAY shuhn] (1) Unlawful seizure; (2) encroachment upon
rights of another.

usurper [yoo SUHRP uhr] (1) One who assumes governmental power illegally;
(2) one who encroaches upon rights of another.

usury [YOO zuh ree] Practice of lending money at a rate of interest higher than
is allowed by statute.

☆ **usury** The charging of interest greater than that permitted by law in return for the
loan of money.

utensil Implement, useful article.

utility (1) Practical value; (2) public service company.

utter (1) To sell; (2) to speak, describe, report; (3) to put into circulation, as, to
utter counterfeit money.

ux. [uks] (uxor) Wife.

uxor [UKS awr] Wife.

uxoricide [uks AW ri sahyd] Killing of wife by husband.

V

v. (also **vs.**) Against, versus.

vacancy Unfilled position, office or premises.

vacant Empty.

vacate To set aside, render void, empty.

vacatur [VAY kuh toor] Setting aside of a legal proceeding by judicial order.

vacuum Condition of emptiness, unfilled space.

vagabond One who wanders from place to place without any fixed dwelling, and who is likely to become a public menace or public charge.

vagrancy Condition of wandering about without working.

☆ **vagrancy** In Uniform Crime Reports terminology, the name of the UCR category used to record and report arrests made for offenses relating to being a suspicious character or person, including vagrancy, begging, loitering, and vagabondage.

vagrant One who wanders about without fixed residence and lawful means of support.

vague Indefinite, obscure.

valid Legally sufficient, meritorious, justifiable.

validate To confirm, make legally binding, ratify.

validity Legal sufficiency.

valuable (1) Having monetary worth or value; (2) having desirable characteristics.

valuable consideration Compensation, performance, or promise of performance, given as an inducement to another to obtain some right, interest or benefit.

valuation Act of determining monetary worth or price.

value Estimated or actual monetary worth of anything.

vandal One who destroys or defaces property of others without justification.

vandalism Destruction or defacement of property of others without justification.

☆ **vandalism** In Uniform Crime Reports terminology, the name of the UCR category used to record and report arrests made for offenses of destroying or damaging, or attempting to destroy or damage, the property of another without his consent, or public property, except by burning.

variance (1) Discrepancy between two matters, state of disagreement; (2) modification in application of zoning regulation to permit a use otherwise prohibited.

variation Alteration, modification.

vassal [VAS uhl] (1) Under feudalism, one giving servitude to a superior lord; (2) person completely subordinate to another or to some influence.

vehicle (1) Means of transportation; (2) agent of transmission, as, a newspaper may be a vehicle for transmission of current information.

☆ **vehicular manslaughter** Causing the death of another by grossly negligent operation of a motor vehicle.

vel non [vel nohn] Or not.

venal [VEE nuhl] Corruptly obtainable.

venality [vee NAL i tee] Willingness to be bribed or corrupted.

vend To sell.

vendee One to whom something is sold.

vendetta (1) Blood feud; (2) prolonged and bitter feud.

venditioni exponas [ven di tee OH nee eks POH nuhs] (you expose to sale)
Title of writ addressed to sheriff or similar officer to perform his duty in sale of
property to satisfy a court order.

vendor Seller.

venire [vuh NEE ray] (to come) (1) Writ directed to sheriff for summoning jurors;
(2) entire panel drawn for possible jury service.

venire facias [vuh NEE ray FO kee uhs] Common law writ addressed to sheriff,
commanding him to produce jurors for service.

venireman [vuh NEER man] Person called as a juror.

venture -n. (1) Enterprise involving risk; (2) speculation; -v. (3) to expose
to risk.

venue [VEN yoo] Geographical place where some legal matter occurs or may be
determined.

☆ **venue** The geographical area within which a court has jurisdiction; the
geographical area (municipality, country, etc.) from which a jury is drawn and
in which trial is held in a court action.

verbal Oral, spoken.

verdict Decision or finding made by a jury.

☆ **verdict** *recommended statistical terminology* In criminal proceedings, the
decision of the jury in a jury trial or of a judicial officer in a nonjury trial, that
the defendant is guilty or not guilty of the offense for which he or she has
been tried.

verification (1) Confirmation of accuracy or truth; (2) certification before a notary
or other officer authorized to administer an oath of the truth of a statement
being made, subscribed and sworn to.

verify (1) To confirm by oath, affirmation, or proof; (2) to confirm the authenticity
of.

verity [VE ri tee] Truth.

versus [VUHR suhs] Against.

very -adj. (1) Actual, true, absolute; -adv. (2) extremely, to a high degree;
(3) In actual fact.

vessel Craft used for navigation or transportation by water.

vest (1) To take legal effect; (2) to place into possession; (3) to endow
with authority.

vested Accrued, settled, not contingent.

vested interest Legal right or title which has come into being and may be
transferred.

vested right Legal status in which a person has such property right as will be
protected by governmental action.

veteran (1) Person formerly in military service; (2) person with experience
acquired by long service.

veterans' preference Special consideration in civil service selection given to
persons honorably discharged from military service.

veto (I forbid) (1) Disapproval or non-approval by a chief executive of pending
legislation; (2) act of prohibiting something.

vex To annoy, harass, tease, worry.

vexatious [vek SAY shuhs] Troublesome, lacking reasonable justification, distressing.

via [VAHY uh] By way of, through means of.

viable Able to live, grow, develop or be put into use.

vicarious Serving in place of something original, acting as a substitute.

vice -n. (1) Inherent fault or defect; (2) immoral conduct or habit, evil behavior; -pref. (3) in place of, succeeding.

vice versa [VAHY suh VUHR suh] In changed order, conversely.

vicinage [VIS uh nuhj] Neighborhood, adjacent district.

vicinity Nearness, proximity.

vicious (1) Evil, depraved, foul, infamous; (2) savage, untamed, fierce; (3) corrupt, degenerate.

☆ **victim** A person who has suffered death, physical or mental anguish, or loss of property as the result of an actual or attempted criminal offense committed by another person.

☆ **victimization** In National Crime Survey terminology, the harming of any single victim in a criminal incident.

vide [VEE day] See, as, vide supra means "see above".

videlicet [vi DEL uh set] (abbreviated **viz.**) That is to say, namely.

vie [vee (n.), vahy (v.)] -n. life; -v. to compete, contend, challenge.

vi et armis [vee et AHR mis] By force and arms.

view -n. (1) Observation, inspection, examination; (2) inspection by jury or by a court of some place or premises involved in a legal proceeding; -v. (3) to inspect examine, observe, consider attentively.

vigilant Watchful, cautious, alert.

vigilante [vi ji LAN tee] One of a group of citizens who volunteer to suppress crime and punish criminals without delay.

vigor Strength, force, energy.

vigorous Strong, energetic, active.

vile Mean, contemptible, repulsive.

village Usually, a municipal corporation whose area is smaller than a city.

villain (1) Scoundrel, rascal; (2) depraved person who commits evil acts; (3) person who deliberately does serious harm to others.

vinculo matrimonii [VEENGK yoo loh ma truh MOH nee ee] Bonds of matrimony.

vindicate (1) To justify, avenge; (2) to exonerate, free from guilt; (3) to demonstrate accuracy or truth of something challenged as inaccurate or untrue.

vindication Exoneration, justification.

vindictive (1) Seeking revenge or retribution; (2) nasty, spiteful.

violation Infringement of law, breach, transgression.

☆ **violation** I. The performance of an act forbidden by a statute, or the failure to perform an act commanded by a statute. II. An act contrary to a local government ordinance. III. An offense punishable by a fine or other penalty but not by incarceration. IV. An act prohibited by the terms and conditions of probation or parole.

violence Force, physical abuse, intense action.

violent Vehement, characterized by strong physical force, furious.

vir [veer] Man.

vires [veer ays] Powers.

virtuous Of good moral character, chaste, pure.

vis [vis] Force.

visa [VEE zuh] Official endorsement placed on a passport indicating its examination and grant of authority to travel as indicated.

visible Capable of being seen, distinct, conspicuous.

visitation right Right of non-custodial parent after separation or divorce to companionship of child or children of the marriage for a limited time as determined by mutual agreement or court decree.

visitor (1) One who goes to see another at some place; (2) person appointed to make formal call for inspection or supervision.

vital (1) Essential to life; (2) energetic, animated; (3) of great importance.

vital statistics Public records of birth, death, marriage and health.

vitiate [VISH ee ayt] (1) To destroy, make void; (2) to injure, impair.

viva voce [VEE vuh VOH chay] Orally, by word of mouth.

viz. [viz.] (**videlicet**) Namely, that is to say.

vocabulary Collection of words or of words and phrases.

vocation (1) One's business or means of earning a living; (2) strong inclination toward some kind of work or action.

vociferous Loud, noisy, boisterous.

void Null, having no legal effect.

voidable That which may be nullified but is otherwise effective.

voir dire [vwor DEE ray] (to speak the truth) Preliminary examination of a witness or juror to test competency for service as witness or juror.

volenti non fit injuria [voh LEN tee nohn fit in JOO ree uh] With consent, there is no injury.

voluntarily Freely, of one's own will.

voluntary Spontaneous, done of one's free will.

☆ **voluntary commitment** In corrections usage, admission to a correctional, residential, or medical facility or program for care or treatment without a court commitment and by personal choice.

☆ **voluntary manslaughter** Intentionally causing the death of another, with provocation that a reasonable person would find extreme, without legal justification.

volunteer -n. One who renders a service without having any legal interest or obligation to do so; -v. to offer spontaneously.

vote Formal designation of choice on a question such as election of a candidate.

voter One who has right to record his choice in an election.

voting trust Procedure by which trustees are designated for stockholders, to exercise the stockholders' rights in casting ballots on corporate matters.

voucher Document which supports a business transaction as proof.

voyeur [vwo YUHR] Individual whose sexual desire is focused upon seeing the sexual acts or organs of another; sometimes referred to as a "peeping tom".

vs. Versus, against.

vulgar (1) Uncouth, unrefined, indecent; (2) having common or ordinary meaning.

W

wage (1) Salary; (2) payment by an employer for labor or services usually at an hourly or daily rate (referring chiefly to physical labor).

wage earner One receiving wages or salary for his income.

wager Bet.

wagering contract Agreement between parties without exchange of consideration, and dependent upon happening of an uncertain event or condition.

wages Amount paid by an employer for performance of labor or services, usually at an hourly or daily rate (referring chiefly to physical labor).

waive To give up voluntarily, relinquish, refrain from.

waiver Intentional surrender or renunciation of a known right or privilege.

wanton [WON tuhn] (1) Reckless, characterized by disregard of consequences, unrestrained; (2) lewd, sensual.

wanton and reckless misconduct [WON tuhn and REK les mis KON dukt] Intentional performance of an act likely to cause harm to others.

war Armed conflict between two or more political bodies or nations.

ward (1) Person, such as a minor, who is under another's supervision; (2) geographical division of a city for political and administrative purposes.

warden (1) Guardian, keeper; (2) person having charge of a prison; (3) officer having specified duties, such as game warden, fire warden or grand jury warden.

warehouse Place for storage of goods.

warehouse receipt Document, usually negotiable, issued by an establishment which stores goods, indicating receipt there of and title to the goods.

warning Notice of danger or adverse consequences.

warrant -n. (1) Authorization, justification; (2) formal document issued by competent officer, giving authority and direction to another to perform a described act, such as a warrant of arrest or search warrant; -v. (3) to authorize, justify; (4) to guarantee, especially as to quality of merchandise; (5) to assure good title to a purchaser by express condition.

☆ **warrant** In criminal proceedings, any of a number of writs issued by a judicial officer, which direct a law enforcement officer to perform a specified act and afford him protection from damage if he performs it.

warrantee Person to whom a warranty is given.

warrantor One who makes a warranty.

warranty Statement expressly or impliedly guaranteeing something; usually a collateral obligation by a seller concerning subject matter of the sale.

warranty deed Formal instrument conveying title to real property, wherein grantor represents that he holds title in fee simple, free of all liens and encumbrances, and will defend title against any claims.

wash sale (1) Transactions which negate each other, such as broker executing buy and sell orders for same securities; (2) fictitious sale of securities without any actual change of ownership, usually intended to influence trading.

waste -n. (1) Injury to or destruction of property by a tenant; (2) defective or superfluous material; -v. (3) to consume without purpose; (4) to devastate, bring to ruin.

watch (1) Period of time allotted for performance of duty, as by a member of ship's crew; (2) state of vigilance.

watchman Person assigned to protect property against fire, theft or other damage.

watered stock Instruments of corporate ownership issued for less than their par value.

way (1) Street, thoroughfare; (2) route, path; (3) means, manner.

waybill Description of shipment made by carrier, containing description of shipment, consignor, consignee, route, charges and other information.

way of necessity Right of passage over land of grantor when the grantee's land is completely surrounded and without access to streets or roads.

ways and means Methods for raising revenue.

wayward minor Person below age of legal capacity to commit a crime but otherwise within statutory definition of one whose conduct is delinquent or criminal so as to subject him to legal custody or supervision.

wealth Aggregate worth of things of value.

weapon Any instrument used or designed to be used in fighting.

wear and tear Injury or depreciation in regular use.

wedlock Marriage.

☆ **weekend sentence** Regular repeated periods of imprisonment on any specified day or days of the week.

weight Measure of heaviness.

weight of evidence Preponderance of proof.

welfare (1) Well-being, happiness, prosperity; (2) public assistance.

Westlaw Computer database and computerized legal research system developed by West Publishing Company.

wharf Structure on navigable water alongside which vessels can be loaded or unloaded.

wharfage Charge made for use of a wharf for loading or unloading cargo.

whenever (1) As long as; (2) as soon as; (3) in every case.

whereas (1) When in fact; (2) since.

whereby (1) By which; (2) as a result of which.

whereupon (1) After which; (2) closely and proximately following.

wherever In every place or circumstance.

while During, as long as.

☆ **white-collar crime** Nonviolent crime for financial gain committed by means of deception by persons whose occupational status is entrepreneurial, professional or semi-professional and utilizing their special occupational skills and opportunities; also, nonviolent crime for financial gain utilizing deception and committed by anyone having special technical and professional knowledge of business and government, irrespective of the person's occupation.

white slave Female held for immoral purpose, usually in interstate commerce.

whoever No matter who.

whole Entire, complete, intact, sound, strong, undamaged.

whole blood Line of descent from same two parents.

wholesaler Merchant who sells to retailers, jobbers or other merchants.

wholesome Sound, health-promoting, beneficial.

wholly Completely, entirely, solely.

whore (1) Prostitute; (2) female who indulges in promiscuous sexual intercourse.

widow Woman who has survived death of her husband.

widower Man who has survived death of his wife.

wife Female partner in a marriage.

will -n. (1) Wish, desire, determination; (2) written instrument by which a person makes disposition of his property to take effect upon his death; -v. (3) to bequeath, devise; (4) to determine, decide, desire.

willful (wilful) Deliberate, intentional, stubborn.

☆ **willful homicide** The intentional causing of the death of another person, with or without legal justification.

willingly Voluntarily, intentionally.

wind up To terminate, liquidate, bring to a conclusion.

wiretap -v. To overhear or record a telephonic or telegraphic communication intentionally, without consent of either party, by some mechanical means; -n. a device for this purpose.

withdraw To remove, take back, relinquish.

withdrawal (1) Act of removal, retraction; (2) detachment.

withdrawal of juror Procedure by which, on consent of the litigants, one juror is removed from the jury and thereafter the court terminates the proceeding because the jury is no longer complete.

withhold (1) To retain that which belongs to another; (2) to restrain, refrain, keep back.

within Into, inside of.

without Outside of, beyond, lacking.

without delay At once.

without justification Lacking reasonable excuse.

without prejudice Preserving all legal rights and claims for later determination.

without recourse Term affixed to a negotiable instrument by an endorser as notification that he assumes no responsibility for payment of the instrument.

without the state Outside the state.

with prejudice Binding and determinative so as to bar a subsequent proceeding on the same issue.

witness -n. (1) Person who offers or may offer evidence in a legal proceeding; (2) one who observes something; -v. (3) to subscribe one's name to an instrument as an aid in establishing its authenticity; (4) to observe, furnish evidence.

☆ **witness** In criminal justice usage, generally, a person who has knowledge of the circumstances of a case; in court usage, one who testifies as to what he has seen, heard, otherwise observed, or has expert knowledge of.

wittingly Knowingly, intentionally.

woolsack [WUHL sak] (1) Originally, official seat of Lord Chancellor of England in the House of Lords; (2) office of a judge.

words Vocabulary, tools of speech.

words of art Specialized terms applicable to a particular field and having a specific meaning and usage in that context.

work (1) Labor, exertion, effort; (2) product of creative effort, as, a literary work.

workhouse Correctional institution for minor offenders.

working capital (1) Cash available in a business for current use; (2) that portion of current assets of a business which is in excess of current liabilities.

workmen's compensation Statutory system by which employees are compensated for injury arising out of or in the course of their employment (sometimes known as workers' compensation).

worldly (1) Pertaining to current and earthly existence, as distinguished from spiritual affairs; (2) pertaining to practical concerns.

worth Value, utility, wealth.

worthless Having no value, unproductive.

worthy Deserving, meritorious, estimable.

wound Bodily injury involving breaking or tearing of skin, usually by a hard or sharp instrument.

wrath Intense anger.

wreck -n. Something destroyed or made useless; -v. to destroy, ruin, frustrate.

writ [rit] Formal legal instrument issued out of or in behalf of a court, commanding person named to perform or refrain from performing a specified act.

☆ **writ** A document issued by a judicial officer ordering or forbidding the performance of a specified act.

writ of error [rit uv E ruhr] Legal instrument by which a party seeks appellate review in an action at law, based upon alleged error in the proceedings or Judgment of the court.

writ of error coram nobis [rit uv E ruhr KAW ruhm NOH bis] Formal legal instrument, and proceeding thereunder, by which a court is asked to vacate a judgment it has entered in a criminal action, based upon alleged error in its proceedings.

writ of habeas corpus [rit uv HAY bee uhs KAWR puhs] Writ used to produce a person in custody before a court to determine legality of his detention.

☆ **writ of habeas corpus** In criminal proceedings, the writ which directs the person detaining a prisoner to bring him or her before a judicial officer to determine the lawfulness of the imprisonment.

writ of prohibition [rit uv proh hib ISH uhn] Formal legal document issued by a higher court, directing a lower court to discontinue legal proceeding pending therein.

writing (1) Act of placing marks upon paper or other medium; (2) surface containing words.

wrong (1) Violation of law, invasion of legal right; (2) unfair or immoral act.

wrongdoer One who acts unfairly, immorally or illegally.

wrongful (1) Illegal; (2) unfair.

wrongful death Killing of a person without legal justification.

wrongfully (1) In violation of law; (2) unjustly, unfairly.

Y

yard (1) Unit of volume for material in bulk equal to cubic yard; (2) unit of linear measure equal to 36 inches; (3) land area adjacent to a building or group of buildings; (4) commercial storage area.

year (1) Generally, twelve calendar months; (2) period required for one revolution of earth around sun.

yearbooks Reported cases in English law, from the time of King Edward I (1272) to Henry VIII (1509).

yeas and nays [yayz and nayz] Affirmative and negative votes upon an issue.

yellow dog contract Employment agreement offered and maintained on condition that employee will not join or belong to a labor union.

yield -n. (1) Return, income, result, revenue; -v. (2) to provide a result; (3) to surrender, relinquish, submit; (4) to provide as profit or interest.

youth (1) Period between childhood and maturity; (2) person, usually male, between childhood and maturity.

☆ **youthful offender** *recommended statistical terminology* A person, adjudicated in criminal court, who may be above the statutory age limit for juveniles but is below a specified upper age limit, for whom special correctional commitments and special record sealing procedures are made available by statute.

Z

zealot [ZEL uht] One who vigorously supports a cause.

zone Area or district allocated for a particular purpose.

zoning Governmental restriction of buildings and their uses according to location.

zoning laws Statutes prescribing use to which land in a given area may be put, and regulating size and nature of buildings.